Roland Baumgartner
Peter-Lukas Meier

Unparalleled diversity

Dear readers, dear visitors setting off
on the Grand Tour of Switzerland,

People say that opposites attract: at first this might not strike you as an expression which can be applied to a country, yet it is entirely appropriate for Switzerland. For it is precisely these contrasts that make our country so captivating and that inspire visitors, both from Switzerland and abroad, to explore it.

The Swiss population lives in large cities the size of Zurich (over 400,000 inhabitants) or minute villages with a nonetheless rich past, such as Marmorera, a hamlet of only 31 souls in the Canton of Graubünden. Likewise, our lakes might be immense (Lake Geneva, 580 km²) or tiny (Mauensee, 0.55 km²), but they are all very popular walking destinations. The Paul Klee Centre in Bern is relatively recent, while Abbey of Saint-Maurice is currently celebrating 1,500 years of existence. For shopping, our towns and cities are overflowing with shops and boutiques where the world's leading brands can be found, but our countryside also has a great deal to offer those who like local crafts and regional specialities. The town of Chaux-de-Fonds stands out for being built on a grid, while Chur and many other places are distinctive for their carefully preserved ancient and winding streets. Palm trees abound in Ticino, while permanent snow covers the high peaks of Valais, two neighbouring cantons. And what about our country's four official languages?

So much to experience and explore in such a small country

Switzerland is a unique and remarkable holiday destination; it owes this in part to the country's small size since the variety and concentration of tourist attractions is sure to enthral visitors, whether from Switzerland or abroad, who can enjoy them without travelling long distances.

All this has led to the introduction of a tourism offer which helps eager-to-explore visitors to choose their itineraries and destinations. This offer is even more attractive since today's tourists increasingly prefer the idea of a circuit to visiting a single place.

Our country's tourist authorities have identified and exploited this potential to promote Switzerland in a new way, with a single and carefully thought-out circuit which takes in all its regions: the Grand Tour of Switzerland. This itinerary offers an opportunity to discover the diversity of our country through over 200 sites and tourist attractions which are relatively close to each other and located within or very close to this corridor for exploration. Nature, culture, architecture, leisure and entertainment, lakes and mountains, gourmet pleasures and urban walks: this circuit contains all the ingredients to satisfy the most varied expectations.

Johann N. Schneider-Ammann
Federal Councillor and Head of DEFR (Federal Department of Economic Affairs, Education and Research)

Perfect unity in terms of infrastructure and quality of service

The Grand Tour of Switzerland promises not only a journey rich in contrasts, but also the guarantee of flawless quality from start to finish in something which has made our country famous throughout the world: first class infrastructures and reliable, competent service providers attentive to customer requirements. In hotels, restaurants, tourist offices and other organisations, every effort will be made to ensure that the Grand Tour leaves each and every visitor with excellent memories of Switzerland.

I strongly encourage you to make this journey. This publication will help you to determine which sections of the itinerary inspire you most and to plan your journey to suit every mood and ensure that every instant is enjoyable and memorable. This is the perfect way to reconnect with the true spirit of holidays!

Johann N. Schneider-Ammann
Federal Councillor and Head of DEFR
(Federal Department of Economic Affairs,
Education and Research)

Martin Sturzenegger
President of the Grand Tour of Switzerland Association

Jürg Schmid
CEO of Switzerland Tourism

Dear readers,

In Switzerland almost everyone has, at least once in their life, stood and admired the Matterhorn. The thundering Rhine Falls, which spectacularly unleash up to 700 cubic metres of water per second, are just as well known. Likewise, the Kapellbrücke (Chapel Bridge) in Lucerne will instantly come to mind if you're asked to name a famous wooden bridge, and you have doubtless already photographed some of the exceptional flora and fauna in the Swiss National Park. You might also, at some time, have been one of the 300,000 annual visitors to Chillon Castle. Of course, you also know that if you wish to spend a holiday in a southern ambience, you have no need to leave Switzerland, and like many of us you might well have already explored the treasures to be found within one of Basel's 40 museums.

But the Grand Tour of Switzerland, which links the great tourist attractions via a circuit encompassing the whole of the country, is not in any sense intended "just" for foreign tourists. It has also been designed to surprise and enthral the inhabitants of this country and give them the opportunity to visit or return to the "great classics", as well as to discover the valleys, alpine pastures, villages and other lesser known sites which are nonetheless very definitely worth going out of your way to see.

For example, did you know that you can take Europe's steepest funicular to Lake Ritom in the Piora Valley, where you will find a mountain restaurant serving the most succulent Ticino delicacies? Have you heard of the lake of Saint-Léonard, Europe's largest navigable underground lake? Have you ever visited St. Martin's Church in Zillis and admired its unique painted ceiling? Or experienced the thrill of crossing the bridge at Mostelberg, the longest suspension footbridge in Europe? Discover the charming and modest Werdenberg, Europe's smallest town and a vineyard in Saillon which measures just 1.67m². At the other end of the spectrum, the Grand Chalet in Rossinière and the box-hedge maze in Evionnaz are the largest of their kind in the world.

The Grand Tour of Switzerland offers an itinerary which doesn't take the fastest routes, but the most picturesque. And there are many of them. For example, take the Tremola road on the south-facing slope of the St. Gotthard Pass, which for two hundred years has been reputed to be one of the most beautiful alpine routes. Or the Corseaux to Lutry section, which crosses the enchanting landscapes of Lavaux, and the route between Ardon and Saillon, with its succession of charming winegrowing villages so typical of the canton of Valais. And don't forget to explore the road from Melide to Montagnola which will show you the romantic side of Ticino, or the one from Zernez to Silvaplana where the "garden of the Inn" (a literal translation of the name "Engadin") unfolds its many facets. On the other side of the country, you can enjoy vast horizons as you follow the Rhine from Eschenz to Tägerwilen.

You'll find that it's not the journey by car which is important here, but discovering the many gems, all close to one another, which lie along the way. The itinerary takes on a purpose in its own right; by inviting the traveller to explore countless places along the way it offers the best of Switzerland in a nutshell.

We wish you a pleasant journey and many exciting adventures!

Contents

Leg	Sections of the Grand Tour itinerary	Page
	Passionate about Switzerland	9
	The 25 sections of the Grand Tour itinerary	11
	Bern region, Emmental – Lucerne	
1	Bern – Lucerne	15 – 23
	Lucerne – Lake Lucerne region	
2	Lucerne – Schwyz	29 – 37
3	Schwyz – Zurich	39 – 47
	Zurich region	
4	Zurich – Schaffhausen	51 – 59
	Eastern Switzerland – Liechtenstein	
5	Schaffhausen – St. Gallen	63 – 69
6	St. Gallen – Wildhaus	71 – 77
7	Wildhaus – Davos	79 – 87
	Graubünden region	
8	Davos – St. Moritz	91 – 99
9	St. Moritz – Andeer	101 – 107
10	Andeer – Bellinzona	109 – 113
	Ticino region	
11	Road from Chiasso to Bellinzona	117 – 125
12	Bellinzona – Furka	127 – 133

Leg	Sections of the Grand Tour itinerary	Page
	Valais region	
13	Furka – Visp	137 – 143
14	Zermatt, the Visp and Saas Valleys	147 – 153
15	Visp – Martigny	155 – 163
	Romandy – Geneva region	
16	Martigny – Montreux	167 – 173
17	Montreux – Saint-George	175 – 183
	Geneva region	
18	Road from Geneva to Saint-George	189 – 195
	Southern Jura	
19	Saint-George – Yverdon-les-Bains	199 – 205
20	Yverdon-les-Bains – Neuchâtel	207 – 213
	Basel region – northern Jura	
21	Road from Basel to Neuchâtel	217 – 225
	Neuchâtel – Fribourg region	
22	Neuchâtel – Fribourg	229 – 235
23	Fribourg – Château d'Oex	237 – 245
	Bernese Oberland region	
24	Château-d'Oex – Interlaken	249 – 255
25	Interlaken – Bern	259 – 267

Useful information for the journey	273
Index of places	275 – 277
My personal impressions of the Grand Tour	281 – 285
Impressum – Legal notice	288

Appendix: 1:500,000 scale tourist map showing the Grand Tour of Switzerland

Passionate about Switzerland

1,000 miles, or 1,600 kilometres, of roads and sublime landscapes which are some of the most beautiful in the world. No other itinerary could match the Grand Tour of Switzerland in terms of diversity of landscape and wealth of cultural heritage over such a short distance.

1,600 kilometres on the road, from the federal city of Bern to Lake Lucerne in the heart of Switzerland, then from the economic capital Zurich on to Lake Constance and the very rural region of Appenzell. The hues that inspired the artist Giovanni Segantini and the first alpine passes signal our arrival in the Engadin valley. A tome could be devoted to these passes alone, but we continue on our way until we reach the palm trees of Lake Maggiore before crossing other legendary passes to reach the canton of Valais. After a little detour via the Matterhorn, near Zermatt, we arrive in Romandy on the shores of Lake Geneva. Then we head north to the Jura and Neuchâtel. It would, of course, take just half an hour to return straight to Bern, but this would be to overlook one of the most charming sections of our Grand Tour: the picturesque Gruyère area, Château-d'Oex and its hot air balloons, and Simmental with its farms and their magnificent window box displays. Another small detour takes us to the Eiger, the Mönch and the Jungfrau and close to the village of Grindelwald. We then follow the shores of Lake Thun and drive through the very rural Gürbe Valley before returning to our point of departure, Bern.

Variety guaranteed

On the map, the Grand Tour of Switzerland covers 1,600 kilometres. But the distance is much greater if you include the various suggested detours and halts located in the vicinity of the itinerary. The Grand Tour is divided into 25 legs. You can cover it in just 16 days, taking just a very short time to discover the breathtaking variety of Switzerland's landscapes. For our country offers a change of fabulous scenery every few kilometres, separated by just a mountain pass or a few metres change in altitude. This impression of variety also naturally springs from our four linguistically and culturally distinct regions. But beyond the natural surroundings and the language spoken, architectural styles, the nature of dwellings and agriculture, flora and geology ceaselessly change along the way. The Grand Tour varies from an altitude of 196 metres at Ascona to its highest point of 2,429 metres at the Furka Pass. Between the two, there is infinite diversity.

Request stop

You can explore so many new places by car. This is why we recommend 400 activities and places, whether small or large, legendary or less well known. By meeting the men and women of Switzerland and absorbing their culture you will make this Grand Tour a memorable experience. Our remarkably varied traditions are alive and well, as is our gastronomic heritage. You will discover authentic specialities in every canton (such as "capuns" in Graubünden and "choléra" in Valais), or even in every town (Zurich style shredded veal or Lausanne saucisson) and village (Aigle les Murailles wine in Yvorne). Stop off along the way to enjoy local specialities or indulge in a gourmet feast, and savour your Grand Tour to the hilt.

Follow the guide!

The itinerary we describe is the official "Grand Tour" of Switzerland. The maps in this guidebook show you its exact route. We have chosen "national" and "local" roads so that you can immerse yourself in these varied regions and landscapes and take the time to visit the sites along the way, so no motorways are included.

Enter your destination into your sat-nav, select the "avoid motorways" option and replace "fastest route" by "scenic route". The names of these preferences might vary according to brand but the principle is the same, and all sat-navs use the same maps. Let yourself be guided automatically across Switzerland.

You can also download the Grand Tour of Switzerland map. You will find the download code on the official Grand Tour of Switzerland 1:275 000 scale map published by Hallwag Kümmerly+Frey. The entire Grand Tour of Switzerland route can be downloaded in GPX format for your sat-nav device from the Switzerland Tourism homepage.

Take your time

The Grand Tour of Switzerland is not a one-way itinerary. Followed in the opposite direction, its landscapes and panoramas will look entirely different. It's worth giving it a try!

We have one last piece of advice for the road: forget about performance! Switzerland and its Grand Tour are so magnificent and so varied that they are well worth spending extra time to explore. Set aside three days instead of just one for a particular section, for example, or concentrate on just one region of the country. You can return the following year to complete the tour. Don't worry: Switzerland's beauty spots will still be there!

The 25 legs of the Grand Tour itinerary

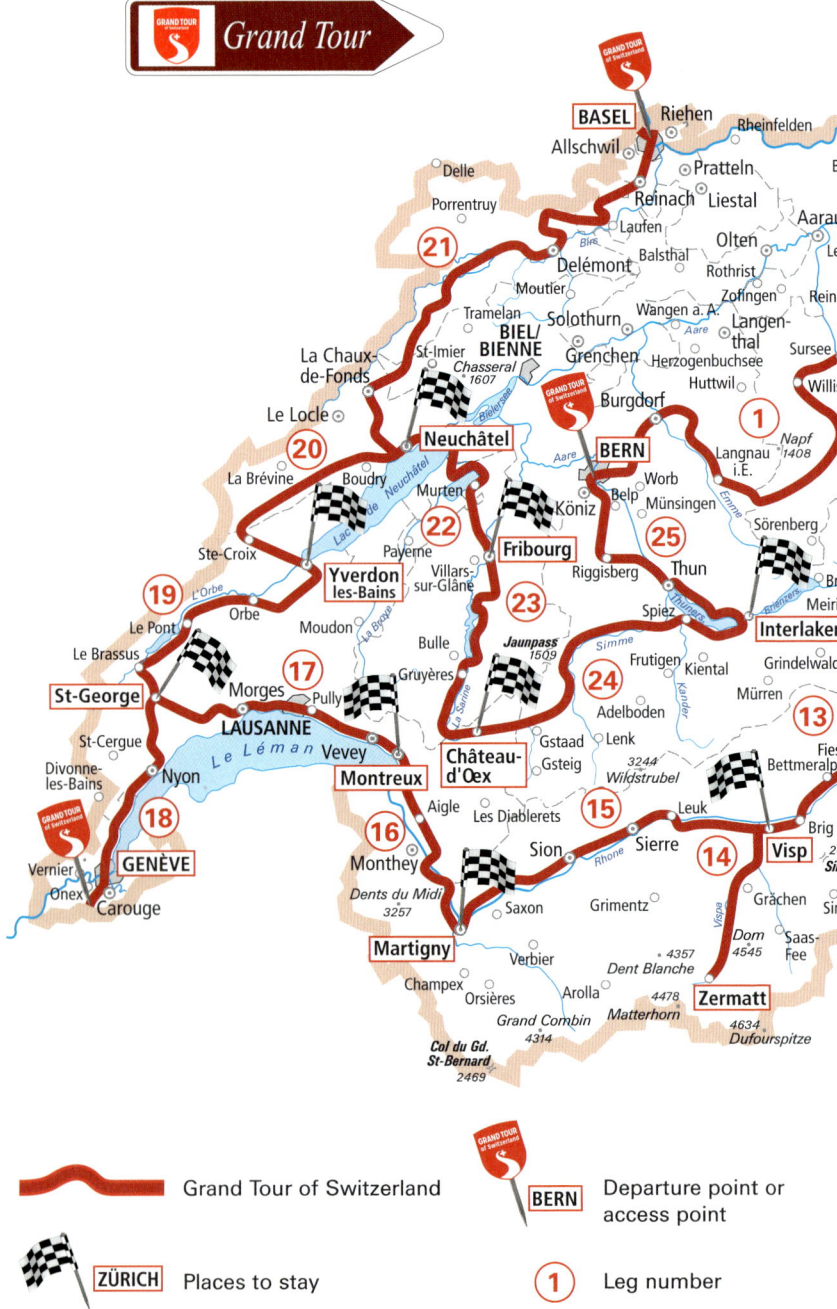

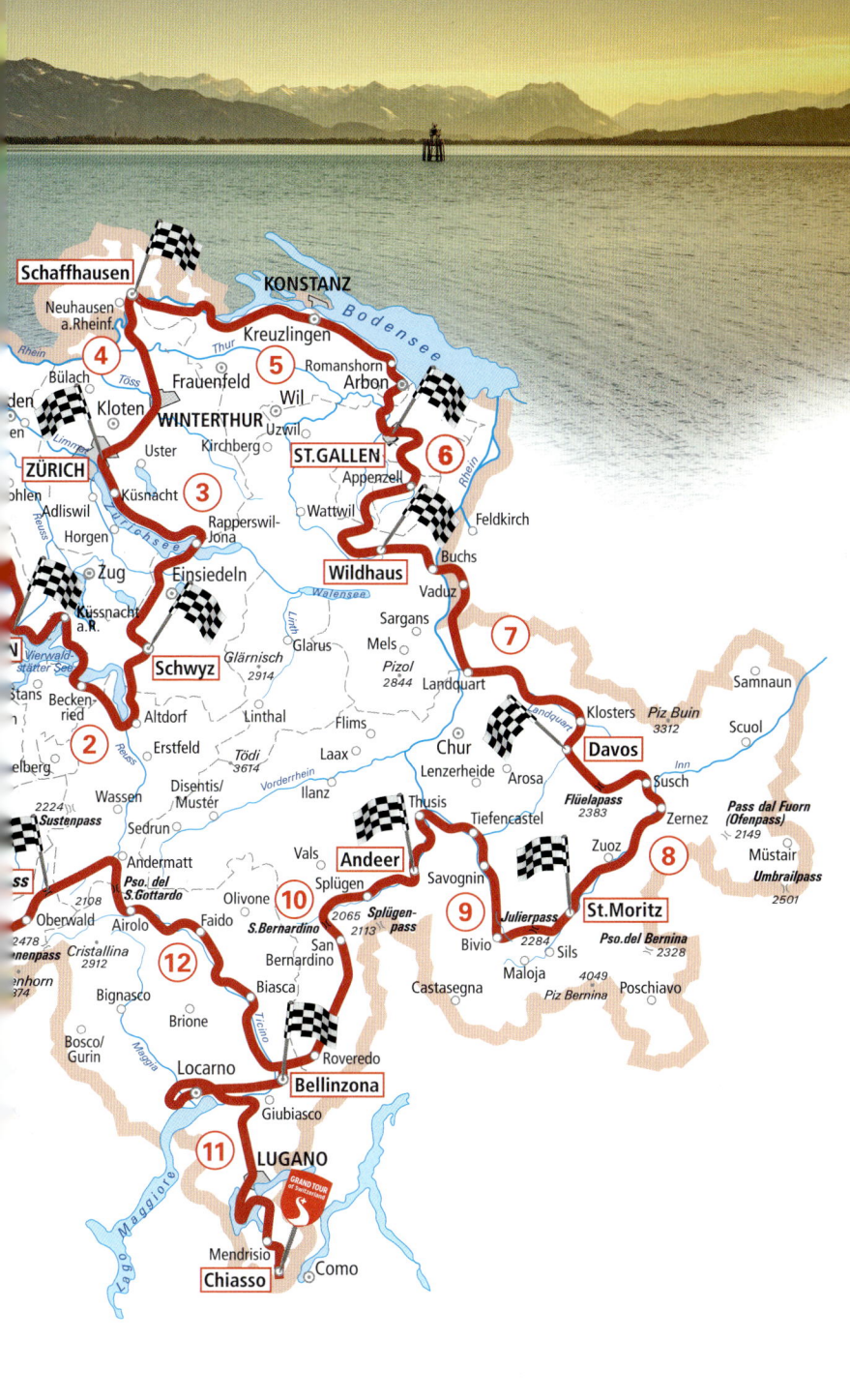

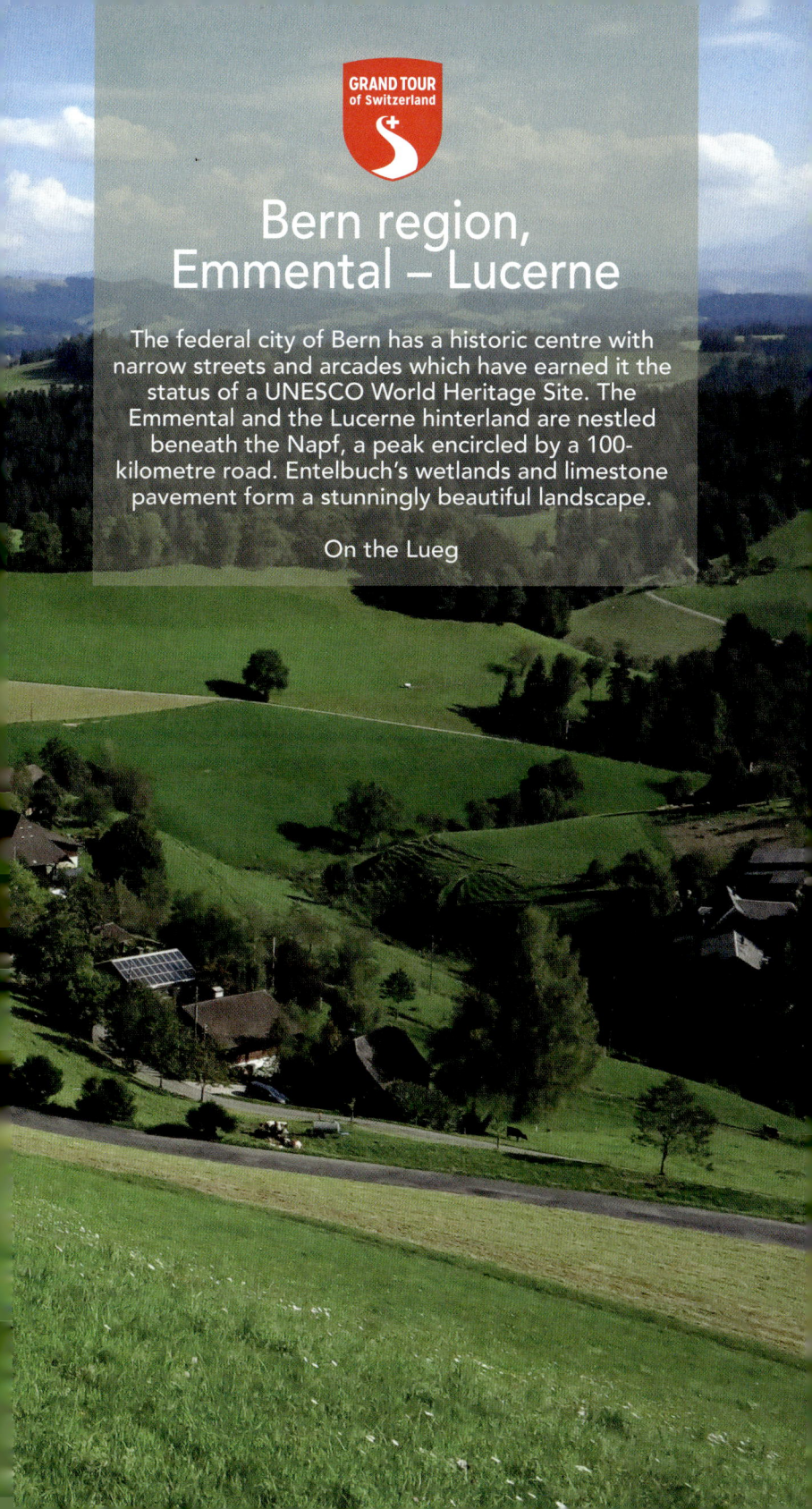

GRAND TOUR of Switzerland

Bern region, Emmental – Lucerne

The federal city of Bern has a historic centre with narrow streets and arcades which have earned it the status of a UNESCO World Heritage Site. The Emmental and the Lucerne hinterland are nestled beneath the Napf, a peak encircled by a 100-kilometre road. Entelbuch's wetlands and limestone pavement form a stunningly beautiful landscape.

On the Lueg

The Old City of Bern, Kramgasse, the Zytglogge clock tower (1)

Federal Palace, Bern

Bern Rose Garden (2)

Paul Klee Centre, Bern

Bern Bear Pit (2)

Leg 1

Bern – Lucerne

Emmental, Entlebuch, the Lucerne hinterland, Lake Sempach, the Seetal

Our Grand Tour of Switzerland starts with the capital, Bern. The Federal Palace (Parliament), the historic alleys of the city which was home to the Dukes of Zähringen and the Bear Pit form our first remarkable site: the Old City of Bern, a UNESCO World Heritage Site. Once past the Young Boys Football Club's new stadium you reach green countryside and a rolling landscape. Our first leg is fairly long but offers rich and very diverse landscapes and cultural sites. The imposing Burgdorf Castle can soon be seen on the horizon, standing watch over the peaceful and well-preserved town which lies below. Cross over the Lueg, which affords stunning views of the Pre-Alps and the snow-capped peaks in the Bernese Alps, to visit the Affoltern cheese dairy. Incidentally, do you know why there are holes in Emmentaler PDO? It would take several days to explore everything the area has to offer: traditional farms, the Gotthelfhaus, the potteries in Langnau, Kambly's Bretzeli and the Entlebuch Biosphere.

On arriving in the Lucerne hinterland we reach the vibrant market town of Willisau. The Grand Tour goes through its historic centre, which is well worth a visit. Twelve kilometres further on you get to the very ancient municipality of Sursee, near which stands the gigantic former radio transmission tower of Beromünster (216m). We soon reach the Seetal, with Lake Hallwil and Lake Baldegg. Don't miss a visit to Hallwyl Castle before continuing onwards to Lucerne.

① The Old City of Berne (World Heritage Site)

The Federal Palace, the Zytglogge clock tower, six kilometres of shaded arcades (Lauben), sandstone façades steeped in history, sculpted Renaissance fountains, a famous cathedral and an impressive roofscape which can be admired from the bell tower: welcome to what is indisputably Europe's most beautiful medieval city and a World Heritage Site since 1983.

② Bear Pit and Rose Garden

From the historic centre of the lower city, cross Nydeggbrücke Bridge to reach the old Bear Pit. It was supplemented by a park in 2009: Bern's mascot certainly deserved a garden with swimming pool on the banks of the River Aare! After taking your time to watch the bears, you can enjoy a local beer at the Altes Tramdepot, or walk on to the Rose Garden which offers a panoramic view of the Old City.

③ Dählhölzli zoo and adventure park

Cross Monbijou Bridge to reach Dählhölzli, where Bern's zoo is to be found with its enclosures bordered by woodland and the river. To the north, near Thunplatz, a treetop adventure park awaits you right in the town. Not far from the park you can also enjoy the Ka-We-De wave pool, and on the opposite bank of the Aare, the Marzilibad. This swimming pool is surrounded by an extensive lawn where swimmers can stretch out and relax. Or you might prefer to go for a dip in the river, with a direct view of the Federal Palace…

View of the Bernese Alps from the Gurten (4)

Ranflüh, Emmental

Burgdorf Castle (6)

The Gotthelf Centre (8)

The road from Emmental to Entlebuch

A typical Emmental farm (9)

Leg 1

④ A mountaintop with a view over the town and the Alps
The Gurten, which is traffic free, is a mountain to the south of Bern. It can be reached from Wabern by a panoramic funicular railway. Well-known since 1977 for its annual festival, its many activities and facilities make it worth a visit all year round (restaurant, picnic areas, electric cars, model railway with steam engine, castle to climb, Frisbee area and bowling game).

⑤ Solothurn, a baroque gem on the banks of the Aare
Switzerland's most beautiful baroque town was the place of residence of ambassadors from the court of France until the 18th century. Its finest landmark is St. Ursus Cathedral, whose façade was funded by Louis XIV, and which features a monumental Italian-style staircase. The narrow streets of the old town are also flanked by fine town houses, fountains and towers. —> 23 km

⑥ Burgdorf: castle and Franz Gertsch Museum
Before you make your way into the Emme Valley, stop off to see the largest and best preserved of the castles dating from the era of the Dukes of Zähringen. History lovers will be enchanted by Burgdorf, as much for the three museums housed in the Castle as for the unique atmosphere of the old centre. The world-renowned Franz Gertsch Museum contains several giant portraits by this master of hyperrealism.

⑦ The Lueg and Emmental cheese dairy
After Burgdorf, the Grand Tour climbs into the Emmental hills with their beautiful landscapes and prosperous-looking farms. The Lueg memorial pays tribute to 54 Bern Cavalry soldiers who died during the 1918 influenza epidemic. There is a panoramic view over the Emmental, the valley which produces most of the legendary cheese of the same name. In Affoltern you can visit the traditional Küherstock cheese dairy which dates from 1741, where milk is heated over an open fire, and the modern dairy which produces a tasty PDO Emmentaler. **More information on page 268.**

⑧ Lützelflüh: Gotthelf Centre
Visiting the old rectory will take you back to the times of Albert Bitzius. The pastor was also an author with the pen name of Jeremias Gotthelf, and visitors can see his comfortable sofa as well as his much more austere study. The Gotthelf Centre has a shop and café. It is closed in winter.

⑨ Farms in the Emmental and regional museum
These prosperous-looking farms with flowered window-boxes and pretty gardens are certainly eyecatching. Typical of the valley, they are built from wood in traditional style with an adjoining stable. You will notice their impressive hipped roofs sloping down very low on either side, their decorated attics "Spycher" and small outbuildings known as "Stöckli", originally intended for the older generation. In Langnau, the superb "Chüechlihus" chalet houses a museum of local crafts, with a particular focus on ceramics.

On the Lueg, view of the Alps (7)

Mooraculum (11)

The Kambly experience, Trubschachen (10)

An encounter on the road to Menziken

The small town of Willisau (13)

Leg 1

⑩ Trubschachen: The Kambly experience

Kambly's history started in 1910 with traditional "Bretzeli" waffle biscuits. The Trubschachen visitors' centre, on the Grand Tour itinerary, retraces the biscuit factory's 100-year history. You can watch master confectioners at work and taste a wide selection of biscuits in the shop before buying your supplies for the year! A tour by electric bicycle coupled with a smartphone application starts from Langnau and gives you the opportunity to learn all about the top-quality produce grown in the Emmental and used by Kambly. **More information on page 269**

⑪ Entlebuch, a UNESCO biosphere reserve

Switzerland's first biosphere reserve lies between Wolhusen and the hamlet of Wiggen. It includes the spectacular Schrattenfluh limestone pavement, vast wetland landscapes and flora and fauna of national significance. Visitors can enjoy extremely varied interests here: the energy route, the Kneipp trail, Ramoos charcoal burners and the Heiligkreuz pilgrim church.

⑫ In the land of Aeolus, god of wind

Wind turbines feature prominently in the landscape to your right. The size of the new Lutersarni turbine is staggering: 120 metres high (i.e. the same height as Prime Tower in Zurich) with a rotor spanning 80 metres in diameter. It is currently the largest wind plant in central Switzerland. Its annual production provides enough energy for 600 four-person households. —> 6 km

⑬ Small town of Willisau and gold panning in the Napf area

The Willisau area is renowned for its "Willisauer Ringli" biscuits (made with honey and shaped like a ring), but the little medieval town is well worth the detour in its own right for its two large gates, historic monuments and unparalleled atmosphere. This leg might also make your fortune, for there's gold in the Napf uplands! There are several excursions on offer to learn about gold panning. Good luck!

⑭ The small town of Sursee and Lake Sempach

This historic small town in the Lucerne region is not very well known but is worth a visit for its town hall and covered market in a late gothic style. The Basel Gateway and Upper Gateway are the remains of former fortifications. Sempach was the scene of a triumphant victory by the first Confederates against the Austrian occupiers in 1386. In summer its lake, with several very pleasant beaches, is worth stopping at.

⑮ Art and culture at the Beromünster radio tower

From 1931 until late 2008 the Beromünster medium wave transmitter (531 kHz) broadcast Germanlanguage radio programmes in Switzerland. It played a pivotal role against Nazi propaganda during the Second World War. The Blosenbergturm is 216 metres high and can be seen from a great distance. The technical buildings which stand next to the road have been transformed by Werner Zihlmann, a Sursee artist, into a centre for art and culture.

Hallwyl Castle (16)

Heidegg Castle (19)

Muri Abbey (18)

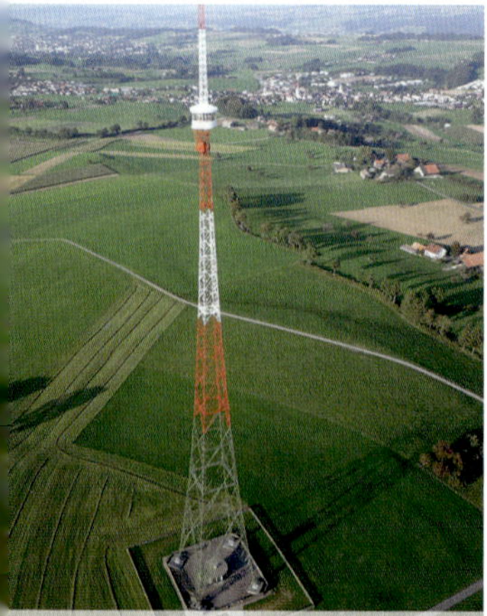

Former Beromünster radio tower (15)

Habsburg family crypt (18)

Leg 1

Hallwyl Castle
(16) The lords of Hallwyl chose a well-protected spot as their home for nearly 800 years. Entirely surrounded by water, this 13th century castle has lost none of its appeal. The tour is accompanied by an audio guide and includes several short videos. The Grand Tour passes just in front of the Castle.

Cruise on Lake Hallwil
(17) The lake near the castle is a very popular destination for excursions. It is encircled by a 22 kilometre pathway which offers an opportunity to explore the mostly undeveloped shoreline, or even take a dip. But the most pleasant way to see the lake is without doubt to take a cruise aboard one of the regularly scheduled motorboats.

Muri Abbey, home to the Habsburgs
(18) History lovers will enjoy the small detour via the Lindenberg, the highest point in the Canton of Aargau, and Muri. This former Benedictine abbey features a cloister, a crypt and Switzerland's largest cupola. Its history is closely linked to that of the Habsburgs. Entrance is free of charge to the abbeychurch of St. Martin with its five organs, gardens and fountains. Those who wish to learn more can visit the new museum, with an iGuide and application for the tour.
—> 12 km

Heidegg Castle, museum and rose garden
(19) Just beyond Lake Hallwil the smaller Lake Baldegg appears in view on the right. Considered to be "dead" a few decades ago due to its excessive phosphorus content, it is now kept alive with added oxygen. Heidegg Castle, the emblem of the Lucerne Seetal area, offers panoramic views. The museum housed in its square tower is open in summer. You can take your time to explore its charming rooms and rose garden and why not, enjoy a glass of wine from the estate's own vineyard.

Bern – Lucerne
Bern region, Emmental – Lucerne

The route

Leave from Berne, drive through the Emmental, around the Napf via Entlebuch and the Lucerne hinterland, Lake Sempach and Lake Hallwil, the Seetal then on to Lucerne and Lake Lucerne.

Distance: 181 kilometres

Photo opportunity: A remarkable view of the Bernese Alps from the Lueg memorial. The magnificent farms in the Emmental with their colourful flower and vegetable gardens. The leg draws to a close with the highly photogenic Hallwyl Castle.

How do the holes form in PDO Emmentaler? They are not made by hand and mice play no part in it either! Cultures of specific bacteria are in fact added to the milk. Fermentation breaks down the lactose and lactic acid and releases carbon dioxide in the process. The thickness of the wheel keeps the gas imprisoned within the cheese, where it forms holes.

Worth a detour

Bern: The Paul Klee Centre, an undulating building designed by Renzo Piano, with museum, meeting rooms and events venue – www.zpk.org

Affoltern im Emmental: Emmentaler cheese dairy, modern and traditional methods, immense restaurant – www.emmentaler-schaukaeserei.ch

Sörenberg: children's activity park in the Rossweid wetlands – www.mooraculum.ch

Wolhusen: tropical greenhouse and plants, Mahoi restaurant – www.tropenhaus-wolhusen.ch

Tourist information

Bern Tourism – www.bern.com
Bahnhofplatz 10a, 3011 Bern; +41 (0)31 328 12 12

Tourismus Emmental – www.emmental.ch
Bahnhofstrasse 44, 3401 Burgdorf; +41 (0)34 402 42 52

The Entlebuch biosphere reserve – www.biosphaere.ch
Chlosterbüel 28, 6170 Schüpfheim; +41 (0)41 485 88 50

Sempachersee Tourismus – www.sempachersee-tourismus.ch
Centralstrasse 9, 6210 Sursee; +41 (0)41 920 44 44

Tourismus Lenzburg Seetal – www.seetaltourismus.ch
Kronenplatz 24, 5600 Lenzburg; +41 (0)62 886 45 46

Bern – Lucerne

Bern region, Emmental – Lucerne

Official Partner of

1600 kilometres sheer driving

Welcome to the Home of quattro.

LeasingPLUS
Package includes: service and maintenance, tyres, courtesy car + insurance

www.audi.ch

GRAND TOUR of Switzerland

Lucerne – Lake Lucerne region

If you are thinking of walking around the whole Lake with all its arms, be prepared for a 150-kilometre hike! The landscapes of central Switzerland are outstandingly varied, from the Swiss Plateau to the glaciers of Titlis and Gemsstock. There's nothing like a tour on a paddle steamer to discover early Switzerland and the birthplace of the Confederation.

The Gersau-Beckenried car ferry

Kapellbrücke (Chapel Bridge,) Lucerne (1)

The Wasserturm, Lucerne (1)

Lucerne Culture and Congress centre (KKL) (2)

Lake Lucerne: flotilla of paddle steamers (3)

Leg 2

Lucerne – Schwyz

Lucerne – Lake Lucerne region

Lucerne is one of Switzerland's most popular tourist destinations and makes a perfect base for many exciting excursions. The 14th century Kapellbrücke (Chapel Bridge), rebuilt in 1993 after a fire, and the futuristic KKL congress centre designed by Jean Nouvel form a fascinating contrast. Let's start by following the north shore of Lake Lucerne via Küssnacht, before reaching the famous Rigi mountain at Weggis and Vitznau. We continue to skirt around the lake until we reach Gersau, where we take the car ferry. 20 minutes later the "Tellsprung" sets us down on the opposite shore at Beckenried in the canton of Nidwald. There are various possible excursions from here, for example to the Niederbauen, a nearby peak which is well worth the visit.

To reach Flüelen you will have to take the Seelisberg motorway tunnel, the only road which will take you to Uri. The first part of the Axenstrasse takes you to Tellskapelle (Tell's Chapel), built on the spot where our national hero is said to have escaped, with a courageous leap, from his enemy's boat. It offers a magnificent view over the lake, where you can watch vintage paddle steamers as they make their way towards Rütli meadow, where the Conferates of Uri, Schwytz and Unterwald swore to unite against the cruel Habsburg bailiffs in 1291. Lake Uri is in fact none other than Lake Lucerne! It must be said that its shape is a little complicated, with its many arms. Just a few kilometres further on we reach Schwyz, at the foot of the two Mythen mountains.

① Lucerne: Kapellbrücke and the Musegg towers

Kapellbrücke is without doubt one of Switzerland's most photographed monuments. Its massive, 34 metre high octagonal tower, the Wasserturm, is one of Lucerne's emblematic landmarks. Built around 1300 at the same time as the town's fortifications, it has been used during its history to house the town's archives, treasury and prison. Its roof is now home to alpine swifts in summer. Another of the town's emblems, the Musegg towers, are partly accessible on foot. They too were part of the fortifications.

② Lucerne Culture and Congress Centre (KKL)

This impressive building designed by the acclaimed French architect Jean Nouvel is situated on the shore of the lake, next to the station. Its innovative architecture, like the functions and events which take place there, is very important for the town. The concert hall is renowned for its outstanding acoustics. The building has a distinctive roof with a 45 metre overhang.

③ Lake Lucerne's flotilla of paddle steamers

What about exchanging your car for a paddle steamer? Five Belle Époque steamers are waiting for you in Lucerne. What could be more nostalgic than to hear the captain call his commands and the foghorn boom out? 38 kilometres of routes across the lake, 34 landing stages and stunning landscapes await you when you set sail on Lake Lucerne.

Pilatus, Lake Lucerne (4)

CabriO: the Stanserhorn cable car with open top deck (5)

Hollow Way (7)

Beckenried/Klewenalp (11)

Car ferry (9)

Leg 2

Pilatus: in the dragon's den
(4)

You can travel up the rock face by a cable car which looks somewhat like a helicopter or a historic rack-and-pinion railway (the steepest in the world with a 48% slope)… and there you are at the summit of Mount Pilatus. You will find a historic listed hotel there, with a terrace and gallery with a view over Lucerne, not to mention illustrations of dragons by Hans Erni. Younger visitors will enjoy the Fräkmüntegg tree-top adventure park and summer toboggan run.

Stanserhorn: CabriO-Bahn
(5)

The lower Stans railway station is linked to Lucerne and Beckenried. The journey upwards starts with a traditional funicular railway with open wooden carriages. Then there's a change of setting, and century: at the Kälti intermediate station passengers board the CabriO, a cable car with an open top deck, for an exhilarating ride with the wind in their hair and an unobstructed view. There are no overhead cables as they are positioned at the side of the cabin. A candlelit dinner is served at the summit of the Stanserhorn every Friday and Saturday evening. —> 14/9 km

Queen Astrid's chapel
(6)

In August 1935 the Belgian royal couple was staying as they often did on the Horw peninsula. Whilst out driving, a tragic accident occurred just outside Küssnacht at the foot of Mount Rigi, which cost young Queen Astrid (formerly Princess Astrid of Sweden) her life. A chapel was built in her honour on the banks of Lake Lucerne and it was formerly a very popular destination with Belgians.

Küssnacht: the Hollow Way (Hohle Gasse)
(7)

"This is the hollow way that he must take / To reach Küssnacht, there is no other route", William Tell is reputed to have said as he waited in ambush for the Bailiff Gessler between Lake Zug and Lake Lucerne. It was on this ancient trade route that he shot and killed his enemy with his famous crossbow. This historic place, an important part of the national legend, features a modern information pavilion.

Mount Rigi, known throughout the world
(8)

From Küssnacht, a first cable car takes you to Seebodenalp which is well known for its vintage motorbike race. Above Weggis there is a second cable car while at Vitznau the rack-and-pinion railway station is right next to the landing stage. So there is certainly no shortage of transport to Mount Rigi – and that's nothing new! A first inn was built there in 1815 after it became popular with poets and natural scientists. In 1873, Europe's first mountain train reached the top of this panoramic summit in a cloud of steam.

The Hammetschwand Lift (10)

Titlis, Engelberg

The Alp Tritt alpine hut, Niederbauen (12)

National Council chamber (14)

... the same view (14)

Leg 2

⑨ Two "noses" and a car ferry

After Vitznau, the Grand Tour passes by the "Upper Nose" (Ober Nas), where the waters of Lake Lucerne pass through an 850 metre wide strait. If all the water was pumped out of the lower lake there would be a 100 metre high waterfall here, without the upper lake ever drying out. In just 20 minutes the Tellsprung takes you and your car from the Förstli (Gersau) landing stage to Niederdorf, near Beckenried on the south shore (canton of Nidwalden).

⑩ The Hammetschwand Lift

Here it is at last, that brightly lit point that we could see at night from Lucerne! An almost vertical rocky path leads from Bürgenstock and Honegg car parks down to the lake. To return to the top, we take Europe's highest outdoor lift. It starts inside the mountain and reappears barely a minute later at the summit of the Hammetschwand. —> 10 km

⑪ Klewenalp and Stockhütte

The Klewenalp cable car is well known to motorists who see it crossing over the motorway shortly after it leaves the lower station at Beckenried. There are several restaurants and even a hotel up on the alpine slopes. Many visitors enjoy returning to Beckenried via Stockhütte and Seelisberg first with the cable car, followed by CarPostal bus then boat.

⑫ Niederbauen, Alp Tritt alpine hut, wildlife trail

The village of Emmetten lies on the road to Seelisberg. Visitor can reach Niederbauen from here by gondola lift and cable cars. The Alp Tritt alpine hut is also worth a detour, particularly for Hermann's mountain cheeses. The Niederbauen is also a starting point for paragliding and a trail to observe Oberbauenstock wildlife. —> 5 km

⑬ Seelisberg and its lake

From Emmetten, the road continues to Seelisberg in the canton of Uri. It ends in a cul-de-sac, at least as far as vehicles are concerned. Pedestrians can take the funicular railway down to the Treib landing stage, while walkers can set off on the "Swiss Path" towards Bauen. The small Lake Seelisberg, campsite and beach, is an enchanting spot. —> 12 km

⑭ The painting in the National Council chamber

So what exactly does the painting in the Federal Palace auditorium represent, and can we visit the place it was painted? The answer to that second question is yes. To admire the Cradle of the Confederation in real life, and a bird's eye view of the Rütli meadow, you have to climb up to Marienhöhe, about twenty minutes further up from Seelisberg. But don't expect to see a trout stranded on the rock: the one in the painting was an "April fool's" joke by the painter, in reference to the opening day of the Federal Palace on 1 April 1902. You return to Beckenried by the Seelisberg motorway tunnel. —> 12 km

The "Swiss Path" with Lake Uri, the Gitschen, the Uri Rotstock and Oberbauen (20)

Zwyssig memorial, Bauen (16)

Tellsplatte, Lake Uri (18)

William Tell memorial, Altdorf (17)

Axenstrasse, Brunnen (18)

Leg 2

⑮ Flüelen and the Lorelei Islands

On exiting the southern end of Seelisberg tunnel (9.3 kilometres long) you will discover a superb vista of the Uri Alps. To your left you can see the Lorelei Islands. Artificially built with 3.3 million tons of rock extracted when the Gotthard base tunnel was excavated, this small archipelago is Lake Lucerne's corner of paradise. The charming Seedorf beach is worth a detour.

⑯ Bauen and the Swiss Psalm

It is only since 1956 that a made-up road has linked the pretty village of Bauen to Seedorf. Before that, travellers had the choice between a mule track and boat. The Gotthard motorway is about one kilometre distant, running under the mountain. Fig and palm trees grow in Bauen due to the relatively mild climate of this sheltered bay. The house in which Father Alberik Zwyssig, composer of Switzerland's national anthem, was born is in the village centre.
—> 10 km

⑰ In William Tell's footsteps

Altdorf is the capital of the canton of Uri and the homeland of our national hero, William Tell. Places linked to this legendary figure are concentrated within a small area: a famous memorial and theatre, a themed pathway leading to the Tell fountain and the museum in Bürglen, the small town where Switzerland's liberator was born.

⑱ Tellsplatte on Lake Uri

The Axenstrasse, which links Flüelen to Brunnen, is a very busy road and it is advisable to make several halts. Don't miss the Tellsplatte, shortly before you reach Sisikon. It is said that this is where Tell managed to escape the clutches of the infamous Gessler by jumping from his boat. The chapel standing on the shore of the lake contains four frescoes: "the Rütli Oath", "the Shooting of the Apple", "Tell's leap" and "the Death of Gessler in the Hollow Way".

⑲ Rütli

A little further on, on the opposite side of the lake, is the birthplace of the Swiss Confederation. History tells us that on 1 August 1291, emissaries from the first cantons (Uri, Schwyz and Unterwalden) gathered together in Rütli meadow to form an eternal alliance. The simplest way to reach Rütli is to take a boat from Brunnen.

⑳ The Swiss Path

This pleasant hiking circuit around Lake Uri was created to celebrate the Confederation's 700th anniversary. Its 35 kilometres will take you from Rütli to Brunnen via Flüelen and Tellskapelle (Tell's Chapel). All the Swiss cantons are represented, starting with the original ones. Even the distance is proportionate to the population, with 5 millimetres per inhabitant!

The route

This section in the centre of Switzerland focuses on Lake Lucerne and the legendary figure of William Tell. Follow the road around Mount Rigi until you reach Gersau, cross Lake Uri by car ferry and explore the surrounding area as far as Brunnen and Schwyz.

Distance: 72 kilometres

Photo opportunity: After Vitznau, Lake Lucerne's many inlets around the "Ober Nas". Steep, rock face on the Axen, near Flüelen on Lake Uri. The new road goes through a tunnel; stop when you reach the Axenegg and continue on foot to admire the old road.

Did you know? The Swiss army knife was invented in 1890 for the Swiss army. Intended to help soldiers in all sorts of different situations, it held a blade and various tools in a light and compact form. To find out all about this legendary knife, visit the Victorinox museum and shop in Brunnen.

Worth a detour

(A) **Lucerne:** Swiss Museum of Transportation and film theatre – www.verkehrshaus.ch

(B) **Engelberg:** Cable cars at Titlis and exploring the glacier – www.titlis.ch

(C) **Buochs:** Canoeing on Lake Lucerne – www.kanuweg.ch

(D) **Brunnen:** Victorinox Knife Museum and Swiss Knife Valley Visitor Centre – www.swissknifevalley.ch

(E) **Morschach:** Swiss Holiday Park, water park – www.swissholidaypark.ch

Tourist information

Lucerne Tourism
Zentralstrasse 5, 6002 Lucerne
+41 (0)41 227 17 17; www.luzern.com

Lake Lucerne Navigation Company
Werftestrasse 5, 6002 Lucerne
+41 (0)41 367 67 67; www.lakelucerne.ch

Nidwalden Tourismus
Postfach 1045, 6371 Stans
+41 (0)41 610 88 33; www.nidwalden.com

Uri Tourismus
Schützengasse 11, 6460 Altdorf
+41 (0)41 874 80 00; www.uri.info

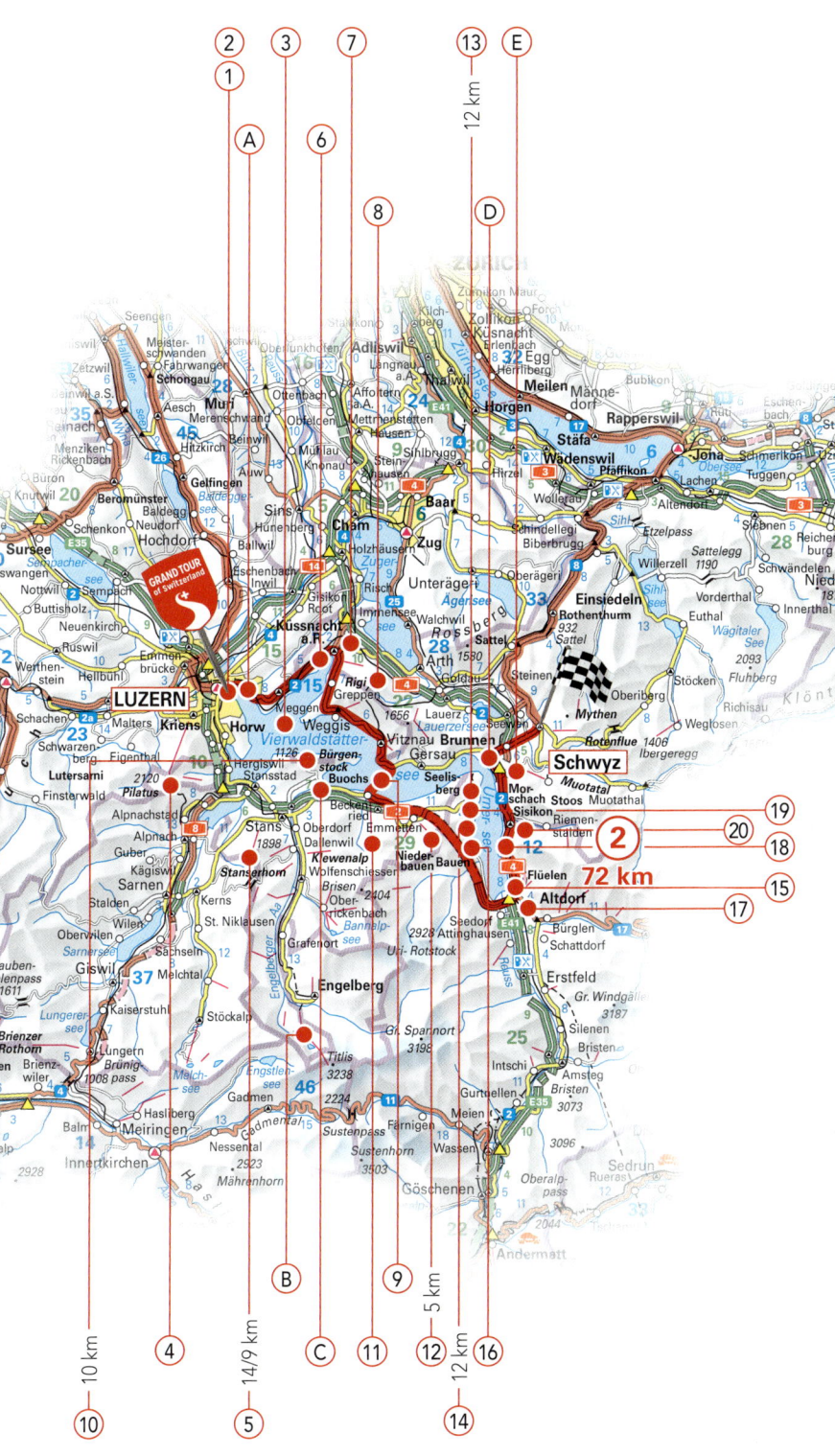

Lucerne – Schwyz
Lucerne – Lake Lucerne region

Sattel, between Schwyz and Rothenthurm

The Bethlehem House (2)

Schwyz (1)

High altitude path on Mythen (3)

Grosser Mythen (3)

Leg 3

Schwyz – Zurich

From Schwyz to Lake Zurich

We wave goodbye to Schwyz, with its large square and impressive town hall. The road starts to climb immediately towards Sattel and Rothenthurm's listed upland wetlands. It's thanks to Rothenthurm that wetland protection was included in the Federal Constitution. At Biberbrugg, don't resist the temptation to turn off and have a look at Einsiedeln Abbey. At Schindellegi we get our first view directly to the north of Lake Zurich, which we will continue to see until the end of the leg.

But for the moment, we make our way towards Pfäffikon and, via the road over the dam, to St. Gallen on the other side of the lake. The historic town of Rapperswil, with its 14th century castle, port and over 20,000 rose bushes, makes a relaxing place for a break before taking to the road again along the lake towards Zurich. Take your time: for one thing it's a fairly busy road, but most importantly there are some magnificent viewpoints over the lake which will make it impossible to resist stopping regularly to take photos! The shore has been nicknamed the "gold coast" in reference to its sumptuous villas and their rich owners. If the Lake Lucerne leg gave you a taste for car ferries, you can always cross over to the south shore at Meilen. You can catch up with the official Grand Tour itinerary by crossing the River Limmat by the first bridge. You will arrive in the Bellevue district.

Schwyz: at the foot of the two Mythen peaks

Schwyz, the eponymous capital of the canton, was mentioned for the first time in 972. In 1642 the town was almost entirely destroyed by fire. One of the very few houses to escape the flames is called the Bethlehem House and dates from 1287. The large square is Schwyz's nerve centre, where you can see the town hall with its painted facades, several impressive buildings and the parish church of St. Martin. A small weekly market is held there each Saturday.

Three important museums

The Ital-Reding estate is located on the Muotathal road and comprises a manor house, the Bethlehem House and a farm building (which now houses the canton's library). The museum is open from May to October.

The Forum of Swiss History occupies the former arsenal and provides a modern multimedia exhibition. Along with three other museums (the Landesmuseum in Zurich, the Château de Prangins on the shore of Lake Geneva and the Sammlungszentrum at Affoltern am Albis) it forms the Swiss Museum group. The recently re-opened Museum of the Swiss Charters of Confederation retraces the legend and reality of Swiss history. Did the Federal Charter of August 1291 really mark the official birth of the Confederation?

Upland moor landscape, Rothenthurm (10)

Edge of the wetlands near Bennau

Fronalpstock, Stoos (5)

Sattel-Hochstuckli (7)

Revolving gondola, Ägerisee (7/9)

Leg 3

The Mythen
③ The two majestic Mythen peaks, emblematic of Switzerland's birthplace, overlook the Schwyz basin. A steep path will take you from Holzegg (reached by cable car from Alpthal or the new cable car from the Rotenfluh) to the Grosser Mythen restaurant, 500 metres higher. —> 5 km

Rotenfluh and the Mythen region
④ A cable car has been in service to carry passengers up to the Rotenfluh since 1957. The new gondola lift now takes you from Rickenbach to the highest point at an altitude of 1,427 metres. This is the quickest way to enjoy the Mythen region, in both summer and winter.

Stoos: The Fronalpstock and the Klingenstock
⑤ The Fronalpstock plateau above Brunnen offers panoramic views and is accessible from the Muotathal and the traffic-free resort of Stoos, by funicular and chairlift. Experienced hikers will enjoy the spectacular ridge path which goes from the Klingenstock chairlift to the Fronalpstock. It is well made and part of it is protected with a safety chain. The cheese board served by Wisel at the Alp Laui alpine hut is worth a detour! —> 7 km

Muotathal: the Hölloch cave system, virgin forest and huskies
⑥ The remote Muota valley offers roaring waterfalls, fast-flowing torrents, a virgin forest (Bödmeren) and husky kennels. But for many visitors, the highlight is a visit to the spectacular "hellhole", the Hölloch cave system which is one of the world's largest, with 195 kilometres of galleries explored so far. The less daring will enjoy exploring one of three themed hiking trails: Frog and Weather, Jokes, and Creation. —> 13 km

Sattel-Hochstuckli
⑦ Shortly before reaching Rothenthurm plain you will see the Sattel-Hochstuckli leisure park on your right. The coloured gondolas which take visitors up to Mostelberg revolve twice on their own axis on the journey up. There is a small leisure park at the upper station with bouncy castle, trampoline and a summer toboggan run. The station's Skywalk is Europe's longest suspension footbridge at 374 metres in length.

Schwyz – Zurich
Lucerne – Lake Lucerne region

The battle of Morgarten (8)

Rothenthurm upland moors (10)

Chapel of the battle of Morgarten (8)

Near Biberbrugg

Wooden footbridge, Rapperswil (12)

Rapperswil (13)

Leg 3

⑧ The battle of Morgarten
In 1315, the young Confederates fought their first battle for freedom facing the Hochstuckli. To celebrate the 700th anniversary of this battle, an information centre was be opened in 2015 between Sattel and Ägerisee with a chapel, memorial and themed hiking trails. The complex retraces the battle of Morgarten and explores its historical, social and political implications.

⑨ Ägerisee
This small lake close to Morgarten lies in a landscape of hills and moraine between the Zugerberg and the Höhronen. Arctic char fished in the lake is served in local restaurants. There are many places around the lake to relax or swim in summer and a scheduled boat service links seven landing stages. —> 5 km

⑩ Rothenthurm upland moors
The trough-shaped valley which separates Rothenthurm from Biberbrugg contains Switzerland's largest area of wetlands. This vast landscape is not only an essential reservoir for flora and fauna but also a great place to spend a day out and get back to nature. Forests of pine and spruce, peat bogs, low marsh and the meanders of the River Biber with its characteristic vegetation all contribute to the charm of this region.

⑪ Einsiedeln Abbey and the black Madonna
This place of pilgrimage has attracted believers for over 1,000 years. The Chapel of Grace stands inside the baroque abbey, under a painted vaulted ceiling, and contains a black Madonna. In addition to the monks' cells the abbey also has a seminary, ten workshops, a cellar for the estate's wine and a recently renovated stable block, as the monks also raise horses. —> 6 km

⑫ Dam road, wooden footbridge and the Heilig Hüsli
Pfäffikon, in the canton of Schwyz, can be reached from Rapperswil, in the canton of St. Gallen, by a dam across Lake Zurich. In the Middle Ages, pilgrims on the Way of Saint James would cross with a simple floating pontoon. Today a modern, 841 metre wooden footbridge runs along the dam from the Hurden peninsula to the Heilig Hüsli, a small chapel built on an islet, and Rapperswil. With a handrail: you can't stop progress!

⑬ Rapperswil, town of roses on the shore of Lake Zurich
Rapperswil-Jona, on the shores of Lake Zurich, has a crest depicting two roses, but there are several thousand of them in the town's four rose gardens. The hill where the castle stands offers a panoramic view from the Glarus Alps to the Zürcher Oberland. On the lake, scheduled boats like the Stadt Rapperswil paddle steamer make the crossing to Zurich.

Einsiedeln Abbey square (11)

Near Schindellegi

Navigation on Lake Zurich (14)

Lützelsee lake (16)

On the shores of Lake Zurich (14)

Leg 3

A trip on Lake Zurich
(14) In former times Lake Zurich was used exclusively for transport of goods and people, but nowadays it is a highly sought-after residential and leisure area. The best way to enjoy its scenery is to take a trip on the lake, giving you the ideal excuse in summer to take a dip, or relax in a café on one of its beaches.

Bubikon Commandery
(15) This impressive site, dating from 1192, is the best preserved base in Switzerland of the order of the Knights Hospitaller. The courtyard, buildings, museum and café are open to visitors from April to October. The knights' hall, chapel, cellar and other areas are available for private events. —> 5 km

Lützelsee lake
(16) The characteristic moraine landscape between Rapperswil and Wetzikon was formed by the Rhine- Linth glacier. It is believed that the lake was formed where there had been an enormous block of dead glacial ice. Today it is a paradise for storks, nature-lovers and swimmers. You will also notice floating "gardens" on the lake, formed from reeds which have broken away from the shore.

The route

From the Mythen to the Höhronen, from early Switzerland to Lake Zurich. Take the road over the dam to Rapperswil then drive up the "gold coast" to the centre of Zurich.

Distance: 65 kilometres

Photo opportunity: Rothenthurm's upland moors have forged a place in history, firstly at the time of the Alemanni and again in 1987 with a citizen's initiative for wetland protection.

Did you know? The Via Jacobi is the Swiss section of the European pilgrim's trail, the Way of Saint James. Churches, abbeys and chapels line its route. The wooden footbridge (built in 2001) which links Rapperswil to Hurden, is on the Grand Tour itinerary.

To savour: Schafböcke, whose rounded form evokes that of a lamb lying in the grass, are traditional biscuits associated with the Einsiedeln pilgrimage. They are made with honey but unlike gingerbread, are filled. Shaped in wood or clay moulds, they are cooked at a high temperature so that they are golden on the outside but soft inside.

Worth a detour

(A) **Schwyz:** Museum of the Swiss Charters of Confederation, Charter of 1291 – www.bundesbriefmuseum.ch

(B) **Pfäffikon SZ:** Alpamare with water slides, wave pools, and wellness centre – www.alpamare.ch

(C) **Rapperswil:** Knie children's zoo, offers many activities – www.knieskinderzoo.ch

(D) **Seegräben:** Jucker Farm with shop and activities – www.juckerfarm.ch

Tourist information

Info Schwyz Tourismusbüro
Bahnhofstrasse 4, 6431 Schwyz
+41 (0)41 810 19 91; www.info-schwyz.ch

Morschach-Stoos Tourismus
Stooshorn 1, 6433 Stoos
+41 (0)41 818 08 80; www.morschach-stoos.ch

Einsiedeln Tourismus
Hauptstrasse 85, 8840 Einsiedeln
+41 (0)55 418 44 88; www.einsiedeln-tourismus.ch

Verkehrsverein Rapperswil-Jona
Fischmarktplatz 1, 8640 Rapperswil
+41 (0)55 220 57 57; www.vvrj.ch

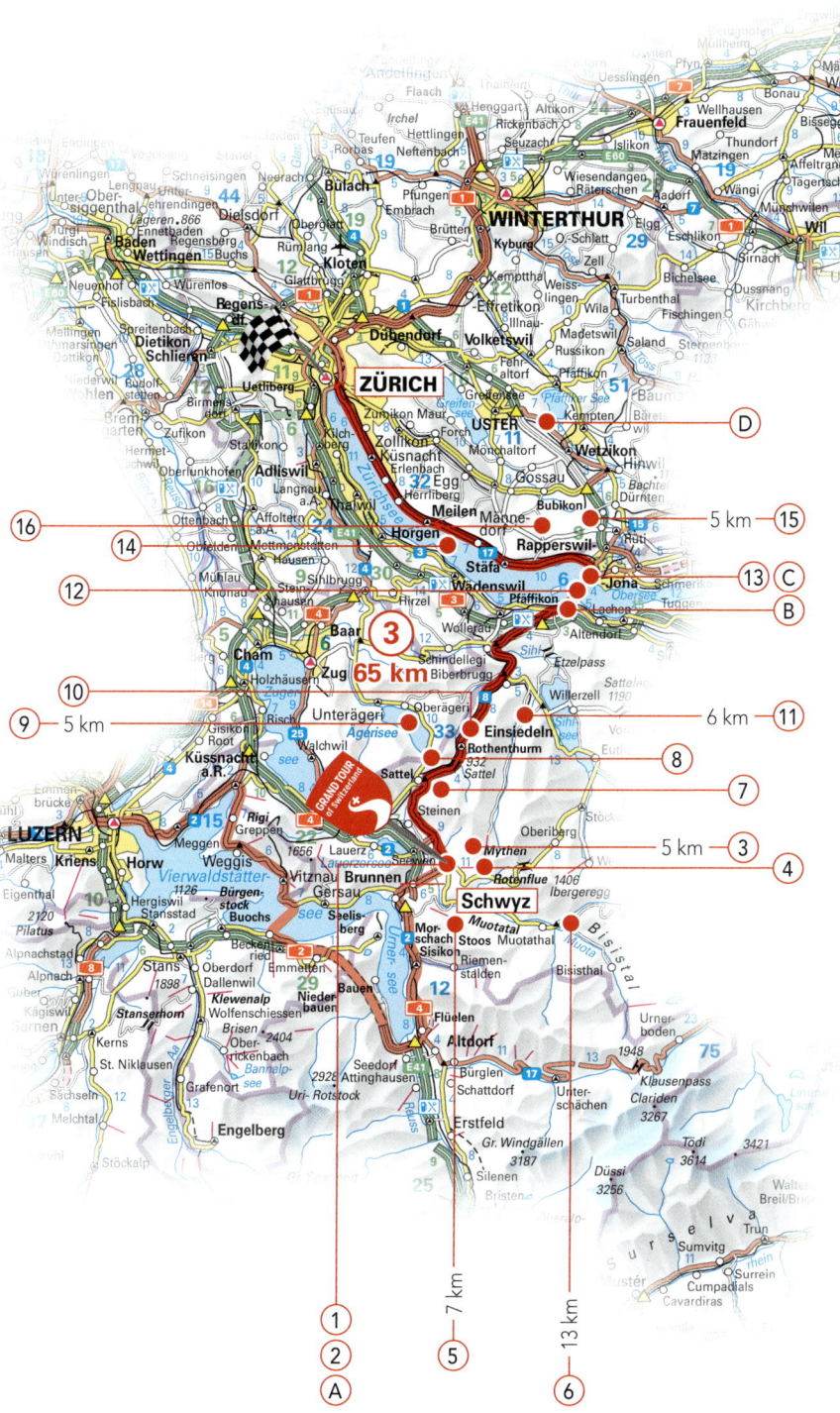

Schwyz – Zurich
Lucerne – Lake Lucerne region

GRAND TOUR of Switzerland

Zurich region

There is far more to Zurich than its airport, banks and Bahnhofstrasse. There are a thousand things to explore in the Niederdorf quarter, on the Rennweg or on the banks of the River Limmat and the lake. Winterthur is also worth a visit, with its museums and rich heritage. Lastly, the Weinland has superb half-timbered houses, castles and look-out towers.

River Limmat and the cathedral

Fraumünster Church, Quaibrücke bridge, Lake Zurich (1)

Zurich Cathedral (1)

The Niederdorf quarter (1)

Shopping in Zurich (1)

Navigation on the River Limmat (2)

Leg 4

Zurich – Schaffhausen

Northwards from Zurich towards Schaffhausen

Zurich is often seen simply as a chic and glamorous city, through the prism of its Bahnhofstrasse, Paradeplatz and zoo, without forgetting FIFA's headquarters. But that would be to forget that Switzerland's financial capital is also rich in picturesque areas on both sides of the Limmat, such as the Niederdorf quarter right in the city centre. Why not take the time to get to know Switzerland's largest city a little better through its cultural scene, events and museums?

We also find culture at Winterthur, just a few minutes away by car (exceptionally taking the motorway from Zurich Unterstrass). Live shows, cabarets and theatres abound here. This former industrial city, home to Sulzer, has been forced to reinvent itself over the last few decades. It has become an innovative city with an abundance of museums (the Oskar-Reinhart collection, Technorama, the Swiss Foundation of Photography).

But let's not spend all our time in towns! The road from Andelfingen to Schaffhausen takes us into the countryside at last. Take a look at the half-timbered houses in the Zurich winegrowing area at Marthalen, then make a little detour via the former abbey at Rheinau. Just outside Schaffhausen you will come across Laufen Castle (car park) and the Rhine Falls. Time to get out your camera!

① Zurich: Old Town, churches, Lindenhof and Bahnhofstrasse

Zurich's Altstadt (Old City) should not be missed under any circumstances. Here are some suggestions for an itinerary. The Grand Tour takes you to Niederdorf: guild houses, the famous Öpfelchammer restaurant, shops, café terraces and traditional craftsmen's workshops all contribute to the charm of this vibrant quarter.

To reach the panoramic viewing platform in Grossmünster Cathedral's Karlsturm tower you will have to climb 187 steps. The view is breathtaking – but no pain, no gain!

Take the Rathausbrücke bridge to cross the River Limmat (which had great importance during the industrial era) and enter the Old Town on the left bank.

Climb up to the indisputably romantic Lindenhof to enjoy (another!) fine view of the cathedral. Then onwards for a little window shopping on Bahnhofstrasse via Rennweg.

② A trip on the River Limmat and Lake Zurich

Amsterdam, Bruges and Venice have their canals, and Zurich has the Limmat and its boat trips. The embarkation point is near the Landesmuseum, just a stone's throw from the central railway station. There are three stops along the river (and three others in the harbour) and visitors are treated to a stunning view of the city's main landmarks on each side. All aboard for a relaxing experience in the heart of an urban landscape.

Landesmuseum: The Swiss National Museum (3)

Excursion on the Uetliberg (6)

Kyburg Castle (8)

Polybahn Funicular Railway (5)

Zurich-Kloten Airport (7)

Leg 4

③ Landesmuseum

The fairytale castle which houses the Landesmuseum stands close to Zurich's railway station. It is one of four museums which make up the Swiss Museum Group (with the Château de Prangins, the Forum of Swiss history in Schwyz and the Sammlungszentrum at Affoltern am Albis). It contains the country's largest collection of art: close to one million objects which recount the life of Switzerland from prehistory to modern times.

④ Freitag bags made from recycled materials

What could be uglier than a used truck tarpaulin? But what could be more stylish than a Freitag bag? A shop which offers the world's largest selection of these bags made from recycled tarpaulin (1,600 models on 4 stories) is located close to Hardbrücke railway station. Don't miss it when you're in Zurich.

⑤ Zurich's funicular and rack-and-pinion railways

Who would have thought it? Zurich too has its funicular railways. They are included in the Grand Tour. The Polybahn, inaugurated in 1889, now carries two million passengers per year. A funicular (now transformed into a rack-and-pinion railway) near the Dolder takes people up to the leisure park to escape from the hustle and bustle of urban living. The third funicular, which goes up to the Rigiblick, is 100% automatic. GA travelcards and tram tickets are valid in Zurichberg's three funicular and rack-and-pinion railways.

⑥ Uetliberg

Do you feel like gaining altitude for a bird's eye view over the rooftops? In Zurich, the finest vista over the town, the lake, the Glarus Alps, central Switzerland and even part of the Swiss Plateau can be found at the Uto Kulm hotel's panoramic tower (free entry). The summit is 20 minutes from Zurich station by the Uetlibergbahn. You can also reach Waldegg by car and continue by train.
—> 12 km

⑦ Zurich-Kloten Airport

The Grand Tour waves goodbye to Zurich close to the international airport. The airport's observation decks are equipped with multimedia binoculars, and information screens give information on airport operations and the aircraft on the runway. The public even has access to a tower from where they can glimpse the pilots in their cockpits. The Skymetro, which takes passengers to terminal E, glides on a 0.2 mm air cushion and is pulled by steel cables. That makes it a kind of cable car! —> 6 km

⑧ Kyburg Castle

Just before you reach Winterthur, stop off at Kyburg to learn what it was like to live in a castle. Belonging to the counts of the same name, the castle subsequently passed into the hands of the Habsburgs and then the Zurich bailiffs, who lived there until 1798. If you've ever wondered what a knight wore under his armour, or how a medieval fort was built, this new interactive museum is a must. —> 7 km

Münstergasse in Zurich

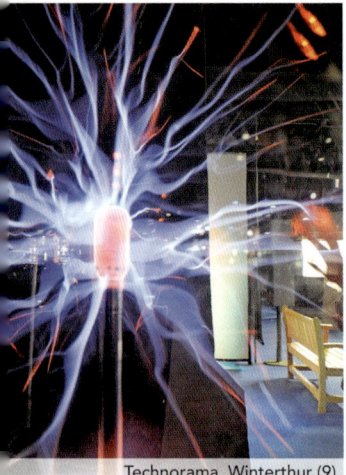
Technorama, Winterthur (9)

Zurich zoo

View from the north to south tower, Winterthur church

Leg 4

⑨ Winterthur: science is fun at Technorama

More than 500 experience stations explain, in simple terms, natural phenomena from electricity to magnetism, as well as sensory perception and even maths! Test, try, interact, create… this is a handson experience! The science centre is entirely suitable for children. It contains a self-service restaurant and picnic areas.

⑩ Winterthur Kunstmuseum

Culture, history and natural science are quite at home in Winterthur. It is home to no less than 17 museums, including the Kunstmuseum (Fine Arts Museum). The latter houses several impressionist masterpieces and modern works of art in the main building. The new building, in a radically different style, is the work of Basel-based architects Gigon and Guyer. Its temporary exhibitions present the work of little-known (but perhaps for not much longer) contemporary artists.

⑪ The Oskar-Reinhart Museum and Collection

The Oskar Reinhart am Stadtgarten Museum is housed in a former college and since 1951 has exhibited some 600 paintings by Swiss, German and Austrian artists as well as 7,000 engravings and drawings from the 15th to the 20th century. The Ferdinand Hodler paintings are particularly noteworthy.

The Am Römerholz Collection, for its part, occupies Oskar Reinhart's former home, a villa surrounded by mature trees in a magnificent garden in the upper part of Winterthur. This remarkable 20th century collection includes not only Impressionist paintings by Renoir, Cézanne and Monet but also superb paintings by Old Masters such as Rubens, Goya and Bruegel.

⑫ The Irchel

Shortly after Winterthur we reach the Irchel on our left, a small wooded upland area wedged between the Töss, the Thur and the Rhine. Its highest point is only 694 metres but it played a significant historical role. It was part of the Roman Empire's Rhineland fortifications and was later included in the Zurich chain of watchtowers. The modern Irchel tower (28 metres) has no defensive mission but offers a breathtaking view of the Weinland. A landscape of vineyards spreads out below the Irchel while to the north there are several castles and step-gabled manors. —> 8 km

⑬ Ebersberg, former artillery fort

Fort Ebersberg, also known as Fort Rüdlingen, was a military secret until 2003. It is one of very few to be located near a border in Switzerland and is a monument with historical national significance. It was carved out of the rock (without the help of machines) between 1938 and 1940 to prevent enemy troops crossing the Rhine. You can visit the outside buildings with interpretive displays but the interior is only accessible to groups with a guided tour. —> 9 km

Half-timbered houses, Marthalen (16)

Watchtower (15)

Wyden Castle

Rheinau Abbey (17)

Husemersee

Leg 4

⑭ Flaach, alluvial plain of the River Thur

Nature lovers would not want to miss making a small detour to the west at Andelfingen. The Swiss Plateau's largest alluvial area (nearly 400 hectares) lies at the confluence of the Thur and the Rhine. A ground-breaking project to preserve landscapes has returned the river to its natural course over the last few kilometres before it joins the Rhine. The Thur is once more free to form meanders and to overflow in times of flood. There is an information centre with restaurant on the banks of the Rhine, near the Flaach campsite and swimming pool. —> 9 km

⑮ Wildensbuch, Zürcher Weinland and watchtower

An old watchtower stands on the other side of the motorway, near Benken. Climb to the top of this 36 metre high wooden tower for an impressive view of Zurich's Weinland region. The tower is accessible on foot (a one kilometre walk) from the village of Wildensbuch, where you can park your car. The Hochwart tower has 186 steps to the top. —> 5 km

⑯ Marthalen: picturesque half-timbered buildings

The region between Winterthur and Schaffhausen is renowned for its red-beamed half-timbered houses. They are in fact traditional wooden frames which have been reinforced with diagonal and horizontal support beams. The village of Marthalen has some very fine examples of this style of architecture.

⑰ Rheinau Abbey and island

A little way short of the Rhine Falls, the river makes a remarkable double loop. A former Benedictine abbey stands on a small island; its baroque-style church can be visited to this day. Services are held there regularly but it also hosts the famous "Rheinau concerts". An on-site hotel has been specially built for the musicians, with practice rooms and halls for orchestras, choirs and other musical ensembles.

The route

Motorway to Winterthur and the Zurich vineyard, then small roads from Andelfingen to the Rhine Falls and Laufen Castle.

Distance: 55 kilometres

Photo opportunity: Two watchtowers (Irchel and Wildensbuch) in a region whose landscapes are relatively little known. Pretty half-timbered houses in the village of Marthalen.

To savour: The Triggel, a Zurich speciality, is a hard, thin little biscuit with a golden surface decorated with a variety of patterns. Triggel connoisseurs let each mouthful melt on the tongue to enjoy the honey flavour to the full.

Worth a detour

(A) **Zurich:** Grossmünster Cathedral – stained glass, tours – www.grossmuenster.ch

(B) **Zurich:** Kunstmuseum (Giacometti, Picasso, Monet, Chagall, Munch) – www.kunsthaus.ch

(C) **Zurich:** The Rietberg Museum (Asian, African, American and Oceanic art) – www.rietberg.ch

(D) **Zurich:** Zoo with 360 different species and Masoala tropical greenhouse – www.zoo.ch

(E) **Zurich:** Boat trips on the lake and the Limmat – www.zsg.ch

(F) **Wintherthur:** Swiss Foundation of Photography – www.fotomuseum.ch

Tourist information

Zurich Tourismus
Im Hauptbahnhof, 8001 Zurich
+41 (0)44 215 40 00; www.zuerich.com

Zurichsee Schifffahrtsgesellschaft
Bürkliplatz, 8001 Zurich
+41 (0)44 487 13 33; www.zsg.ch

Winterthur Tourismus
Im Hauptbahnhof, 8401 Winterthur
+41 (0)52 267 67 00; www.einsiedeln-tourismus.ch

ProWeinland
Thurhaldenstrasse 14, 8451 Kleinandelfingen
+41 (0)52 317 47 14; www.zuercher-weinland.ch

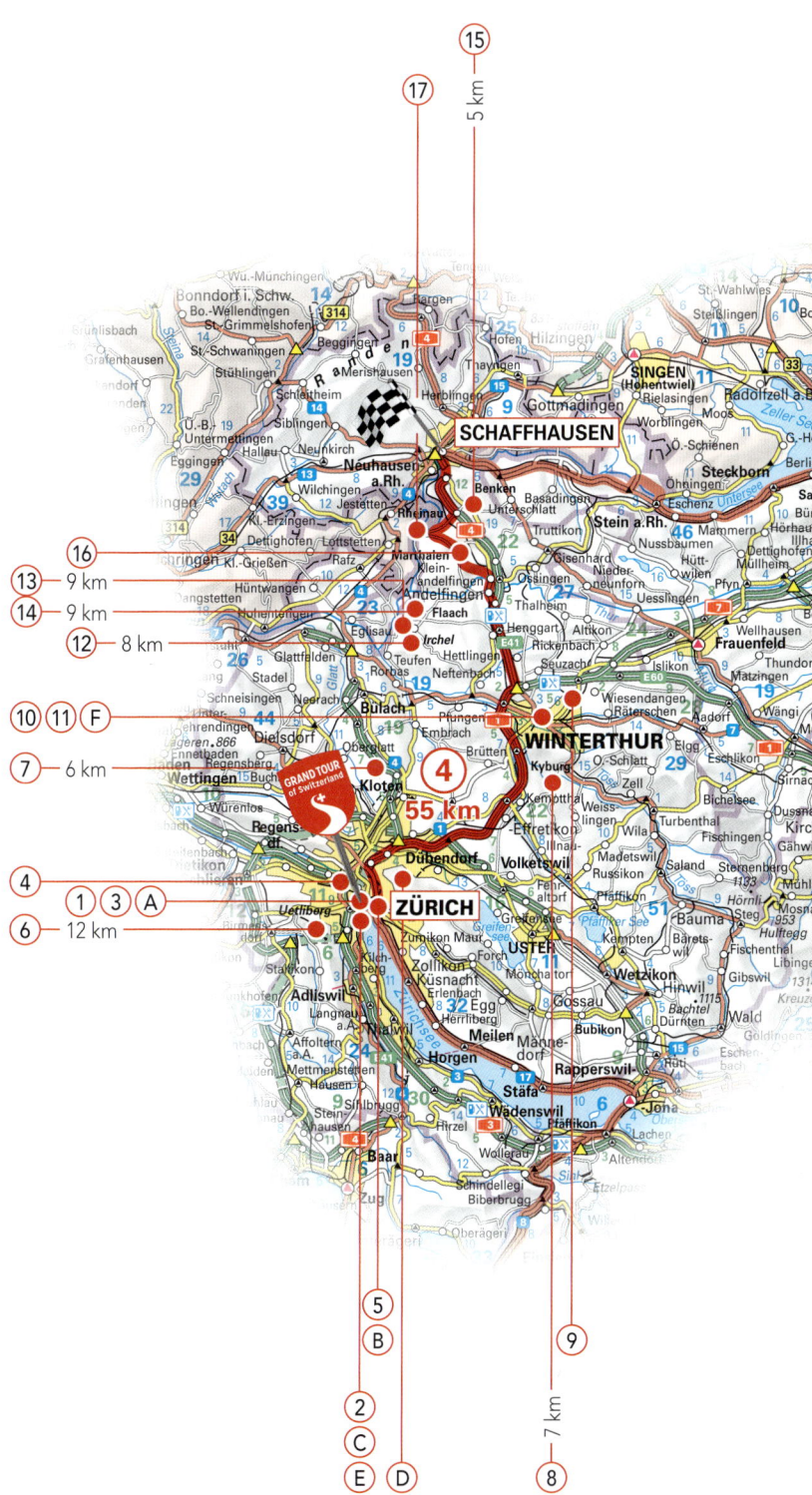

Zurich – Schaffhausen
Zurich region

Eastern Switzerland – Liechtenstein

What if Eastern Switzerland became a canton? The question sometimes makes waves in the worlds of politics and media. In the meantime, Eastern Switzerland offers the Rhine Falls, the orchards of Thurgau, the city of the Prince-Abbots of St. Gallen and – beyond the Appenzell hills – the impressive Alpstein range, Toggenburg, the Rhine Valley and the Glaris region.

The road to Schwägalp, Toggenburg

Rhine Falls (1)

Schaffhausen Old Town (2)

Boats on the Untersee

The Munot fortress, Schaffhausen (2)

Randen observation tower, Beringen (3)

Leg 5

Schaffhausen – St. Gallen

The Upper Rhine, Untersee and Lake Constance

After a fabulous stay in Schaffhausen, with its spectacular Rhine Falls, pretty oriel windows in the Old Town, many gourmet restaurants and the Munot Fortress, it's time to move on along the Rhine towards Stein am Rhein. Leave your car in one of the many car parks at the gates of this historic town and wander at your leisure through its narrow streets. With its perfectly preserved medieval centre, Benedictine abbey and impressive Hohenklingen Castle, Stein am Rhein's reputation has long since spread beyond Switzerland's borders.

We then follow the lower shore of Untersee, passing Napoleon's Castle on the way and then Steckborn before we reach Kreuzlingen, a town on the shore of Lake Constance. On your left lies Lake Constance (known colloquially as the Swabian Sea by our German neighbours) and on your right Mostindien, Thurgau's apple-growing region. The Grand Tour then takes you to Romanshorn (where the ferry leaves for Friedrichshafen) and Arbon, a little-known gem with a maze of narrow streets and splendid half-timbered houses. This is where you take your leave of Lake Constance, unless you decide to continue to the village of Altenrhein to visit the Hundertwasser market, for example. You now cross a rolling, wooded landscape as you make your way towards the former ecclesiastical principality of St. Gallen. This section of the route is particularly enchanting in springtime, when the apple and pear trees are in blossom.

① Rhine Falls: 700,000 litres of water

On average, 700,000 litres of water cascade over these 150 metre wide and 23 metre high falls, each second! Welcome to one of Europe's largest waterfalls. You can watch this impressive (and roaring) spectacle from Laufen Castle or Wörth castle on the opposite bank. Visitors can take a small boat to an islet surrounded by a mist of spray.

② Schaffhausen: Old Town and Munot fortress

A maze of narrow streets, a cultural heritage which is both gothic and baroque and a multitude of fountains: Schaffhausen takes you 1,000 years back in time. Oriel windows and richly-decorated façades make the pedestrian-only Old Town one of the most picturesque in Switzerland. It is overlooked by the circular Munot fortress, which dates from the 16th century and has become the town's emblem. Every evening at 9 pm the tower guard rings a bell which in former times signalled the closing of the town's gates and inns.

③ The Randen

North of Schaffhausen is a small part of the Jura mountains called the Randen. This natural reserve is notable for its combination of wooded areas and agricultural land. The wildflower meadows on south-facing slopes contain sun-loving plants, including some rare varieties of orchid. —> 10 km

Stein am Rhein (5)

Stein am Rhein (5)

Steckborn (8)

Diessenhofen (4)

The Napoleon Museum (9)

Leg 5

④ Boats on the High Rhine, Untersee and Lake Constance

Boat of all sizes run scheduled services between Schaffhausen, Untersee, Lake Constance and the Alter Rhein (old Rhine). The smallest boats link Schaffhausen to Kreuzlingen on the High Rhine and Untersee via Stein am Rhein, Steckborn and Constance. The larger ones sail from Meersburg to Lindau in Germany via Kreuzlingen and Rorschach.

⑤ Stein am Rhein

Shortly before arriving at Untersee, where Lake Constance becomes the Rhine once more, the Grand Tour takes you to this small town with well-preserved half-timbered houses, pretty oriel windows and brightly-painted facades. Take the time to visit one of its museums, or just to stroll around this charming and lively town on the banks of the Rhine. In December you'll find a Christmas market and magical atmosphere.

⑥ Hohenklingen Castle

A medieval fortress with a stunning view of the Rhein and the lake stands watch over Stein am Rhein. There is free access to the square tower, inner courtyard and gallery, and the castle also houses a very pleasant restaurant. Hohenklingen is a brisk half hour's walk from the town centre. There is also limited parking space behind the castle.

⑦ Roman and medieval heritage around Stein am Rhein

Stein am Rhein and the surrounding area have many historic monuments which are worth a visit such as the chapel on Werd Island, the church and the Roman fortress of Burg, the very fine abbey church in Wagenhausen and the monastery of St. George. This magnificent example of a Benedictine abbey is both Gothic and Renaissance in style. Its late Gothic cloister is particularly noteworthy as are the Renaissance frescoes in the banqueting hall.

⑧ Steckborn small town, lake and sewing machines

This small town is situated halfway between Stein am Rhein and Kreuzlingen on two tips of land on Untersee. Scheduled boat and ferry services leave from Steckborn for Germany, or navigate the Rhein as far as Schaffhausen. Take a look at the half-timbered houses which are typical of the region, the town hall and the regional museum housed in the Turmhof, the town's emblem. Steckborn was also the birthplace of the famous Bernina sewing machine. A small exhibition is devoted to it at the entrance to the company's premises.

⑨ Salenstein: Arenenberg Castle and Napoleon museum

In the hills above Lake Constance stands the elegant castle where Louis-Napoleon, future French Emperor, grew up. His mother, Hortense de Beauharnais, decorated it with Empire wall hangings, furniture and paintings in memory of her step-father Napoleon Bonaparte. The castle has now been turned into a museum and is open to the public.

Entrance to the port, Constance

Half-timbered house, Arbon (10)

Swimming pool on stilts, Lake Constance (11)

Hundertwasser market (13)

Fruit tree in Thurgau cider country (10)

Leg 5

On the shores of Lake Constance

⑩ To the right you have a fine view of Lake Constance and to the left Thurgau's cider-producing area, Mostindien. Rollerbladers can have a wonderful time skating by the sparkling waters of the lake. At Romanshorn, the port installations are a reminder that goods were transported by water up until 1976. Today there is a ferry link to Friedrichshafen with departures several times a day.

Arbon's Old Town is fascinating, with narrow twisted streets and pretty half-timbered houses (Untertorgasse and Fischmarktplatz) as well as a 16th century castle. The town was also home to Saurer, a former manufacturer of heavy goods vehicles. Some of its finest models, built between 1911 and 1980, are on display at the Saurer museum.

Rorschach beach and historic baths

⑪ If you would like to cool down after this long tour through a historic and picturesque area, just make a detour to Rorschach for a swim. The bath-house on stilts (1924), with its immense roof, is the last of its kind to have been preserved on Lake Constance. This heritage site hosts cultural events on summer evenings. —> 6 km

On the Alter Rhein (old Rhine)

⑫ A pleasure boat also makes the crossing from Rorschach to Rheineck. It starts by crossing the bay and takes 30 minutes to reach the mouth of the old Rhine, near Rheinspitz. The passage through the straight canal which leads to Rheineck offers an excellent opportunity to observe many species of wild birds. You can return to Rorschach by train or car, unless you prefer to take the rack-and-pinion railway to Walzenhausen to explore Appenzell's Joke Trail. —> 7 km

Altenrhein: Hundertwasser market

⑬ Another place to visit in the Rorschach area is Altenrhein's market, a whimsical and dreamlike building with golden domes, bright colours, curved shapes, strange little unmatched windows, ceramic-clad pillars and planted roof. You will probably have recognised Austrian architect Hundertwasser's magical style. —> 11 km

The small town of Bischofszell

⑭ This is our last little outing in the canton of Thurgau before we reach our destination. Bischofszell certainly merits its nickname of "town of roses". It offers an unending supply of new rose gardens, rose weeks, themed parties etc. It is also renowned for its baroque architecture. Its superb town hall (1750) alone is worth the journey, with its pink blush walls and black and gold wrought iron. The old eight arch stone bridge dates to around 1500. —> 11 km

Schaffhausen – St. Gallen
Eastern Switzerland – Liechtenstein

The route

Follow the Rhine, Untersee and Lake Constance as far as Arbon, then take minor roads to cross the lands of the prince-abbots of St. Gallen.

Distance: 98 kilometres

Photo opportunity: Idyllic landscapes around Stein am Rhein then the shores of Untersee. The road leaves Lake Constance at Arbon and crosses the orchards of Thurgau.
Roggwil Castle, Mammertshofen Castle.

Did you know? The name Mostindien, which designates an area to the east of the canton of Thurgau, was invented in 1853 by a humorous weekly paper. "Most" rhymes with "ost" (east) and means "must" (or unfermented juice – from apples, it goes without saying!). As for "Indien", it refers to the shape of the canton, which with a little imagination looks like India.

Worth a detour

(A) **Stein am Rhein** Lindwurm Museum (19th century life) – www.museum-lindwurm.ch

(B) **Stein am Rhein** Miniature train and park – www.steinerliliputbahn.ch

(C) **Lipperswil:** Connyland leisure park – www.connyland.ch

(D) **Rorschach:** Würth Forum, art exhibitions and shop – www.wuerth-haus-rorschach.ch

(E) **Altenrhein:** Aviation museum – www.fliegermuseum.ch

Tourist information

Schaffhauserland Tourismus
Herrenacker 15, 8201 Schaffhausen
+41 (0)52 632 40 20; www.schaffhauserland.ch

Koordinationsstelle Rheinfall (Rhine Falls)
Stokarbergstrasse 125, 8204 Schaffhausen
+41 (0)52 620 49 11; www.rheinfall.ch

Tourismus Stein am Rhein
Oberstadt 3, 8260 Stein am Rhein
+41 (0)52 632 40 32; www.tourismus.steinamrhein.ch

Thurgau Tourismus
Egelmoosstrasse 1, 8580 Amriswil
+41 (0)71 414 11 44; www.thurgau-tourismus.ch

Schaffhausen – St. Gallen
Eastern Switzerland – Liechtenstein

Transhumance festival, Appenzell (9)

Ebenalp (8)

Äscher Guesthouse (8)

On Gallusplatz, St. Gallen (1)

St. Gallen collegiate church (1)

Leg 6

St. Gallen – Wildhaus

Appenzell region and Toggenburg

We cannot leave St. Gallen without a visit to the abbey library, a World Heritage Site since 1983. The cathedral with its baroque style façade is the town's cultural emblem. The abbey buildings house one of the world's oldest and finest libraries. Pass by the lakes where St. Gallen bathed and follow the road which leads upwards to the Appenzell region. The cantons of Appenzell Inner Rhodes and Appenzell Outer Rhodes offer a succession of stunning landscapes. The route may not seem long in terms of distance, but offers a multitude of things to see and do. You will notice that the houses are different and that people here are shorter than elsewhere… which they make up for with their legendary sense of humour. And if it sometimes has a bite to it, it's a quality they share with the Appenzeller Mountain Dog, which is both watchdog and sheepdog. You won't be breaking any speed limits as you enjoy the many panoramic view points, picturesque villages, medicinal herb gardens, museums and convivial inns!

After the Appenzell region we climb upwards to Schwägalp, alpine pastures at the foot of the Säntis, a spectacular summit in the Alpstein range which can be reached by cable car. The leg ends in Toggenburg, the home of double Olympic ski-jumping champion Simon Ammann, with Wildhaus as the final destination.

① St. Gallen: Abbey precinct and library

St. Gallen is a multi-faceted town. The old city centre is partly pedestrian, so you can safely stroll around and admire the town's magnificent oriel windows. The abbey precinct, including the baroque cathedral and famous library, has been a UNESCO World Heritage Site since 1983. The reading room, with its rococo decoration, is simply superb. The collection contains some 160,000 works, many of which are amongst the earliest printed books, and over 400 volumes which date from before the year 1000.

② The three lakes of St. Gallen

When the sun is hot in St. Gallen you don't have to go all the way to Lake Constance to cool down. The Grand Tour takes you to the famous Drei Weieren (Three Lakes) and public bathing houses. These ponds, originally made to provide the Abbey with water or to be used in case of fire, are some of Switzerland's most beautiful natural bathing spots.

③ Appenzell train network

If you think of Appenzell, the region's red trains will also doubtless come to mind. Since 2006, the entire rail network in the hills between St. Gallen and the Rhine Valley has been placed under the management of a single company, Appenzeller Bahnen (AB). The lines concerned are: St. Gallen – Gais – Appenzell, Gossau – Appenzell – Wasserauen, St. Gallen – Trogen, Rorschach – Heiden, Rheineck – Walzenhausen and Altstätten – Gais. Some of the lines are rack-and-pinion railways.

The Bollenwees mountain inn

Eggen high-altitude trail (5)

The Joke Trail (4)

Cow bell factory

Appenzell region

Seealpsee with the Altmann in the background, Alpstein region (8)

Leg 6

④ From Heiden to Walzenhausen: the Joke Trail

When you're driving towards the Appenzell region, if you feel like a laugh, make a detour via Heiden. The nine kilometre Joke Trail takes you to Walzenhausen, and the 80 signs along the way will give you a taste of the region's famous sense of humour through the jokes they tell (in German and dialect).
—> 12 km

⑤ Waldegg: Eggen high-altitude trail and herb garden

Between Vögelinsegg and Teufen, the Grand Tour runs alongside the Eggen range. Stop here to enjoy a walk, a meal at the traditional Waldegg restaurant, or take a look at Dr. A. Vogel's medicinal herb garden and pharmacy. There is a hiking trail interspersed with information boards on local plants between Waldegg and the herb garden.

⑥ Gais: a traditional village and former health resort

In bygone days people came to Gais for the clean air. Nowadays, visitors also admire the large square with scroll-gabled houses, typical of Appenzell's baroque architecture. Gais was famous in the 19th century for its whey health cures. A museum retraces the village's history from 1750 to 1900 through an interesting collection of paintings and drawings.

⑦ The Gäbris: a striking panorama

You can't continue on your way without a small detour to the Gäbris. You will discover an idyllic lake there, and above all a spectacular panorama from the summit (the most southerly in the Swiss Pre-Alps (1,251 m). The Unterer Gäbris mountain inn is delightful. Note the baby-changing table with a direct view of… the cowshed! —> 6 km

⑧ The Alpstein range

The Alpstein range reveals its full beauty between Gais and Appenzell, with the Hoher Kasten, the Ebenalp, the Altmann, the Säntis and on the right, the Kronberg. You can take a cable car from Brülisau to the Hoher Kasten, and another from Wasserauen to the Ebenalp, which is the starting point for hiking trails leading up to the caves (which used to be inhabited) and the famous Äscher mountain hut. The lakes (Seealpsee, Sämtisersee and Fählensee) are all worth making a detour. —> 7 km

⑨ Appenzell's rustic paintings

Appenzell's main street is a traffic-free zone, so you can walk along safely as you admire the brightly-painted façades of the houses. The different patterns, coats of arms and symbols are so varied and so numerous that it would be difficult to imagine what meaning lies behind them. The Löwen-Drogerie for its part is covered in paintings of medicinal plants.

Seealpsee and, in the background, the Säntis and its transmitter (8)

Schwägalp wetland (11)

Säntis cable car (12)

Stein cheese dairy

View of the Hoher Kasten from the Gäbris

Leg 6

From Gontenbad to Jakobsbad: barefoot trail

(10) The barefoot trail leaves from Gontenbad, a hamlet just outside Appenzell. It takes you along the golf course before crossing a landscape of wet meadows and reaching the Kronberg upper cable car station at Jakobsbad. Half way along you can plunge your arms into the water of a fountain, in line with the famous Dr. Kneipp's method, and when you arrive you can cool down your feet in a mountain stream. This walk will surprise you by the different sensations it gives the soles of your feet. You can return to your car by going back along the same path (allow about 90 minutes), or take a red train, which will take you back to your departure point in just 5 minutes.

Adventure and discovery at Schwägalp

(11) Many visitors just park at Schwägalp to take the cable car up to the Säntis. But this alpine meadow is really well worth a longer visit. A new hotel was opened in 2015. Educational trails of every distance and on every theme leave from each side of the pass: wetlands, environment, forest, alpine economy and geology.

The Säntis

(12) Climbing aboard the "Schwebebahn" is an unforgettable experience. This cable car leaves from Schwägalp and passes high above rocky ledges before it reaches the summit. As you look out from the panoramic platform inside the base of the transmitter, try to name each of the peaks you can see around you. Sunset and sunrise on the Säntis are memorable, as are journeys up in the cable car at night with a full moon, or a stay at the Alter Säntis inn.

Who can find the Ofenloch?

(13) To the west of the Schwägalp Pass lies a wild and romantic wooded valley where the River Necker rises. This natural reserve offers you a great adventure: to set off in search of the Ofenloch, an immense cavern in the rock face with 100 metre high waterfalls. It's not for nothing that they call it the "Grand Canyon of eastern Switzerland"!

The seven peaks of the Churfirsten

(14) At Neu St. Johann you suddenly discover a view of the Churfirsten. Many travellers know these seven peaks only from the other side, from Walenstadt lake. This true emblem of Toggenburg forms a chain from Wildhaus to Wil.

Starkenbach: old-style cable car to reach Wildmannlisloch

(15) The first way of getting up to the Churfirsten is by aerial lift at Starkenbach, and it's a real adventure! An old-fashioned wooden cable car takes you to Strichboden, from where it takes just 20 minutes on foot to reach the mysterious Wildmannlisloch (wild man's hole) which children love to explore. The trail continues to the Sellamat and the Iltios, where you can return by the road.

The route

Leaving from St. Gallen, roam through the Appenzell region passing through Gais and the picturesque village of Appenzell. Then skirt around the Alpstein until you reach Alt Toggenburg.

Distance: 71 kilometres

Photo opportunity: The Appenzell hills with the historic site of Vögelinsegg, Speicher, Teufen and Gais. The route from Urnäsch to the Schwägalp Pass (1,278 m), then the Säntis and Neu St. Johann (Toggenburg).

To savour: The recipe for Biber and Biberli goes back about 500 years. These biscuits made with honey are filled with hazelnuts and decorated with different patterns.

Worth a detour

(A) **Stein AR:** The Appenzell cheese dairy, guided tours – www.schaukaeserei.ch

(B) **Appenzell:** Appenzeller beer, tour of the Brauquöll brewery – www.appenzellerbier.ch

(C) **Jakobsbad:** Kronberg cable car, bobsleigh run, treetop adventure park – www.kronberg.ch

(D) **Urnäsch:** Appenzell Folk Art Museum www.museum-urnaesch.ch

Tourist information

St.Gallen-Bodensee Tourismus
Bahnhofplatz 1a, 9001 St. Gallen
+41 (0)71 227 37 37; www.st.gallen-bodensee.ch

Appenzellerland Tourismus AR
Bahnhofstrasse 2, 9410 Heiden
+41 (0)71 898 33 00; www.appenzellerland.ch

Appenzellerland Tourismus AI
Hauptgasse 4, 9050 Appenzell
+41 (0)71 788 96 41; www.appenzell.info

Säntis cable car
Talstation, 9107 Schwägalp
+41 (0)71 365 65 65; www.saentisbahn.ch

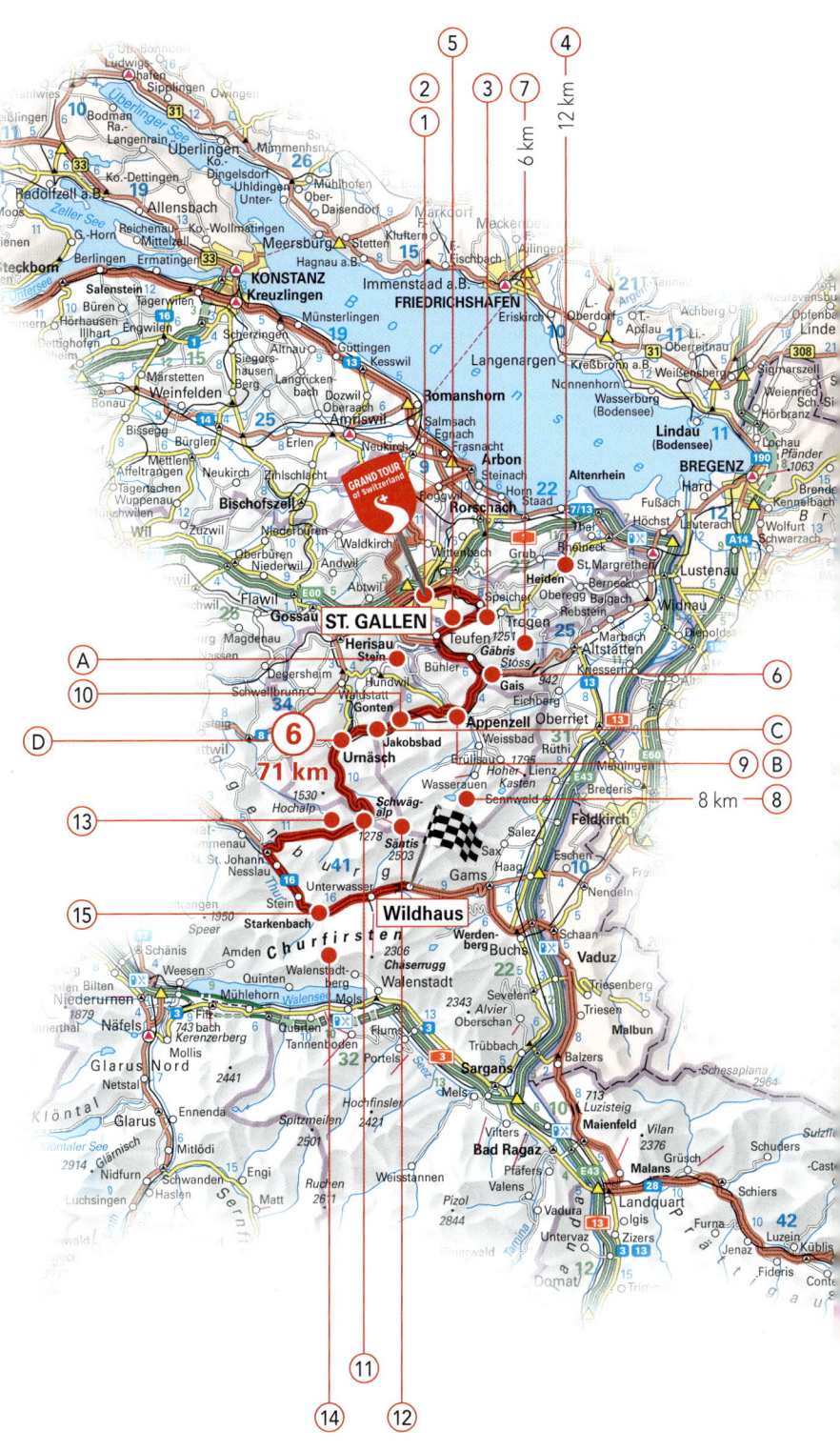

St. Gallen – Wildhaus
Eastern Switzerland – Liechtenstein

Between Toggenburg and the Rhine Valley with Margelchopf in the background

Krinau, Toggenburg

Werdenberg (3)

Wildhaus, Schönenbodensee (2)

Sound trail (1)

Leg 7

Wildhaus – Davos

From the Rhine Valley to the Prättigau Valley

After the slight rise between Alt Toggenburg and Wildhaus the road suddenly descends into the Rhine Valley, which we cross after a short visit to the small fortified town of Werdenberg. Without the slightest formality we now cross into the Principality of Liechtenstein; highlights are the impressive royal castle and the capital of Vaduz, well-known for its banking activity. We then follow a charming road which takes us, via the St. Luzisteig Pass, to the picturesque vineyards of Maienfeld. This is the home of Heidi, Johanna Spyri's young heroine.

When you reach Landquart you are only 16 kilometres from Chur, if you would like to have a look at the canton of Graubünden's pretty capital. The Grand Tour now forks to take you through the "Chlus", and the new road tunnel in Prättigau Valley, which leads to Klosters. Connoisseurs of architecture will make sure to take a look at the impressive Salginatobel bridge, near Schiers. The main road through the Prättigau Valley is lined with picturesque hamlets on each side, and villages to explore such as Fideris and Serneus. But perhaps you would rather climb up to the Sulzfluh, in the St. Antönien Valley?

At Klosters, don't be surprised if you bump into a member of the British royal family. For this is where Prince Charles and his sons learned to ski! Klosters, with its small mountain village atmosphere, makes a charming contrast to neighbouring Davos, better known for its international summit meetings.

Toggenburg mountain trains

The Grand Tour takes you to one of the seven Churfirsten peaks, namely the Chäserrugg (via the north face). Mountain trains and aerial lifts will take you to the Iltios, Alp Sellamatt, the Gamsalp and the Gamplüt. A miniature cable car links Starkenbach to Wildmannlisloch and a chair lift runs from Krummenau to Wolzenalp. Families will particularly enjoy the Toggenburg Sound trail, which features 25 different sound installations which everyone is welcome to try out for themselves.

Wildhaus: Schönenbodensee

This picturesque mountain lake extends an invitation to take some time for… doing nothing at all! This natural lake set in superb scenery near Wildhaus has a jetty, pedalos and a climbing tower. An ideal spot for families and nature-lovers to swim and relax.

Werdenberg, Europe's smallest town

Werdenberg, a short distance from Buchs, is a tiny medieval town with wooden buildings. It has just 34 houses, a castle on a rocky spur (guided tours) and a superb lake. A little further north a small cable car takes you directly to the Stauberenkanzel, from where you can reach the Alpstein.

Gams in the Rhine Valley with the Saxerlücke in the background

Vaduz Castle (4)

The Walser village of Steg (5)

The Älplibahn gondola lift, Malans (10)

Sargans (6)

Spitzmeilen SAC refuge with the Alvier in the background (7)

Leg 7

④ Vaduz, small city and castle

The contrast between historic landmarks (including the 17th century royal castle) and modern award-winning buildings (such as the parliament and the art museum) is what makes Liechtenstein's capital so charming. There are also a large number of gourmet restaurants and cultural sites in Vaduz.

⑤ Walser village of Malbun, Triesenberg (Liechtenstein)

The town of Triesenberg is worth a visit for its museum, which retraces the history of the Walser people who migrated to the region from the canton of Valais and northern Italy in the 13th century. You can travel on to Steg and Malbun (the principality's ski-resort) via a tunnel. You can watch a falconry demonstration here, or go for a day's hike on the Princess Gina trail. —> 13 km

⑥ Sargans: castle and iron ore mine

Sargans Castle, the town's emblem, overlooks the surrounding countryside and offers a panoramic view. Its tower houses the Sarganserland museum and a restaurant. Iron ore was discovered on the slopes of the Gonzen about 2,000 years ago. The mine only stopped operating in 1966. A small number of its galleries are now open to the public. —> 8 km

⑦ Swiss Tectonic Arena Sardona

The history of the Alps can be read like a book at this World Heritage site which lies between the Murgseen, the Pizol and Martinsloch. Unique geological formations bear witness to the immense forces at work on our planet and the collision of African and European tectonic plates. The "Glaris thrust", for its part, proves that the movement of the earth's crust can sometimes thrust younger rocks above older ones. —> 29 km

Wildhaus – Davos
Eastern Switzerland – Liechtenstein

The Tamina Gorge (9)

Iron ore mine at Sargans (6)

Wildsee in the Pizol region (7)

The town of Chur (11)

Salginatobel bridge (13)

Leg 7

⑧ Maienfeld, Heidi's village

This is the village in the Bünder Herrschaft winegrowing area which inspired author Johanna Spyri. The Heidi fountain is surrounded by picturesque houses and even the most reluctant children will enjoy the hiking trail, for they will be walking in the footsteps of Heidi, Peter the Goatherd and little Clara.

⑨ Bad Ragaz: historic bath house and the Tamina gorge

This resort, located at the end of the valley, is popular with visitors who explore the gorge using a very safe path, passing a fountain of thermal water before finally reaching the cave where the spring rises. The healing properties of this mineral-rich water were already well-known to our ancestors. Using a basket on a rope, they would be lowered into the gorge to bathe in the water at a temperature of 36.5°C.

⑩ Malans: cable car for the Vilan

The small yellow cable car leaves from Malans and only runs in the summer. It's an ideal destination for recreation and hiking! Climbing to the summit of the Vilan (2,376 m) will take you only two hours and you will be rewarded by a 360° panorama of the Graubünden Alps. The Älplibahn alpine restaurant, at an altitude of 1,801 m, is well-known for its friendly atmosphere. They will even open in the evenings for a small group (return to the valley included).

⑪ Chur

The Hof, or Bishop's Court, offers a magnificent view over the delightful capital of the canton of Graubünden. The alpine town of Chur is one of the oldest in Switzerland. With a very distinct character and many sights to see, it combines tradition and modernity with great success. There's no shortage of pleasant bars and places to shop. —> 16 km

⑫ Brambrüesch and the Dreibündenstein

The Dreibündenstein is the peak which watches over Chur. It can be reached by cable car and gondola lift. When you reach it you have a panoramic view over the town, the Rhine Valley and the peaks of the Calanda. There are several free-ride trails for mountain-bike enthusiasts on the Pizoggel, where the Swiss championships were held in 2009. Hikers will enjoy climbing the Dreibündenstein, and those who feel up to it can continue to Churwalden or Feldis. —> 17 km

⑬ Salginatobel bridge, a feat of engineering

A few kilometres beyond Schiers, in the Prättigau Valley, the mountain road which leads to Schuders crosses this famous bridge over the Salgina. It was built between 1929 and 1930, just a few years after the ban on motor traffic was lifted in Graubünden (1900-1925). It is a single track, reinforced concrete road bridge. It has been designated a Historic Civil Engineering Landmark, as has the Eiffel Tower. Visitors can follow a marked path to admire it and photograph it from every possible angle!

Monbiel near Klosters, facing the Silvretta Alps (16)

Stafelalp, Davos, looking towards the Jacobshorn region

Prättigau, looking towards Klosters

Partnun, Sulzfluh (15)

Sunniberg bridge near Klosters

Leg 7

Prättigau high-altitude trail

(14) You can walk from Landquart to Klosters along the Austria-Switzerland border, but it will take you four days. The trail follows the contour lines, below limestone cliffs. In the distance you might notice mountain-climbers clinging to the rock face on one of the many rock-climbing routes or the Sulzfluh via ferrata. —> 17 km

Sankt Antönien: Partnun and the Sulzfluh

(15) Now we make another small detour near Küblis to visit the Walser village of St. Antönien. From this very typical valley you can reach Prättigau high-altitude trail as well as the Sulzfluh (2,817 m) thanks to a famous 750 metre via ferrata. Several old smuggling paths will take you into Austria. Partnun, at the foot of the limestone cliffs, has a particularly romantic hotel with candlelit bedrooms and outdoor Jacuzzi. —> 17 km

Klosters: the Silvretta glacier trail

(16) The Silvretta SAC (Swiss Alpine Club) refuge is two and a half hours' walk from Klosters/Monbiel. A well-marked, four-kilometre trail starts just behind the refuge. Its information panels along the way will tell you all about the glaciers, weather and climate change. The refuge has can sleep 65 people (rooms of 4 to 20 beds). —> 15 km

Wildhaus – Davos
Eastern Switzerland – Liechtenstein

The route

Drive down to the Rhine Valley, then up again towards the Principality of Liechtenstein. Cross St. Luzisteig Pass, the Bünder Herrschaft, and then the Prättigau Valley to reach Klosters and Davos.

Distance: 86 kilometres

Photo opportunity: The road down from Alt Toggenburg towards Werdenberg Castle, with its many hairpin bends, offers some fine viewpoints. Picturesque scenery between Balzers (Liechtenstein) and the Bünder Herrschaft, then Malans.

To savour: Each of the 150 valleys in the canton of Graubünden has its own recipe for barley soup, but it's said that the best comes from the Prättigau Valley. They do share some similarities: uncooked barley left to soak overnight, a variety of vegetables and smoked meat.

Worth a detour

(A) **Alt St. Johann:** The Toggenburg Sound trail – www.klangwelt.ch

(B) **Wangs and Bad Ragaz:** Pardiel gondola lift, Gaffia chairlift – www.pizol.com

(C) **Bad Ragaz:** Tamina spa centre – www.taminatherme.ch

(D) **Klosters:** The Madrisa and Madrisa-land cable car – www.madrisa.ch / www.madrisa-land.ch

Tourist information

Toggenburg Tourismus
Hauptstrasse 104, 9658 Wildhaus
+41 (0)71 999 99 11; www.toggenburg.org

Heidiland Tourismus
Valenserstrasse 6, 7310 Bad Ragaz
+41 (0)81 720 08 20; www.heidiland.com

Chur Tourismus
Personenunterführung, 7000 Chur
+41 (0)81 252 18 18; www.churtourismus.ch

Prättigau Tourismus
Sananggastrasse 6, 7214 Grüsch
+41 (0)81 325 11 11; www.praettigau.info

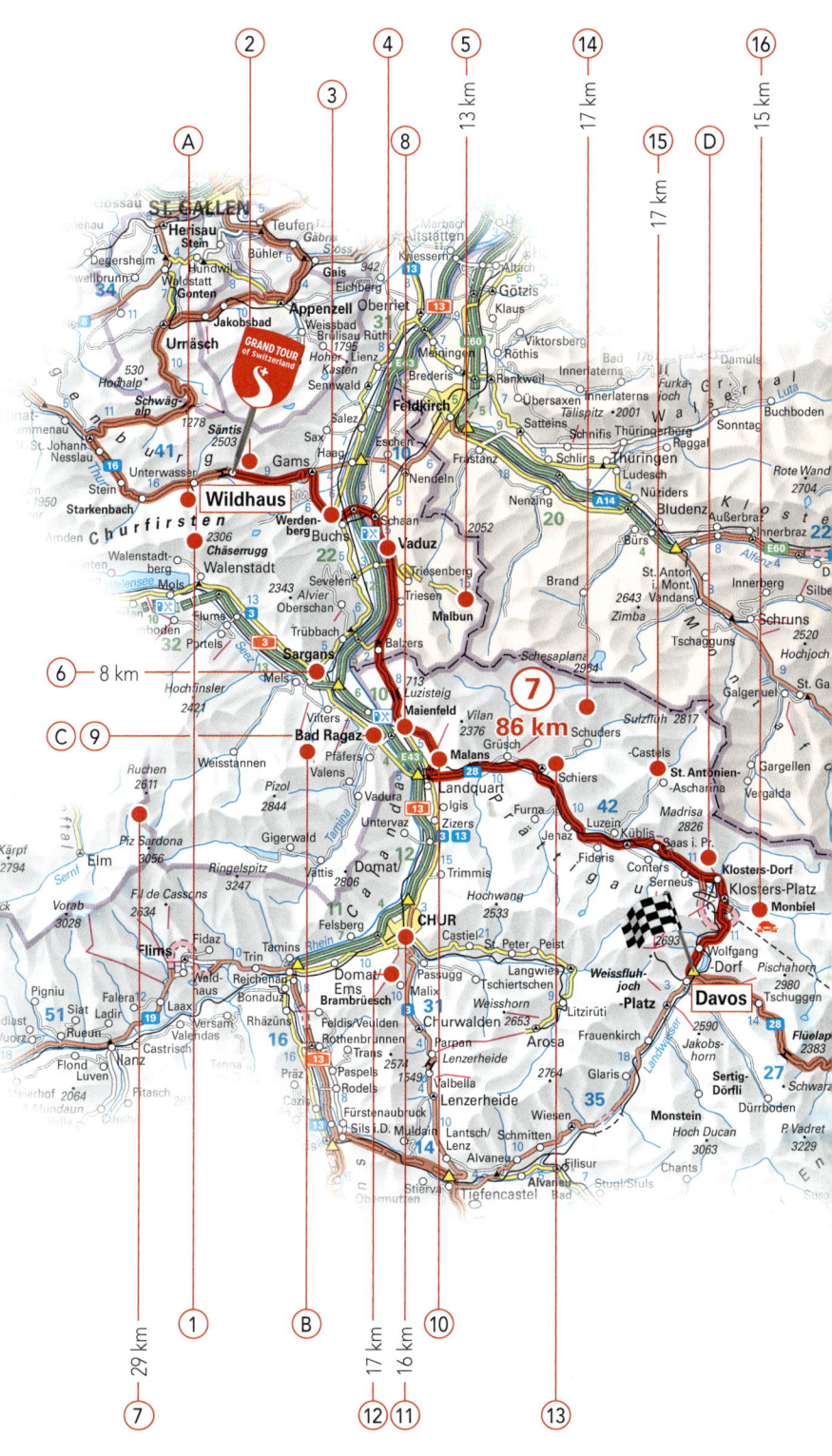

Wildhaus – Davos
Eastern Switzerland – Liechtenstein

Graubünden region

GRAND TOUR of Switzerland

The canton of the "Grey League" – part of the old Roman province of Raetia – stretches from the Bünder Herrschaft to the southern Alps. Three languages are spoken in the region, and life here is conducted along the length of each valley. It's also a departure point for countless hikes and other adventures in alpine pastures and on numerous summits.

The Flüela Pass

Sertig Dörfli (5)

Schatzalp funicular, Davos (3)

Parsenn Weissfluhjoch (1)

Mountain bike free-riding trail (2)

The Schatzalp (3)

Leg 8

Davos – St. Moritz

The Flüela Pass and Engadine

Davos is the most urban of winter sports centres. A former health resort, it still has some sanatoriums but it is now known above all for hosting congresses. It's also one of Switzerland's most popular destinations for skiers and mountain bikers. After driving along the lake, enter the town centre and continue until you reach the Kurpark. From there, follow the Promenade which will take you to the Ernst Ludwig Kirchner museum.

After Davos, the road climbs through a barren landscape with almost no trees until it reaches the Flüela Pass, at 2,383 metres. The pass is closed in winter, when the route via the Vereina Tunnel (which links Klosters to Sagliains) must be used instead. It's a useful alternative, but of course doesn't offer the same views! When you arrive in the Lower Engadine, don't forget to make a short detour via the very picturesque village of Guarda, the spa town of Scuol, and S-charl.

Next, head for the Upper Engadine and Zernez, where you will find the Swiss National Park visitor centre. A day's excursion to the Fuorn Pass and Switzerland's oldest and largest nature reserve is well worth a visit. You then have just 34 kilometres left to reach St. Moritz. The high-altitude valley becomes increasingly wider and more fertile. The stunning landscapes at 1,700 metres above sea level, the pure air and luminosity alone make the journey worthwhile.

① Davos: Parsenn Weissfluhjoch

The mountains which surround Davos are worth a detour. The Weissfluhjoch was particularly wellknown from 1942 to 1996, when it was the base for the Institute for Snow and Avalanche Research. Nowadays, visitors come here for the funicular, which takes them up to Parsenn via the Höhenweg middle station. The route follows the contours of the land and the train reaches speeds of over 30 km per hour.

② Gotschnagrat: mountain bike free-riding trail

Mountain bikers will enjoy Parsenn's free-ride trails, some of which are technically quite challenging. If you take the cable car from Klosters you can explore the free-ride trail which leaves from Gotschnaboden. Inspired by the legendary Whistler A-Line in Canada, this formidable and spectacular six-kilometre trail contains no fewer than 50 bends. Experienced mountain bikers hurtle down it without braking!

③ Time to relax at the Schatzalp

Located 300 metres above Davos, the Schatzalp offers a truly unique experience for nature and history lovers who are looking for a little peace and quiet. It is easily reached via a funicular which has been running since 1899. The former sanatorium inspired Thomas Mann to write his famous novel, "The Magic Mountain". The Alpinum, for its part, is a botanical garden specialised in mountain plants with around 3,500 varieties from all over the world (June – Sept).

Road to the Flüela Pass, Lower Engadine (8)

Kirchner Museum (4)

The narrow "Bärentritt" bridge (7)

Val S-charl (10)

Wiesen viaduct (7)

Tarasp Castle, Lower Engadine

Scuol health spa (9)

Leg 8

④ Davos: The Kirchner Museum
This museum at Davos Platz is devoted to the artist's works and stands at the very place they were painted. The landscapes of Davos inspired Kirchner up until his death in 1938, and the village with its pointed church tower is a recurring theme in his pictures.

⑤ The Walser village of Sertig
The village of Sertig is located on the other side of the Jakobshorn. It can be reached on foot, by car or by CarPostal bus. Its old houses, cowsheds and famous little church are part of the Walser heritage. Food is served at the Bergführer and the Walserhuus. —> 12 km

⑥ Monstein: Silberberg mine and museum
Graubünden's mining museum at Schmelzboden, located at the entrance to a gorge, offers an adventurous experience. Visitors make their way through the narrow galleries, tunnels and furthest corners of the disused Silberberg mine, where lead and zinc used to be extracted. Guided tours are available from Davos. —> 13 km

⑦ Zügenschlucht and the Wiesen viaduct
If you follow the river towards Tiefencastel you will notice the valley getting narrower before the road finally disappears into a tunnel. A stony track then takes you into the Zügenschlucht gorges, along the crystal clear waters of the River Landwasser. Twice every hour a Rhaetian Railways train passes by and enters a tunnel through the mountain before crossing the impressive Wiesen viaduct. —> 17 km

⑧ The Flüela Pass and the Lower Engadine
The most direct route to the Lower Engadine passes through the Flüela Valley and Val Susasca to the east before reaching Susch. You can put your car on the train through the Vereina tunnel between Selfranga and Sagliains, not far from Susch. But the road through the pass is far more beautiful. In summer, a heritage mail coach pulled by six horses takes visitors once a week from Davos-Platz to Flüela Hospice.

⑨ Scuol health spa
This resort in the Lower Engadine is well-known for its hot springs. Mineral water flows from the village fountain and you can enjoy the Bogn Engiadina's spa facilities with water at 34–37°C: outdoor and indoor pools, steam bath, hot tub, saunas and Roman-Irish baths for a treatment lasting several hours. For a complete change of scene you can then go up to St. George's Church, perched high on a rocky spur overlooking the Inn, for a magnificent view over Scuol and the National Park. —> 20 km

Zuoz, Engadine

Guarda (12)

The Swiss National Park (13)

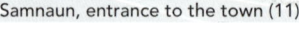
Samnaun, entrance to the town (11)

Chamonna Cluozza, National Park (14)

Champlönch children's trail (15)

Leg 8

⑩ Val S-charl and God da Tamangur, symbol of the Romansch language

A mountain road takes you from Scuol to the picturesque village of S-charl, on the edge of the National Park. This is an ideal spot for walkers and lovers of the outdoors. The Schmelzra Museum shows how lead and silver ore was extracted by hand on the Mot Madlain. Just an hour's walk will take you to God da Tamangur, Europe's highest Swiss pine forest. It was immortalised in a poem, making it symbolic of the survival of the Romansch language. —> 35 km

⑪ Samnaun, duty free – but full of charm

This former smugglers' paradise is located in the north-east of Graubünden, where the borders of Switzerland, Austria and Italy meet. These days, the small and somewhat isolated town of Samnaun in the Lower Engadine is known for being Switzerland's only duty-free area. But it's also popular with hikers, mountain bikers and those who want to enjoy nature. A double-decker cable car provides a service all year round to Ischgl in the Austrian Tyrol. —> 58 km

⑫ Guarda, Schellen-Ursli's village

Many of the villages in the Lower Engadine region between Zernez and the border are well worth a visit. The old houses decorated with sgraffiti are particularly noteworthy. This technique consists of scoring patterns, drawings and inscriptions into a layer of fresh plaster, creating the illusion of paintings. Alois Carigiet, who drew the illustrations for the classic children's story Schellen-Ursli, was inspired by the décor of some of Guarda's most beautiful houses. —> 9 km

⑬ The Swiss National Park

Founded over a century ago, the Swiss National Park was the work of true visionaries. Their goal was to "protect our country's original fauna and flora in a specific region". Today the areas around the Fuorn Pass are still home to ibexes, marmots and mountain hares. Human presence is tolerated on condition that visitors stay on the hiking trails at all times. The best way to prepare your trip to the National Park is to drop into the modern information centre at Zernez.

⑭ Chamonna Cluozza: a night in a refuge

Although there is plenty of accommodation available along the river Inn and in Val Müstair, there are only two establishments within the National Park itself: the Il Fuorn hotel at the Fuorn Pass and the wooden chalet in Val Cluozza. This refuge, located at 1,882 metres above sea level has kept its early 20th century charm and can sleep 63 guests. The accommodation and restaurant are modest, but they are located in the heart of the National Park just three hours from Zernez on foot.

⑮ The Champlönch children's trail (Fuorn Pass)

Families can rent a children's multimedia audio-guide at the National Park visitor centre and set off towards the Fuorn Pass. This educational walk starts at car park number 1. The audio-guide emits a signal and then tells a story about your current location. Children are kept constantly engaged and eager to walk on to the next spot to hear a new story. —> 7 km

Diavolezza and Piz Palü (20)

Val Müstair, looking towards the Fuorn Pass (16)

Müstair Abbey church (16)

The Tschierva glacier, Piz Bernina and Biancograt (19)

Val Roseg (19)

Leg 8

⑯ Müstair: Benedictine monastery and biosphere reserve

Val Müstair (which with the Swiss National Park forms the Alps' first high-altitude biosphere reserve) can be reached from the Fuorn Pass. Charlemagne certainly made an astute choice when he had a church built in this remote valley near the Italian border. The Benedictine Abbey of St. John is also a UNESCO World Heritage Site. —> 39 km

⑰ Celerina: San Gian church, the valley' emblem

Not only are Engadine Airport and the golf course located on the plain near Samedan, so is San Gian Church, which stands prominently on a hill and can be seen from afar. With its two bell towers in different styles, it has become the emblem of Celerina and the region. The church has an interesting interior with a painted ceiling, pointed arches and frescoes.

⑱ Muottas Muragl and Segantini's cabin

The most beautiful viewpoint over the lakes of the Upper Engadine is doubtless to be found between the vast Inn valley and the valley leading to the Bernina Pass. The artist Giovanni Segantini, with his keen sensibility for beautiful landscapes and light, probably shared this opinion. The panorama is particularly impressive at sunset (the train service continues after nightfall). You can even spend the night there, at the Romantik-Berghotel.

⑲ Val Roseg

The best way to reach the Roseg Valley is to take the horse-drawn coach which offers a scheduled service, or to rent a horse and carriage just for you and your family. This traffic-free valley near Pontresina has kept its traditional, old-fashioned character. While you're there, don't forget to pay a visit to the Roseg Gletscher restaurant, which has a reputation for irresistible desserts! —> 3 km

⑳ Diavolezza: mountain scenery from the Palü to the Bernina

Six kilometres before the Bernina Pass, a cable car travels up to the Diavolezza, almost 3,000 metres above sea level. An impressive vista encompassing the Piz Palü, the Bellavista and the Piz Bernina can be seen from the upper station. You can sit and absorb this magnificent sight from a deck chair, or in the hot tub at the hotel. The mountain inn offers double rooms and dormitories. —> 12 km

The route

Cross the Flüela Pass to enter the Lower Engadine and the National Park. Then follow the course of the River Inn via Zuoz and Samedan until you reach St. Moritz and the lakes of the Upper Engadine.

Distance: 65 kilometres

Photo opportunity: After the very charming Lake Davos we pass through a wooded area then an increasingly arid valley (Flüelatal) up to the lakes and the pass. The valley gradually opens up after S-chanf.

To savour: The name of the Engadine's speciality, Bündner Nusstorte (Graubünden walnut pie) is a little confusing as no walnut trees grow in the canton. The recipe was brought back and transformed in the 18th century by Engadine confectioners who had emigrated to Italy and France. The pie is prepared with a sweet shortcrust pastry and filled with a mixture of walnuts, honey, caramel and cream.

Worth a detour

Monstein: Craft brewery –
www.biervision-monstein.ch

Tarasp: Guided tours of the castle in summer –
www.schloss-tarasp.ch

Engadine: Rafting on the Inn –
www.engadin-adventure.ch / www.swissraft.ch

Samedan: Rhaetian Railways –
www.berninaexpress.ch

Tourist information

Destination Davos Klosters
Talstrasse 41, 7270 Davos Platz
+41 (0)81 415 21 21; www.davos.ch

Tourismus Engadin Scuol Samnaun Val Müstair
Staziun Scuol-Tarasp, 7550 Scuol
+41 (0)81 861 88 00; www.engadin.com

Swiss National Park Visitors Centre
Schloss Planta-Wildenberg, 7530 Zernez
+41 (0)81 851 41 41; www.nationalpark.ch

Pontresina Tourismus
Via Maistra 133, 7504 Pontresina
+41 (0)81 838 83 00; www.pontresina.ch

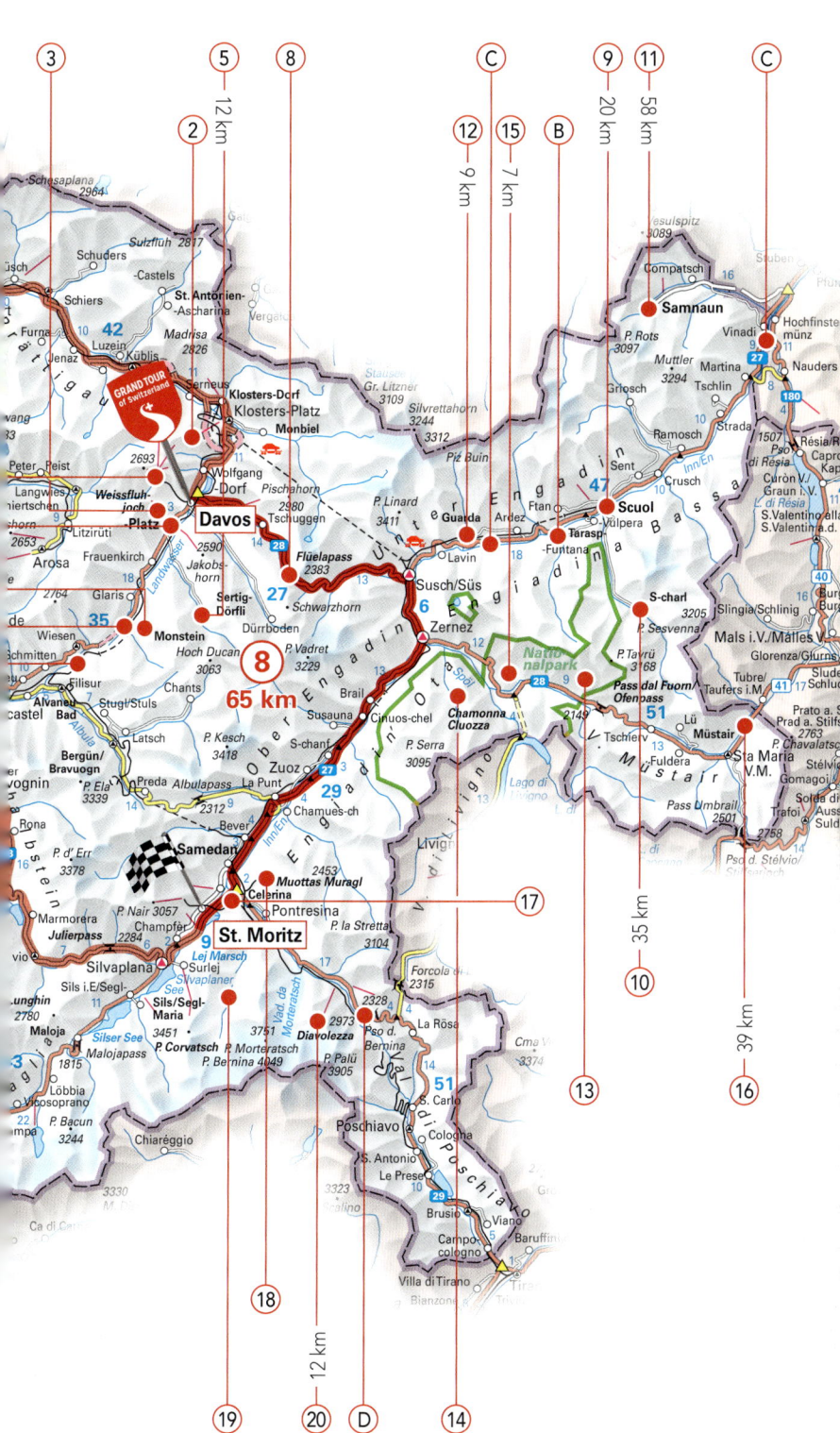

Davos – St. Moritz
Graubünden region

St. Moritz (1)

The Segantini Museum, St. Moritz

St. Moritz

Silvaplana

Corviglia, St. Moritz

Leg 9

St. Moritz – Andeer

Centre of Graubünden and Val Schons

St. Moritz is a town which offers an unusual contrast between luxury cars, mink-clad beauties and exclusive shops on the one hand and the peerless beauty of its surrounding natural environment on the other. It's no coincidence that this landscape has been a source of inspiration for many artists, as it was for Segantini. As we arrive in Silvaplana we turn right and take the road towards the Julier Pass. After 500 metres, photography buffs might like to make a first stop, parking their cars near the first hairpin bend. A superb vista spreads before us over the Upper Engadine and its lakes, the Piz Corvatsch and the Piz de la Margna. From then on, photogenic scenery is almost as omnipresent as the hairpin bends. The road straightens out a little once we reach Bivio. We cross the Oberhalbstein Valley with the famous Alp Flix alpine meadow in the Parc Ela nature park on your right, then Savognin ski resort.

At Tiefencastel we meet up again with the Rhaetian Railways' small red train, a familiar feature in our landscape photos, for example in the Schin gorge which we cross by following the rail track. At Thusis, we face a dilemma. Should we make a detour via the gorges at Ruinaulta (also known as the Rhine Gorge, or Switzerland's "Grand Canyon") or head straight for those at the Viamala? At Zillis, though, we have no alternative but to visit the 12th century church of St. Martin. To fully appreciate its famous painted ceiling, a Romanesque work of art whose 153 panels illustrate scenes from the bible, you will have to lie flat on your back or bring a mirror.

① St. Moritz: 322 days of sunshine per year

This elegant and eminently cosmopolitan resort located at 1,822 metres above sea level has a global reputation. Its name is so prestigious that it has even been registered as a trademark and is protected throughout the world. The Upper Engadine's lakeland plateau enjoys exceptional sunshine (on average 322 days per year) and offers a full range of activities, from water sports to gourmet dining, not to mention hiking, mountain biking, and naturally, shopping!

② Lej Marsch: a small lake to swim in

Several peatland lakes lie within the forest between Pontresina, St. Moritz and Silvaplana. Their waters heat up all summer long, making them ideal for swimming. A famous restaurant stands on the shore of Lej da Staz, but Lej Marsch is without doubt more popular with swimmers. As for, Lej Nair, it is accessible only on foot and offers idyllic scenery.

③ Ascending the Corvatsch

The Corvatsch is the highest point of the Engadine accessible by cable car. The panoramic restaurant offers a stunning view over the mountains. Half-way up, near the Murtèl middle station, you can walk to the Fuorcla Surlej mountain hut. The waters of its small lake reflect the crest of the Piz Bernina.

Excursion on the Corvatsch (3)

Lake Sils (4)

Piz Nair, St. Moritz

Hairpin bends on the Maloja road (6)

The Julier Pass

Bivio at the Julier Pass (8)

Leg 9

④ Lake Sils: boating at the summit

It's well worth spending some time at the enchanting lakes of the Upper Engadine. Windsurfing enthusiasts can discover the famous Maloja wind, others can take a scheduled boat service (at 1,800 metres above sea level!) to the Chastè Peninsula. This was where the writer and philosopher Friedrich Nietzsche wrote his masterpiece "Thus Spake Zarathustra". —> 5 km

⑤ Sils-Maria and Val Fex

If you prefer to be on terra firma you'll find leisure activities just beyond the village of Sils-Maria. The legendary Fex Valley is one of the highest valleys inhabited all year round in Switzerland. Those of a romantic bent can take a horse-drawn carriage to reach the Sonne hotel, which offers not only a magnificent terrace with panoramic views of the mountains, but also delicious local specialities. —> 6 km

⑥ Maloja: glacial potholes and ancient remains

The Maloja Pass, which leads to the Val Bregaglia, is a pass unlike any other: to the north lies the Upper Engadine lakeland plateau and to the south the road twists and winds its way down to Casaccia, 350 metres below. This enchanting landscape has over 30 glacial potholes, the remains of an extremely steep Roman road and a "historic" panoramic tower which is nonetheless young in comparison as it is only just over a hundred years old. —> 11 km

⑦ Piz Lunghin: towards three seas

Very close to the Maloja Pass stands the only mountain in Europe with a three-way watershed: North Sea (Rhine), Mediterranean (Po) and the Black Sea (Inn and Danube). The peak is about three and a half hours' walk from Maloja. —> 11 km

⑧ The Julier Pass: a history of transport

Nowadays this Pass is the main point of entry to the Engadine. The remains of columns at the summit, the early coins found here and the imprint of cart tracks in the stone slabs is evidence of its use as a route between Italy and Lake Constance in ancient times. Mule-drivers would often choose the Septimer Pass, a more dangerous but more direct route. These early logistics experts knew that in order to cover difficult terrain they had to transfer merchandise from oxcarts to mules.

⑨ Parc Ela: Alp Flix and its 2,000 species

From Sur, between Bivio and Savognin, you can follow a narrow road by car or by Bus Alpin up to this little gem of biodiversity at Alp Flix. In a single day, researchers identified over 2,000 species of plants and animals including a new species of midge named "Rhexoza flixella". This mountain pasture is part of Parc Ela, Switzerland's largest regional park, and includes vast wetland areas and forests of Scots pines in a stunningly beautiful landscape. —> 5 km

Ruinaulta, Chli Isla (13)

Riom Castle (10)

The Landwasser viaduct (11)

Church of St. Martin (15)

Viamala Gorge (14)

Leg 9

⑩ Riom Castle: from a prison to a theatre

This impressive castle situated below the resort of Savognin would be hard to miss. Built in the 13th century, it belonged to the bishops of Chur until the valley threw off the episcopal yoke. After the great fire of 1864 all the wood in the fortress was used to rebuild the village and the castle fell into ruins. The roof was rebuilt in 1977 and since 2006 the castle has housed a 220-seat theatre.

⑪ The Rhaetian Railways' Albula line

The train lines between Thusis and Tirano are engineering masterpieces which blend harmoniously into the landscape and form the heart of the Rhaetian Railways UNESCO World Heritage Site. This spectacular line covers 122 kilometres and crosses 196 bridges, 55 tunnels and 20 different municipalities.

⑫ Wooden church at Obermutten

At the start of the Schin gorges, after Solis Bridge, the twisting road branches off towards Mutten and Obermutten. The detour takes you to the crest which separates the Albula and Viamala valleys. This Walser village has the only church in Switzerland to be entirely built from wood. The "Inscha Laada" shop sells a wide variety of regional produce and crafts. The village became prominent in 2011 through a significant Facebook campaign. —> 11 km

⑬ Flims: Ruinaulta (Rhine Gorge)

This impressive 10,000-year-old natural phenomenon lies a little further away from our itinerary. The retreat of the glacier caused the collapse of 10 km³ of solid rock into the valley, blocking the course of the Rhine near Flims. Since then the river has opened a passage through the rock, forming a spectacular gorge which visitors can penetrate thanks to Rhaetian Railways. If you're looking for adventure, white water rafting on the river is an ideal activity; those who prefer to admire the views can go to the "Il Spir" observation platform.
—> 28 km

⑭ Viamala Gorge

The Viamala (literally "bad way") owes its name to its inhospitable nature. Stretching from Thusis to Zillis, with the Hinterrhein running through it, its rocky cliffs are 300 metres high in places. Just a few metres wide, its mysterious atmosphere, the ever-changing colours of its waters and its giant potholes are a constant source of enchantment for visitors. It can be reached from the road by 321 steps with safety rails.

⑮ Zillis in Val Schons: the Church of St. Martin

Zillis is located at the spot where the Viamala Gorge widens up. The Church of St. Martin in the lower part of the village is renowned for its 12th century painted ceiling. With 153 panels, it is the only surviving one of its kind in the world. Feel free to lie on your back or to use a mirror in order to appreciate all the detail!

The route

Cross the Julier Pass to reach the Oberhalbstein Valley, then the Schin Valley as far as Thusis. The byroad then takes you to Val Schons (Schams) and Andeer.

Distance: 72 kilometres

Photo opportunity: The Julier Pass, the most widely-used route to Engadine, goes through some spectacular alpine scenery. The Viamala Gorge between Thusis and Zillis is particularly impressive.

To savour: Bündnerfleisch (or viande des Grisons) is made from lean dried beef cured for several weeks in a mixture of salt and herbs. It is then left to dry for four months. The process is now carried out in modern food dryers but in former times only the dry mountain air was used. The meat is pressed to spread the moisture as effectively as possible. Genuine Bündnerfleisch is never smoked.

Worth a detour

(A) **St. Moritz:** Chantarella, Corviglia, Piz Nair – www.piznair.ch

(B) **St. Moritz:** The Giovanni Segantini Museum (paintings) – www.segantini-museum.ch

(C) **Celerina:** The Bobsleigh Museum – www.estm.ch

(D) **Bergün:** The Albula Railway Museum, near the station – www.bahnmuseum-albula.ch

(E) **Alvaneu:** natural hot spring (34°C), indoor and outdoor pools – www.bad-alvaneu.ch

Tourist information

St. Moritz Tourist Information
Via Maistra 12, 7500 St. Moritz
+41 (0)81 830 00 01; www.estm.ch

Savognin Tourismus im Surses
Stradung 42, 7460 Savognin
+41 (0)81 659 16 16; www.savognin.ch

Rhaetian Railways (RhB)
Bahnhofstrasse 25, 7002 Chur
+41 (0)81 288 65 65; www.rhb.ch

Gästeinformation Viamala
Äussere Bahnhofstrasse, 7430 Thusis
+41 (0)81 650 90 30; www.viamala.ch

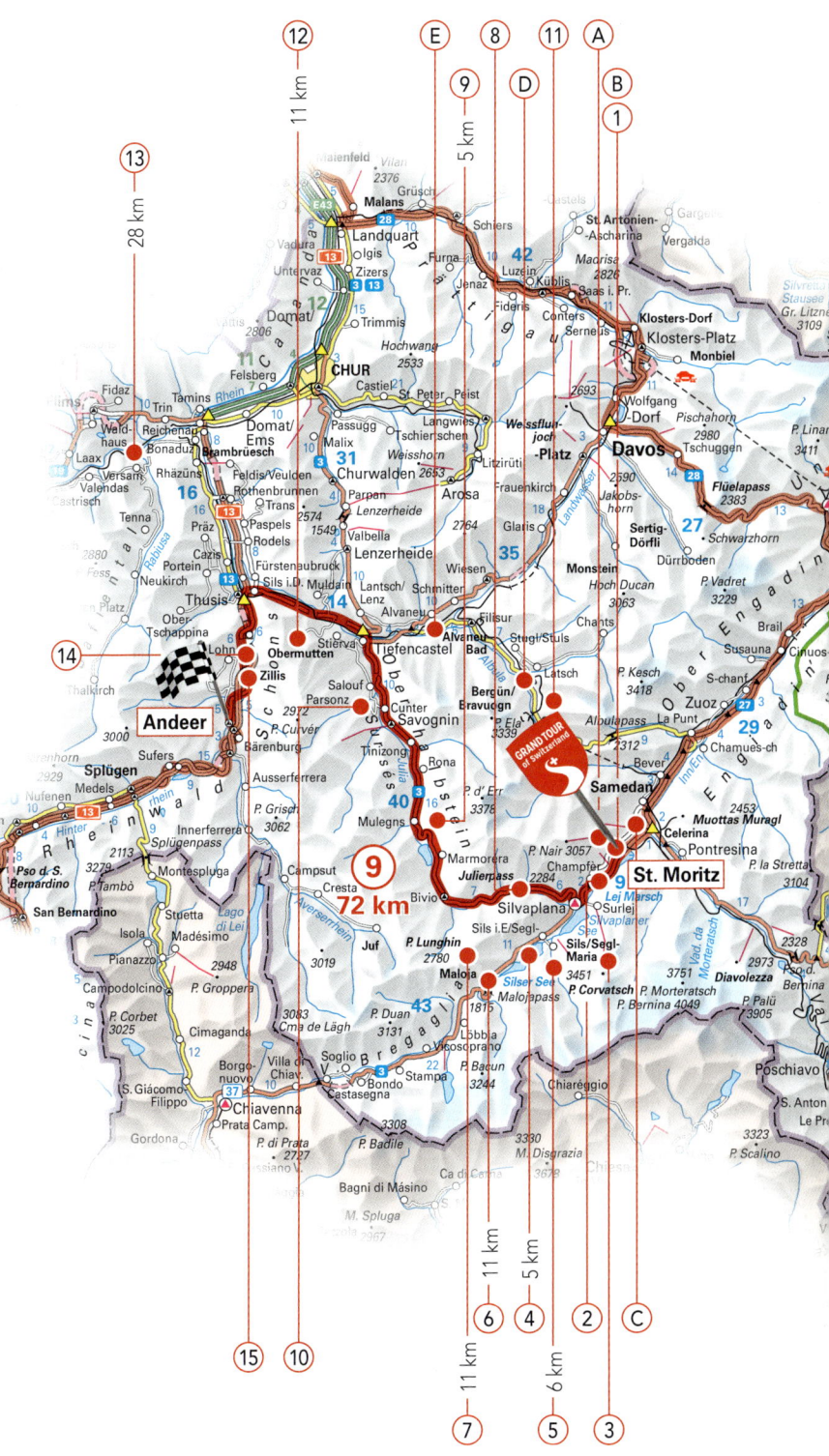

St. Moritz – Andeer
Graubünden region

Sufnersee, the road to San Bernadino

The Walser village of Splügen(3)

Andeer (1)

Rofla Gorge

Village of Splügen (3)

Leg 10

Andeer – Bellinzona

From Graubünden to Southern Switzerland

As this leg starts we are still in the heart of the Beverin nature reserve (with the eponymous peak in the middle) which extends as far as the Safiental. Then when we reach Sufnersee, we enter the territory of the future Adula national park without even noticing. This alpine valley, the Rheinwald, contains the uppermost stretch of the Hinterrhein and the Walser village of Splügen, winner of the Wakker Prize. Don't take the main road and tunnel southwards, but the road to the San Bernadino Pass which contains some 50 hairpin bends just to reach the village of San Bernardino, in Val Mesolcina. Italian is the main language spoken here, but we only enter the canton of Ticino just before our final destination, Bellinzona. Val Mesolcina is still part of Graubünden.

Another 30 tight bends take us through the two levels of San Giacomo before we reach Mesocco. During the journey you can admire the engineering prowess required to build this road which follows the contours of the land closely, particularly as it bypasses the village of Mesocco. When we arrive level with an exit from the express road we turn left to the ruined castle, going towards the bottom of the valley. Don't miss the legendary view southwards from the churches of San Martino and San Rocco in the next village of Soazza.

① Andeer: village of mule-drivers and thermal baths

The old houses in Andeer's main street are well worth taking your time to look explore. This small resort village in Val Schons is renowned for its hot spring and baths, as well as its green-tinted granite which is exported throughout the world. Like Splügen, Andeer was a longstanding hub for transalpine trade: for over 2,000 years, it was on the main route between Graubünden and Italy.

② Juf, Switzerland's highest village

At Rofla Gorge, the road begins to descend towards the Ferrera Valley and Avers. Juf (2,126 m), which lies at the end of the mountain road and the Car-Postal bus line, is the highest village in Switzerland to be inhabited all year long. It has only about 30 residents, belonging to six Walser families, who make their living from agriculture and tourism. Juf has an inn, several holiday flats and even a post office. —> 25 km

③ Splügen, a Walser village on the Hinterrhein

Under no circumstances should you miss the village square, and just a few steps away the fine "palazzi" and Walser chalets which have been coloured dark brown by the sun. Splügen is a typical pass village, which still remembers the mule-drivers of former times who travelled on foot or horseback, carrying salt to Chiavenna and the south and Italian wine to the north.

The San Bernardino Pass (5)

Village of San Bernadino (6)

Santa Maria in Calanca

Val Mesolcina (7)

Parc Adula, Val Camadra (8)

Val Calanca (9)

Leg 10

④ Walser trails: from the canton of Valais to Italy via Graubünden

What reasons impelled the Walsers to leave the Upper Valais in the 13th century and settle in the some of the Alps' highest valleys? Economic hardship, disease, overpopulation? Or perhaps the privileges promised by feudal lords if they transformed their uncultivated lands into farmland. It's impossible to know for sure. But one thing that is certain is that the Walser trails in Valais, the Aosta Valley and Graubünden offer exciting long-distance hiking routes through magnificent and culturally significant natural landscapes.

⑤ The San Bernardino Pass

The tunnel is only 6.6 kilometres long but the road over the Pass which links the Hinterrhein to San Bernardino is a far better choice. It is longer (17 km), but absolutely superb! The Pass was called Vogelberg until a chapel dedicated to San Bernardino of Siena was built in the 15th century. The mule track, with rock slabs and steps, is very well preserved and worth a detour.

⑥ San Bernardino and the Lago d'Isola

Shortly before the pass lies a picturesque wetland landscape with shimmering lakes and glacial striations. We then reach Lagghetto Moesola, a small but charming lake, followed by characteristic marshy terrain, pine forest and flora until we reach the valley and San Bernardino. Lago d'Isola, a reservoir surrounded by alpine forest, is a paradise for lovers of water sports. There is even a 150 metre zip wire over the water.

⑦ Mesocco and Mesolcina

Even though Italian is spoken in this village and valley located to the south of the Alps, they are nonetheless part of the canton of Graubünden. In 1551 the inhabitants gained independence from rule by Milan and chose to join the "Grey League". The imposing ruins of Mesocco Castle bear witness to the strategic importance of this north-south route.

⑧ Parc Adula, a national park project

The Adula (or Rheinwaldhorn) region could well become Switzerland's largest national park. The territory between Val Mesolcina, the Lukmanier Pass, Val Blenio and Vals forms one of the largest natural reserves almost untouched by human influence in Switzerland. Some very high peaks form the centre of the park, with the Greina plateau (and the villages of Olivone and Sumvitg at either side) stretching out in between.

⑨ Val Calanca

Far below Mesolcina, this small and little known valley points northwards. There are 20 kilometres between the entrance to the valley, near Grono, and the last inhabited hamlets. Small villages, almost all with stone roof tiles, nestle in the sunny uplands. Some of them can only be reached on foot or by cable car. —> 10 km

The route

Cross the Rheinwald (from the Latin "vallis Rheni") until you reach the northern entrance to the road tunnel, then cross the San Bernardino Pass and continue until you reach Mesocco and Val Mesolcina, which joins the Ticino plain.

Distance: 86 kilometres

Photo opportunity: near Rofla Gorge the road twists upwards with multiple hairpin bends to the Sufnersee lake and Splügen. The road up to the San Bernardino Pass is one of the most tortuous roads of the Grand Tour.

To savour: "Capuns" are chard or lettuce leaves filled with a stuffing made from eggs, herbs, sausage meat or dried meat. Graubünden inhabitants are past masters in the art of making leaf parcels with vegetable and meat stuffing and the "capuns" from Rheinwald have the reputation of being the best of all.

Worth a detour

(A) **Thusis:** Via Spluga long-distance trail – www.viaspluga.ch

(B) **Andeer:** Rofla Gorge – www.rofflaschlucht.ch

(C) **San Bernardino/the Hinterrhein:** Walser trail – www.walserweg.ch

(D) **San Bernardino – Santa Maria in Calanca:** Sentiero Alpino Calanca, a three-day trail with overnight stays in a refuge – www.sentiero-calanca.ch

Tourist information

Gästeinformation Andeer
Mineralbad, 7440 Andeer
+41 (0)81 650 90 30; www.mineralbadandeer.ch

Gästeinformation Splügen
Bodenplatz, 7435 Splügen
+41 (0)81 650 90 30; www.splugen.ch

San Bernardino, Mesolcina, Calanca
Strada Cantonale, 6565 San Bernardino
+41 (0)91 832 12 14; www.visit-moesano.ch

Andeer – Bellinzona
Graubünden region

Ticino region

"Palme e neve" define this most Italian of Swiss cantons in a nutshell. The shores of its lakes reflect an entirely Mediterranean lifestyle and nonchalance, while life in the mountains is harsh and rural. These fascinating contrasts are mirrored in the Locarno national park project.

Morcote, on the shore of Lake Lugano

View from Monte Boglia over Lake Lugano

Monte Generoso, Kulm Hotel (from 2016)

Wine cellar in Mendrisiotto (1)

A "nevera", in the Muggio Valley (2)

Baptistry at Riva San Vitale (4)

Leg 11

Road from Chiasso to Bellinzona

Access road to the Grand Tour in southern Ticino

The Grand Tour of Switzerland starts at Chiasso's main customs post for our visitors arriving from Italy. The itinerary immediately heads for the mountains and the Muggio Valley. Less well-known but equally interesting are the Breggia Gorge and the Cement trail, near the former cement factory.

We arrive at Lake Lugano near Capolago, the starting point for the little train's scheduled service (from spring 2016) to take visitors to the newly opened hotel on Monte Generoso. The road follows the lake, crosses the Melide causeway and then branches left towards Morcote. This former fishing village offers views of Monte San Giorgio, which abounds with fossils. The road crosses the Collina d'Oro before stopping in Lugano, which should not be missed. You then head for Monte Ceneri and wave goodbye to southern Ticino (Sottoceneri). It might seem paradoxical but the Sopraceneri, or Upper Ticino, includes Switzerland's lowest lying point at 193 metres above sea level, on the shore of Lake Maggiore. Locarno and Ascona, like Lugano, are resorts which radiate southern charm and offer a large number of excursions, for example to the Maggia Valley or the Verzasca Valley, well-known for James Bond's spectacular jump from the dam in the film "Golden-Eye". At Bellinzona, a town with three remarkable castles, we join up with the main itinerary of the Grand Tour.

① Mendrisiotto and Mendrisio

The most southerly tip of Ticino is not simply a transit area between Italy and Switzerland. Its hilly landscapes are ideal for hiking and mountain biking. Special wine routes offer an opportunity to discover the best Mendrisiotto crus. The Palazzo Turconi in the town of Mendrisio (through which the Grand Tour passes) is home to the Università della Svizzera Italiana's architecture academy. Niki de Saint-Phalle's sculpture (the lovebird), stands at the entrance.

② The Muggio Valley

Take a trip back in time when you drive up from Chiasso towards the Muggio Valley and then follow the narrow road to Scudellate. Villages with stone roofs nestle against the cliff in the midst of chestnut groves. On the outskirts of the forest a short walk will take you to carefully-restored stone walls and "nevere", stone icehouses which were used to preserve the milk from the alpine pastures.
—> 8 km

③ Monte San Giorgio: fossil mania

The summit of this mountain to the north-west of Mendrisio rises to less than 1,100 metres but contains a hidden treasure. A Mecca for fossil hunters since the 19th century, it was awarded UNESCO World Heritage status in 2003. 240 million years ago the region formed a 100-metre-deep oceanic basin. The finest fossils which have been found there are kept in the museum at Meride, which has been redesigned by Ticino architect Mario Botta. —> 8 km

Morcote fishing village (5)

View from Monte Lema over the Malcantone (6)

The Monte San Salvatore funicular (7)

On Monte Ceneri

Bay of Lugano (9)

Gandria smuggler's village (8)

Leg 11

4 Riva San Vitale: baptistery

At the southern tip of Lake Lugano stands what might well be Switzerland's oldest religious building. The Riva San Vitale baptistery and its remarkable baptismal fonts date from the 5th century. Part of the black and white marble stone floor is from that period.

5 Morcote fishing village on the shore of Lake Lugano

You mustn't miss a visit to Morcote, with its pretty narrow streets, fine old town houses with arcades and luxurious vegetation. In the past this was essentially a fishing village. In the Middle Ages it was an essential hub for trade with the Duchy of Milan. Parco Scherrer is worth a visit for its palm trees, camellias, wisteria, oleanders, cedars, cypresses, camphor trees and eucalyptuses.

6 Monte Lema, a peak with a panoramic view over the Malcantone

To the west of Lugano, a gondola lift climbs from the village of Miglieglia to an exceptional panoramic viewpoint. On one side the Malcantone spreads out as far as Lugano, Monte Brè and Monte Generoso; on the other side you can see Lake Maggiore with the Valais Alps in the background. The Vetta hotel and restaurant has a superb terrace where guests can enjoy the sun and offers guestrooms and dormitories. The one-day ridge walk to Monte Tamaro is a classic. —> 14 km

7 Monte San Salvatore: Lugano's "sugarloaf"

Monte San Salvatore, Ticino's "sugarloaf mountain" has been accessible without effort since 1890 thanks to the red funicular which leaves from Paradiso near Lugano. Around the year 1200, pilgrims climbed the mountain for the love of Christ who, legend has it, stopped at the summit on his way to heaven. The panoramic platform offers breathtaking views over the roofs of Lugano, the lake and the Alps.

8 Gandria, a charming smuggler's village

Lake Lugano has several arms, one of which lies eastward from the town of Lugano. The picturesque former smuggling village of Gandria is just five kilometres away. Time appears to have stood still for at least a century in this village with its maze of narrow, twisted streets, steep steps, walled courtyards and arcades. Take a seat at one of the inviting terr^aces of the restaurants along the shore to absorb the peaceful atmosphere of the place. —> 6 km

9 Monte Brè, the summit which watches over Lugano

A funicular climbs up in two stages from the outskirts of Lugano to Monte Brè, the panoramic summit which looks out over the Bay of Lugano. The picturesque village of Brè, with its "grotti" (traditional restaurants), can be reached by road. Don't hesitate to take a break at one of the two restaurants at the summit: that's what their terraces are for!

On Monte Tamaro (11)

The Denti della Vecchia (10)

Ascona (13)

Cardada, Locarno (12)

Botta's church, Mogno (18)

Leg 11

Denti della Vecchia: exploring the Colla Valley
⑩ Budding explorers will enjoy a detour via the Colla Valley and the Denti della Vecchia (Teeth of the Old Woman). Mountain bikers can head for Monte Bar, and hikers to Cimadera, where they can walk along the ridge which marks the border with Italy as far as the Denti. The narrow path passes below limestone cliffs which resemble enormous teeth against the blue sky. —> 14 km

Monte Tamaro
⑪ Monte Tamaro stands on your left shortly before the point where the motorway to the south disappears into the Monte Ceneri tunnel. You can take a gondola lift to Alp Foppa, famous for its Church of Santa Maria degli Angeli built by Mario Botta, which offers countless interesting angles for photographs. The middle and upper stations provide access to a summer toboggan run, a zip wire and a tree-top adventure park with a spectacular 15-metre jump. There's plenty here to keep young adventurers happy.

Locarno, Madonna del Sasso, Cardada/Cimetta
⑫ The beating heart of Locarno, on the shore of Lake Maggiore, has always been Piazza Grande, famous for hosting the film festival and the Moon and Stars music festival. The pilgrim church of Madonna del Sasso stands on higher ground at Orselina and offers magnificent views over Locarno. The only place where you can get an even more spectacular view is from the Cimetta (1,671 m), the summit which watches over Locarno. There are also several mountain inns there.

Ascona: an idyllic break on the shores of Lake Maggiore
⑬ Ascona is a small gem on our route through Ticino. This historic town with narrow, twisting streets and old bell tower will also enchant you with its many shopping opportunities. The traffic-free lakeside promenade and its many cafés give a permanent sensation of being on holiday. Author's recommendation: the Jazz Festival in late June.

The Brissago Islands
⑭ Another enchanting spot lies to the south of Ascona: the Brissago Islands. A boat service connects the largest (2.5 hectares) to the shore. It is home to 1,700 species of plants from the Mediterranean, subtropical Asia, Africa, America and Oceania. Irrigated by the lake, protected by the Alps and warmed by the rays of the sun, this park is a small paradise. —> 6 km

Road from Chiasso to Bellinzona
Ticino region

Tenero, Lake Maggiore

Vogorno in the Verzasca Valley (19)

The Walser village of Bosco Gurin (17)

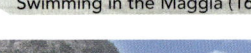
Swimming in the Maggia (16)

Ponte dei Salti, Verzasca Valley (19)

Foroglio, Val Bavona (16)

Grotto, Onsernone Valley

Leg 11

Locarnese national park

(15) The future national park stretches from the Brissago Islands to the Walser village of Bosco Gurin. This region, which was densely populated in the past, made a living from chestnut plantations and exporting straw hats. Some magnificent "palazzi" still bear witness today to the past glory of merchant families. However, many local residents were forced to emigrate, and some sent their children to Italy to become chimney sweeps. In the 20th century, a large proportion of agricultural land was permanently abandoned. The only remaining evidence of this alpine agricultural activity are the drystone terraces and several thousand "rustici" (farmhouses) scattered through the forests, as well as unspoilt villages which are now on the Federal register of listed buildings. —> 9 km

The Maggia Valley: an abundance of granite

(16) The road which leads to the very top end of the Maggia Valley covers 45 kilometres. Shortly after Ponte Brolla we start to see the valley's typical stone houses with flat granite roof tiles and tables, benches and pergolas in gneiss. The village of Avegno, with its houses huddled together, is worth a visit. The "sentieri di pietra" allow those who are interested to discover the valley's other stone buildings. —> 7 km

Bosco Gurin, a Ticino Walser village

(17) When you go from Cevio to Bosco Gurin through the Maggia Valley, you are already closer to Valais than to Lake Maggiore. Or as the crow flies, in any case, as the Formazza Valley in Italy lies between them. The Walser people travelled over the Alpine passes in the Middle Ages to found the only German-speaking village in Ticino here. One of the "sentieri di pietra" offers an opportunity to walk in their footsteps. This one-hour circuit around the village includes the Walserhaus Museum. —> 41 km

Botta's church at Mogno and Brontallo stone village

(18) The Church of San Giovanni Batista designed by Mario Botta stands at the farthest end of the Maggia Valley. It might not be large, but it has gained a global reputation. This surprising church with geometric patterns sculpted in white marble and grey granite is well worth the journey. And since you have come this far, why not take the opportunity to visit Fusio and the stone village of Brontallo? —> 43 km

The Verzasca Valley

(19) The Verzasca Valley meanders over 26 kilometres between Tenero, near Locarno, and Sonogno. Its steep, wooded slopes appeal to romantics and nature lovers. Its rocks, smoothed and polished by the river, offer ideal places to stretch out and sunbathe, natural whirlpools and endless places to swim. Near Lavertezzo, you cross the Verzasca River by the famous Ponte dei Salti (Bridge of Jumps). The dam wall was used in the bungee jump scene in the film "Goldeneye". If you're feeling brave you can emulate 007's feat and leap into a 200-metre void. —> 8 km

The route

Drive from Mendrisiotto to Lugano via Morcote and the lake. Then pass over the Monte Ceneri to reach the Magadino plain and Lake Maggiore, with Locarno and Ascona.

Distance: 105 kilometres

Photo opportunity: The road via Morbio Inferiore and Castel San Pietro is not easy to find but is worth a detour. There are main roads from Melide to Lugano but the Morcote route is far more beautiful.

To savour: "Zincarlìn" from the Muggio Valley is a peppery cheese made from unpasteurised milk. Its distinctive flavour is powerful and quite unique. It weighs about 300 grams and comes in a shape which looks like an upturned cup. The "formaggini" are matured in cellars in the Monte Generoso area. To prevent mould forming, each "zincarlìn" is coated with white wine and salt almost every day for two months.

 41 km

Worth a detour

A **Morbio Inferiore:** Cement trail and Breggia Gorge – www.parcobreggia.ch

B **Capolago:** Monte Generoso, rack-and-pinion train and hotel (reopens in 2016) – www.montegeneroso.ch

 9 km

C **Melide:** Swissminiatur, Switzerland on a 1:25 scale over 14,000 m² – www.swissminiatur.ch

D **Rivera:** Leisure and wellness at the Splash & Spa water park, Tamaro – www.splashespa.ch

E **Gordola:** Parco Avventura (tree-top adventure park) – www.parcoavventura.ch

Tourist information

Mendrisiotto e Basso Ceresio
Via Luigi Lavizzari 2, 6850 Mendrisio
+41 (0)91 641 30 50; www.mendrisiottoturismo.ch

Luganese – Lugano
Riva Albertolli – Palazzo Civico, 6900 Lugano
+41 (0)58 866 66 00; www.luganotourismus.ch

Lake Maggiore Tourist Office
Via B. Luini, 6600 Locarno
+41 (0)848 091 091; www.ascona-locarno.com

Ticino Turismo
Via Canonico Ghiringhelli 7, 6501 Bellinzona
+41 (0)91 825 70 56; www.ticino.ch

Road from Chiasso to Bellinzona
Ticino region

The Old St. Gotthard road, near the pass (12)

Montebello Castle (1)

Piazza Collegiata, Bellinzona (1)

Bellinzona Old Town (1)

New road at the St. Gotthard Pass, Fontana

Leg 12

Bellinzona – Furka

Leventina, St. Gotthard and the Furka Pass

The view over Bellinzona is marked by three impressive castles. The town's carefully-restored old houses bear witness to its Lombardic cultural heritage, but beneath the medieval town's austere appearance lies a dynamic and resolutely modern town with an intensely Italian atmosphere. To reach Montebello and Sasso Corbaro castles, take your car: you might have to ask the way, but you will be rewarded with a panoramic view over the whole of the Magadino plain as far as Lake Maggiore, and one of the best restaurants in Ticino.

From Biasca we continue to the narrow Leventina Valley, where railway and road viaducts seem to jostle for position. After Airolo we take the Tremola, doubtless one of the most well-known roads leading to the St. Gotthard Pass. After Hospental and Realp, we once more embark on a series of hairpin beds which take us up to the Grand Tour's highest alpine pass: the Furka Pass, at 2,429 metres above sea level.

1. Bellinzona, a UNESCO World Heritage Site

Built at a strategic location which allowed them to control access to the valley, the medieval fortifications and Castelgrande, Montebello and Sasso Corbaro castles have become emblematic of Ticino's capital. They have acquired World Heritage status. A wonderful traditional market is held each Saturday in the squares and narrow, winding streets of the Old Town.

2. Monte Carasso and San Bernardo

Monte Carasso, with its former convent which has been turned into a cultural centre, is a well-kept secret. A small cable car takes you up to the chestnut groves and the Monti de Mornera via Curzútt and Pientina. The nearby Romanesque church of San Bernardo is worth a detour.

3. Bellinzona's Matterhorn

The San Bernardino and St. Gotthard roads meet to the north of Bellinzona. Between them stands the Pizzo di Claro (2,727 m), which has been dubbed "Bellinzona's Matterhorn". A small cable car (open all year round) climbs 1,000 metres from the village of Lumino to the crest of the Monti di Saurù. The restored stone houses and mountain restaurant make this a charming place for an excursion.

4. Claro: the Santa Maria Assunta Benedictine convent

Founded in 1490, this convent in the middle of a chestnut grove can be seen from afar on a rocky spur overlooking Claro. The nuns operate a small cable car but passengers will not catch sight of them at any time, not even when they pay for their tickets. Some parts of the convent can nonetheless be visited, and offer a superb view over the Bellinzona area.

Biaschina, Leventina, looking south (5)

On the Furka Pass

Lake Tremorgio (7)

Lake Ritom, Piora Valley (8)

Geren Pass, upper Bedretto Valley

Airolo, view of the Bedretto Valley

Leg 12

⑤ Biaschina: feats of civil engineering

If you take the motorway you miss the view of the tunnels and bridges to the north of Giornico. The 120-metre difference in level on the Biaschina valley floor is due to an enormous rock slide which happened after the last ice age. The railway passes it with spiral tunnels, the by-road with hairpin bends and the A2 motorway with a viaduct which starts to slope upwards at Giornico and a tunnel. Whether you're interested in civil engineering or not, don't miss taking a photo from the old by-road!

⑥ Strada Alta Leventina and Monte Piottino Gorge

On the eastern slope of the Leventina valley are a series of small villages which can only be reached by mountain trails. They are linked together by the famous Stráda Alta, a hiking path which takes several days to complete. The valley's second difference in level (150 m) is the Monte Piottino, which separates the Mid Leventina from the Upper Leventina Valley. The Dazzio Grande (large customs post) to the side of the Monte Piottino Gorge (which can be explored on foot) has been turned into a cultural centre with museum and restaurant.

⑦ Lago Tremorgio: a crater lake?

A very discreet little cable car runs from Rodi-Fiesso up to Tremorgio Lake. The lake's round shape looks like a volcanic crater, but it isn't one. You can walk around the lake on foot, and an ideally located "grotto" lies just above it. To the west the high altitude trail leads to Pesciüm (Airolo).

⑧ Lago Ritom, Alp Piora

The alpine pastures between Airolo and the Lukmanier Pass are popular with nature-lovers. In summer the old funicular to the SBB (Swiss Federal Railways) hydroelectric station climbs an 87.8% slope to take you up to Lago Ritom. The mountain restaurants on its shores have made a name for themselves by serving delicious Ticino specialities, as has the alpine cheese dairy a little further up.

⑨ Airolo and Pesciüm

Airolo, a former mule-drivers village, lies at the southern exit of the St. Gotthard tunnel (A2 motorway) opened in 1980. The railway reached the village in 1882. On the other side of the Pass and the Tremola a cable car takes visitors up to Alp Pesciüm which offers an impressive panorama over the St. Gotthard area. The Bedretto Valley and Lago Tremorgio high altitude trails leave from here, as does the hiking path from Cristallina to Lago di Robièi.

⑩ The Bedretto Valley: towards the Nufenen Pass

If you continue straight on from Airolo (instead of turning right towards the St. Gotthard Pass) you will find yourself in the long Bedretto Valley before reaching the Nufenen Pass and the Goms Valley beyond. Lying between the St. Gotthard and the Cristallina ranges, the Bedretto Valley is a paradise for relaxing, walking and mountain biking. —> 13 km

The Tremola's legendary hairpin bends (11)

The St. Gotthard Pass (12)

The Furka Pass

Andermatt with the village of Hospental in the distance (13/14)

Furka steam train (16)

Leg 12

⑪ Tremola: a challenging route to the St. Gotthard Pass

Switzerland's longest landmark stretches between Airolo and the St. Gotthard Hospice: 13 kilometres, 900 metres difference in altitude, 37 hairpin beds and several million cobblestones. The Tremola, a former coaching road, is a popular choice for all those who enjoy driving.

⑫ The St. Gotthard Museum and Sasso San Gottardo

Take your time to absorb the bleak granite and gneiss landscape at the St. Gotthard Pass. It stands on the line of the main European watershed, where different climates and cultures meet. You can learn more about this unique place in the St. Gotthard Museum, which occupies a former coaching inn. The St. Gotthard fortifications were for a long time a key part of Switzerland's national defence. The caverns now house the Museo Sasso San Gottardo.

⑬ Hospental, a mule-drivers village in the Urserental

This former mule-drivers village to the north of the St. Gotthard Pass was the starting point for trails in every direction, as an inscription in the chapel reminds us: "This is the parting of the ways. Friend, where do you go now? Down to the eternal city of Rome? Towards the German Rhine and holy Cologne? Or rather far to the west, to France"? It's said that the Russian general Suvorov stayed at the St. Gotthard hotel in 1799 (still in existence today).

⑭ Andermatt and Gemsstock

Andermatt was a staging post on the road to the pass until the railway tunnel and then the road tunnel came into operation. Its wooden chalets with stone basements and paved roads with granite slab insets are characteristic of the region. Developer Samih Sawiris's modern buildings make an interesting contrast. You can travel up to Gemsstock (nearly 3,000 metres above sea level) in the middle of the St. Gotthard range by cable car.

⑮ Schöllenen Gorge: the Teufelsbrücke (Devil's bridge) and the Suvorov memorial

How can you build a bridge at such a spot unless the devil lends a helping hand? The French and Russian armies fought in the region in the late 18th century. A memorial sculpted in the rock face pays tribute to the victims. Russian president Dmitry Medvedev visited the memorial in 2009 —> 5 km

⑯ The Furka steam train

The Furka railway line was built between 1912 and 1925 and in the past was used by the Glacier Express. Nowadays, steam engines pulling restored heritage carriages take visitors up the rack and pinion sections from Realp to Oberwald (Goms) via the Furka Tunnel and Gletsch, from June to September.

The route

Cross the Leventina valley on the by-road until you reach Airolo, then follow the old road up to the St. Gotthard Pass. Keep going northwards towards Hospental then continue up the Urseren Valley until you reach the Furka Pass.

Distance: 98 kilometres

Photo opportunity: The Leventina Valley's two levels offer an opportunity to admire some feats of engineering (road and rail). The Tremola's hairpin bends and those on the Furka road are spectacular.

To savour: "Spampezie" are a Leventina speciality. These pastries are filled with a melt-in-the-mouth mixture of hazelnuts, honey, butter and grappa. The sculpted wooden moulds used to make them are true works of art.

Worth a detour

(A) **Pollegio:** Rail tunnel for alpine transit, Gottardo Sud Visitors Centre – www.infocentro.ch

(B) **Airolo:** Caseficio del Gottardo, cheese dairy, museum, shop and restaurant – www.cdga.ch

(C) **The St. Gotthard Pass:** Historic fortress and exhibition about sustainability – www.sasso-sangottardo.ch

(D) **Four springs trail:** A hike over several days to the sources of the Rhine, the Reuss, the Ticino and the Rhône – www.vier-quellen-weg.ch

Tourist information

Bellinzona Turismo
Palazzo Civico, 6500 Bellinzona
+41 (0)91 825 21 31; www.bellinzonaturismo.ch

Leventina Turismo
Via della Stazione 22, 6780 Airolo
+41 (0)91 869 15 33; www.leventinaturismo.ch

Andermatt-Urserntal Tourismus
Gotthardstrasse 2, 6490 Andermatt
+41 (0)41 888 71 00; www.andermatt.ch

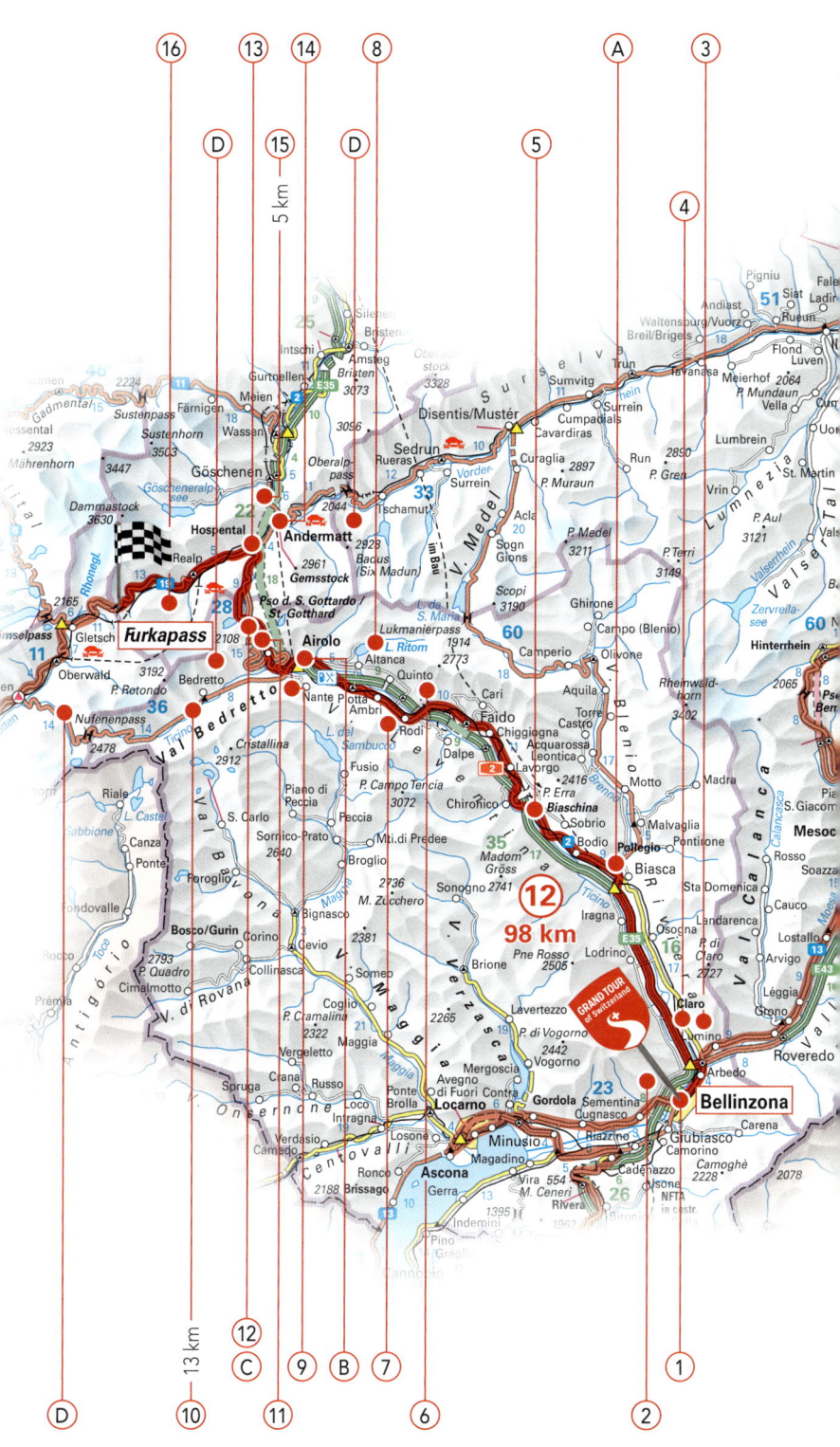

Bellinzona – Furka
Ticino region

Valais region

The Valais region offers 180 kilometres of road between the Furka and Lake Geneva. But it also comprises countless small valleys leading down to the Rhône Valley, sun-drenched villages on the plains and in the mountains, 45 peaks over 4,000 metres above sea level and a distinctive, bilingual culture. This canton is richly varied and enchanting.

The Weisshorn from the valley between Zermatt and Randa

Mountain roads such as those leading to the Furka, Grimsel and Susten Passes

The Furka Pass (1)

An old altitude marker at the Furka Pass (1)

Belvédère hotel (2)

Road to the Grimsel Pass

Leg 13

Furka – Visp
Along the upstream Rhône

Let's stop awhile at the Furka Pass, the highest mountain pass in our Grand Tour. We see a bleakly beautiful landscape with glacial rocks to the left and the Furkahorn to the right. Shortly after the pass we come across six hairpin bends leading to the Grimsel Pass. In all there are eight before we reach Gletsch, former outpost of the Rhône glacier. In summer a small blue train climbs the slope before disappearing into a tunnel in a huge puff of steam: this is the old Furka train, brought back to life by a handful of rail enthusiasts.

After all these zigzags the road straightens out considerably once we reach Oberwald in the Goms district. We have now reached the homeland of the famous gourmet and hotelier César Ritz, who came from Niederwald. There is a choice of cable cars to take us up to the Aletsch area. The Eggishorn and Bettmerhorn summit stations are ideal for observing the great glacier. Nature lovers for their part will enjoy exploring the Aletsch forest, starting from Riederalp. In Brig, the capital of Upper Valais, the spirit of Kaspar Jodok von Stockalper (one of the first great Swiss entrepreneurs, 1609 – 1691) still lingers. The inner courtyard of the palace he built is infinitely more impressive in real life than on Google Street View! Only a few kilometres are now left before the final destination, Visp.

① The Furka Pass
Whereas the St. Gotthard Pass provides a north-south route through the central Alps, the Oberalp and Furka passes link two longitudinal valleys which were formed by geological or tectonic constraints: the Vorderrhein, via Urseren, and the Rhône in the Upper Valais. Anyone who enjoys driving in mountainous terrain will love the Furka Pass (2,429 m) with its many hairpin bends and changing vistas.

② The Rhône glacier: ice tunnel and lake
Ever since the wide pass road was opened 150 years ago, visitors have thronged here by the thousands to admire a unique view of the Rhône Glacier. In 1914, mail coaches already recorded 19,102 passengers. At the time the glacier flowed right down to the bottom of the valley and Gletsch. This is no longer the case but you can still visit the ice cave near the Belvédère hotel and the recently formed lake.

③ The Grimsel Pass and CarPostal
Shortly after crossing the Furka Pass you can see the hairpin bends in the road on the other side of the valley which links Gletsch to the Grimsel Pass. This is the route to the Haslital, in the Bernese Oberland where the River Aare rises, with its reservoirs and pumping stations for the hydroelectric plant. CarPostal's yellow buses travel along several routes which include two or three passes, including the Nufenen, St. Gotthard, Furka and Susten Passes. —> 6 km

Gletsch, Rhône Glacier in the background

Münster, Goms Valley (5)

Oberwald, Goms Valley

Gluringen church, Goms Valley

Ried-Mörel, view towards Goms

The Great Aletsch Glacier

Leg 13

④ Grimselwelt: hydroelectric plant, trains and hotels

The Grimsel and Susten area doesn't just offer passes, however spectacular they may be. The Oberhasli hydroelectric plant has opened several of its trains and facilities to the public including the Gelmerbahn funicular, Europe's steepest with a 106% slope. The Hählen Platten steps, above Handegg, are a point of particular interest on the former Grimsel mule track. —> 12 km

⑤ The Goms Valley: traditional villages, chalets and whitewashed churches

From the Glacier du Rhône hotel in Gletsch (whose restaurant used to overlook the tip of the glacier) a steep road with hairpin bends leads to the 17 kilometre-long Goms Valley which was formed by the Rhône during the ice age. You can enjoy a variety of activities in this wide valley: navigating the first few kilometres of the Rhône by dinghy, hiking on a high-altitude trail – and cross-country skiing in winter.

⑥ Ernen mountain village, at the entrance to the Binntal

For several centuries this village near Fiesch was on the trade route once plied by mule trains. Ernen is no longer on the main road, but its past glory is still evident in its fine old buildings. The Tellenhaus is decorated with frescos illustrating the story of William Tell, including the apple incident. These are believed to be the oldest in Switzerland. Nowadays Ernen is famous for its music festival.

⑦ Binntal: regional nature reserve

This valley of hidden treasures is above all known for its mineral deposits. But its villages and hamlets with sun-scorched chalets are so well preserved that they have been designated as heritage sites of national significance. The Twingi Gorge with its long tunnel, the village of Schmidigehischere and the historic Ofenhorn hotel are all worth visiting. —> 12 km

⑧ Fiesch-Eggishorn: The Jungfrau-Aletsch Swiss Alps

In 2001, the Jungfrau-Aletsch area was the first alpine site to be given UNESCO World Heritage status. It stretches from the Grimsel to Kandersteg and Goppenstein. The impressive Eiger, Mönch and Jungfrau range lies at the centre with the Great Aletsch Glacier. Visitors have a choice of cable car lines to reach higher ground, such as the one which links Fiesch to the Eggishorn, where the whole length of the glacier can be admired.

⑨ Bettmeralp: the Great Aletsch Glacier

Another way to reach the glacier is via the Bettmeralp resort (the cable car leaves from the lower station at Betten) and the Bettmerhorn gondola lift. A multimedia exhibition presents the fascinating world of the glacier. There is a panoramic viewpoint just a few steps from the upper station, but if you would like to take a closer look it would be a pity not to follow the trail which goes past the famous Märjelensee before returning to Bettmeralp via Fiescheralp (4 hr 30 mins).

Villa Cassel, Riederfurka (10)

Suspension footbridge, Aletsch (10)

Aletsch Glacier and forest (10)

Stockalper Palace, Brig (12)

Former hospital, the Simplon Pass (13)

Leg 13

⑩ Riederalp: Aletsch Forest and footbridge to the Upper Aletsch Glacier

The third cable car line takes you to Riederalp, again on the sunny Aletsch plateau. From there you can walk to Villa Cassel (nature conservancy centre) on the Riederfurka. The nearby Aletsch Forest is a unique nature reserve which offers photographers some superb views of the Aletsch Glacier through mature Swiss pines. It takes about four hours to walk to the suspension footbridge and up to Belalp.

⑪ Belalp: hotel, chapel and view of the glacier

The Belalp hotel dates from the early days of tourism in the Alps since it was built in 1858. It stands with its chapel at the very spot where it seems as if the Aletsch Glacier is hurtling towards you. The first tourists might have had to travel by mule but today a road links Naters/Brig to Blatten, where you can catch a cable car to take you above the tree line. The hotel is located at the Aletschbord viewpoint, at just half an hour's walk from the cable car station. —> 7 km

⑫ Brig: Stockalper Palace and fort with Museum of the Swiss Guard

Brig is well-known for the vast 17th century Stockalper Palace with its three towers each crowned with a golden dome. Several of its rooms as well as the impressive inner courtyard are open to visitors. An underground fort, built in 1939/1940, lies on the opposite bank of the Rhône. It now houses not only a "village" which can accommodate 200 people but also an exhibition devoted to the Pontifical Swiss Guard.

⑬ The Simplon Pass, a historical landmark

The pass is charged with history and the spirit of Kaspar Jodok von Stockalper, a prominent figure in the history of Valais seems to linger here. This politician, merchant, banker, builder and officer was granted the privilege at a very early age (in 1634) of transporting merchandise via the Simplon Pass. The Stockalper tower in Gondo, the coaching inn, the mule track and the former hospital are testimonies to his power. His example inspired Napoleon Bonaparte to order a large hospice to be built at the pass in 1801. —> 23 km

⑭ Mund, the saffron-growing village

The mountain village of Mund lies on the right side of the valley between Brig and Visp, 500 metres above the Rhône. It has cultivated saffron crocuses on its sunny slopes since the 15th century. Local restaurants use this "red gold" in a number of specialities. To learn more about it, follow the themed trail or visit the charming saffron museum. —> 8 km

The route

Leave the Rhône glacier behind you and drive towards Gletsch and Oberwald, then continue up the wide Goms Valley to Fiesch before reaching Brig and Visp.

Distance: 67 kilometres

Photo opportunity: The journey between the Furka Pass and the Belvédère hotel, then Gletsch, is particularly photogenic. After Fürgangen, near Deisch, you will glimpse a breathtaking view over the Rhône Valley and the mountains around Visp.

Did you know? César Ritz, "the king of hoteliers and hotelier to kings" (as he was called by Edward VII when he was still Prince of Wales), was born in Niederwald. This son of farmers from the Goms Valley left his mark on the luxury hotel industry and founded the Ritz-Carlton hotel chain. Many restaurants in the region pay tribute to him with special menus.

Worth a detour

(A) **Niederwald:** In the footsteps of César Ritz, hotelier to kings – www.caesar-ritz.ch

(B) **Riederalp:** The Aletsch Pro Natura Center at Villa Cassel on the Riederfurka – www.pronatura-aletsch.ch

(C) **Simplon:** The Simplon Pass on the trade route between Italy and Switzerland – www.viastockalper.ch

(D) **Brigerbad:** Switerland's largest open air thermal baths with waterslide and river – www.thermalbad-wallis.ch

(E) **Bern – Brig:** Lötschberger, BLS's RegioExpress tourist train on the mountain line and the southern Lötschberg ramp – www.loetschberger.ch

Tourist information

Obergoms Tourismus
Furkastrasse 53, 3985 Münster
+41 (0)27 974 68 68; www.goms.ch

Aletsch Arena
Postfach 4, 3992 Bettmeralp
+41 (0)27 928 41 31; www.aletscharena.ch

Jungfrau-Aletsch (world heritage site)
Kehrstrasse 12, 3904 Naters
+41 (0)27 924 52 76; www.jungfraualetsch.ch

Brig Simplon Tourismus
Bahnhofstrasse 2, 3900 Brig
+41 (0)27 921 60 30; www.brig-simplon.ch

Furka – Visp
Valais region

Car train Simplon Brig–Iselle di Trasquera (I).

Travel quickly and comfortably through the Simplon Tunnel in just 20 minutes.

sbb.ch/en/car-carryingtrain

The Matterhorn, Zermatt (1)

The Glacier Trail (4)

Zermatt, a car-free town (1)

The Klein Matterhorn gondola lift (2)

Breithorn, Valais (3)

Leg 14

Zermatt, the Visp and Saas Valleys

Journey to three valleys

The Matterhorn is an absolute must. Nobody can remain indifferent to "Horu", as it is known locally, which was climbed for the first time in 1865 by the English mountaineer Whymper. Zermatt is car free, so we reach the town by shuttle train from Täsch, with a departure every 20 minutes. Nestled in a landscape of glaciers and high mountains, Zermatt offers an opportunity to explore the eternal snows of the Gornergrat and the Klein Matterhorn (Europe's highest ski area) by train.

Saas-Fee, another car-free village offers an equally enchanting and varied alpine experience. The Métro Alpin funicular will take you to the world's highest revolving restaurant.

If you're travelling with children, take them for a trip in the fairy-tale gondola lift from Hannigalp to Grächen. To discover the traditional face of the Valais region, take the mountain road from Stalden to Törbel, a typical village with wooden houses scorched by the sun. There is a wonderful view from the cemetery over the Dom and the Mischabel range (4,545 m), the highest range entirely located in Switzerland. You return through the magnificent landscapes of the Moosalp to Visp, unless you decide to go directly down to central Valais.

Zermatt: The Matterhorn

① At the end of Zermatt Valley, the Matterhorn (called "Horu" in the Valais dialect) is the main focus of attention. Since the first ascension exactly 150 years ago it has attracted several thousand mountaineers year after year. But many more than that are captivated by the view of this majestic mountain with its summit swathed in a small cloud. What better backdrop for a little souvenir selfie?

The Klein Matterhorn: Matterhorn glacier paradise

② No cable car will take you higher than this. First of all you take a gondola lift to the Trockener Steg station, via Furi and Schwarzsee. From there, a dizzyingly high cable car built in 1979 continues up to the Klein Matterhorn station, carved out of the rock. 38 summits over 4,000 metres above sea level, 14 glaciers, cinema lounge, ice rink, toboggan run, restaurant, shop and even a mountaineers' lodge await you!

Breithorn, 4,164 metres

③ This is an ideal opportunity to climb your first 4,000 metre summit with a mountain guide. The Klein Matterhorn mountain station is barely a stone's throw from the icy summit of the Breithorn. Roped to your guide and equipped with crampons, you first cross the Breithorn plateau before zigzagging up to the snowy ridge. The air gets thinner, so take your time. Two hours later you will reach the summit at 4,164 metres above sea level. Congratulations.

Hamlet of Zmutt, Zermatt

The Gornergrat funicular (5)

The lake hiking trail (6)

Jungen, above St. Niklaus (7)

Grächen family resort (8)

Leg 14

④ Glacier Trail, Matterhorn Trail and the Gorner Gorge

If you enjoy mountain hiking, take the Glacier Trail, a themed trail which leads from the Trockener Steg station to the Schwarzsee at the foot of the east face of the Matterhorn. The Matterhorn Trail from Schwarzsee to Zermatt via Zmutt is as its name suggests entirely devoted to the Matterhorn. And from Furi you can walk to the "glacier garden" and the suspension footbridge over the Gorner Gorge.

⑤ Zermatt: the Gornergrat rack-and-pinion railway

Every 24 minutes a train on the rack-and-pinion line leaves Zermatt station for the most beautiful belvedere in the Monte Rosa range, where it arrives half an hour later. From this panoramic platform 3,135 metres above sea level you can see the Gorner glacier and fabulous snow-capped summits as far as the Matterhorn. Sunset views from the Kulmhotel are legendary, as is the reflection of the Matterhorn in the waters of the Riffelsee on calm days.

⑥ Sunnegga, Blauherd, Rothorn and the lakes hiking trail

It's said that the most perfect view of the Matterhorn's pyramidal summit can be seen from here. Leaving from Zermatt, take the underground funicular (a 1,521-metre tunnel) which climbs up to the Sunnegga station at a speed of 12 metres per second. The very popular lake walk from Blauherd takes you from the Findel Glacier valley via three lakes (Stellisee, Grindjesee and Grünsee) and the Fluhalp mountain restaurant before reaching Riffelalp, where you can catch the Gornergrat train.

⑦ Sparren, Jungen and Schalb: three little-known hamlets

Zermatt Valley is deep and narrow, and since the great rockslide of 1991 near Randa, is permanently monitored. The pretty hamlets of Sparren, Jungen and Schalb (Embd) lie on sunny terraces further down the valley and are all accessible by small cable cars.

⑧ Grächen: a family resort and its "bisses"

On the other side of the valley the family holiday village of Grächen stands on another sunny terrace. Just outside the village you have a good view up the valley towards the Matterhorn. The bisses are irrigation channels which have been used for centuries to carry water from the Ried Glacier to the fields. They can be explored on short, easy walks and are a firm favourite with children.
—> 8 km

⑨ Hannigalp: children's wonderland

Ten gondola cabins decorated with scenes from fairy tales transport passengers to a magical kingdom peopled with fairies and princesses. The SiSu family park offers a variety of attractions: animal park, native American fort, Archimedes water spiral and tubing run. Hannigalp is located 500 metres above Grächen, where Zermatt Valley and the Saas Valley meet. —> 8 km

A torrent in Zermatt Valley

Good mountain roads in Valais side valleys

High-altitude trail, Saas-Fee

A pleasant encounter, Zermatt

Kreuzboden, looking towards Saas-Fee

Moosalp (15)

Leg 14

⑩ Balfrin high-altitude trail from Grächen to Saas-Fee

Hannigalp is also the departure point for a high-altitude trail to Saas-Fee via Balfrinalp. This is a fairly demanding hike taking seven hours, but the effort is rewarded with a stunning panoramic view over the glaciers and four-thousanders. At times the path hugs the rock face with a vertiginous drop below and at others crosses scree slopes and alpine meadows. —> 8 km

⑪ Saas-Fee: the Mittelallalin experience

Take the world's highest underground funicular, the Métro Alpin, to enjoy views from the world's highest panoramic restaurant surrounded by snow and ice. Some might like to continue up to their first four-thousander, the Allalinhorn (4,027m), while others might prefer to visit the 5,000 m³ ice pavilion or enjoy a 360° view over the Mischabels range from the revolving Threes!xty restaurant in a cool musical ambience. —> 16 km

⑫ Spielboden: the marmot trail

Marmots are a firm favourite with children and adults alike. You have the opportunity to get to know these amusing and not-so-shy little creatures better on the path between the Spielboden gondola lift station and the Gletschergrotte restaurant. If you throw them carrots and walnuts they immediately collect them to store away for the winter. —> 16 km

⑬ Saas-Grund: Kreuzboden and Hohsaas

You will be able to see eighteen four-thousanders on the Hohsaas themed trail (1.4 km), which gives a detailed presentation of each peak. The cable car climbs 840 metres to Kreuzboden, then an additional 750 metres to reach Hohsaas. Things to see and do include a trout lake, a children's zoo with Chinese pigs and miniature goats, go-karts and giant kick-scooters to ride down to Saas-Grund. —> 13 km

⑭ Walser trail: from Kreuzboden to Visperterminen

Two very popular high-altitude trails leave from Kreuzboden. One of them leads to Furggstalden via the Almagelleralp, the other to Gspon (4 hrs) and Visperterminen (+3 hrs) via Heimischgarten Chapel following the Great Walser Trail, which offers some spectacular views. —> 13 km

⑮ Törbel, Moosalp, Unterbäch: crossing the mountain

When you leave Zermatt Valley and the Saas Valley you can branch off when you reach Stalden and follow a remarkably picturesque road to Bürchen, via Törbel and Moosalp. Then continue to Zeneggen and Visp, unless you prefer to go via Unterbäch, a trail-blazing village for voting rights for Swiss women, to arrive directly in Ergisch and Turtmann in the Rhône Valley. —> 15 km

The route

From Visp, drive up the valley on the by-road. When you reach Stalden, fork off to Zermatt Valley or the Saas Valley (places of interest are presented in the opposite order).

Distance: 60 kilometres (to Täsch and back)

Photo opportunity: From St. Niklaus you start to see the first summits of the Breithorn and the Klein Matterhorn at the end of Zermatt Valley. The Matterhorn can only be seen once you arrive in Zermatt, which you reach by shuttle train from Täsch.

To savour: Rye has been grown in Valais for centuries as the valley's climate is particularly suitable for this crop. Bread had to keep for several months since the communal ovens were only lit two or three times a year, giving rise to the famous Valais rye bread. It can also be made with walnuts or dried fruit, which are both particularly delicious.

Worth a detour

Täsch: Zermatt Shuttle from the covered car park, leaving every 20 minutes (traffic prohibited to Zermatt) – www.matterhorngotthardbahn.ch

Zermatt: Matterhorn Museum – Zermatlantis, the growth of Zermatt, the triumph and tragedy of the first ascension – www.zermatlantis.ch

Saas-Fee: tree-top adventure park and zip wire crossing the Fee Gorge/Feeblitz rail toboggan run/alpine gorge – www.saas-fee.ch/aventure

Tourist information

Zermatt Tourismus
Bahnhofplatz 5, 3920 Zermatt
+41 (0)27 966 81 00; www.zermatt.ch

Zermatt Bergbahnen (aerial lifts)
Schluhmattstrasse 28, 3920 Zermatt
+41 (0)27 966 01 01; www.matterhornparadise.ch

Gornergrat Bahn
Bahnhofplatz 7, 3900 Brig
+41 (0)848 642 442; www.gornergratbahn.ch

Saas-Fee/Saastal Tourismus
Obere Dorfstrasse 2, 3906 Saas-Fee
+41 (0)27 958 18 58; www.saas-fee.ch

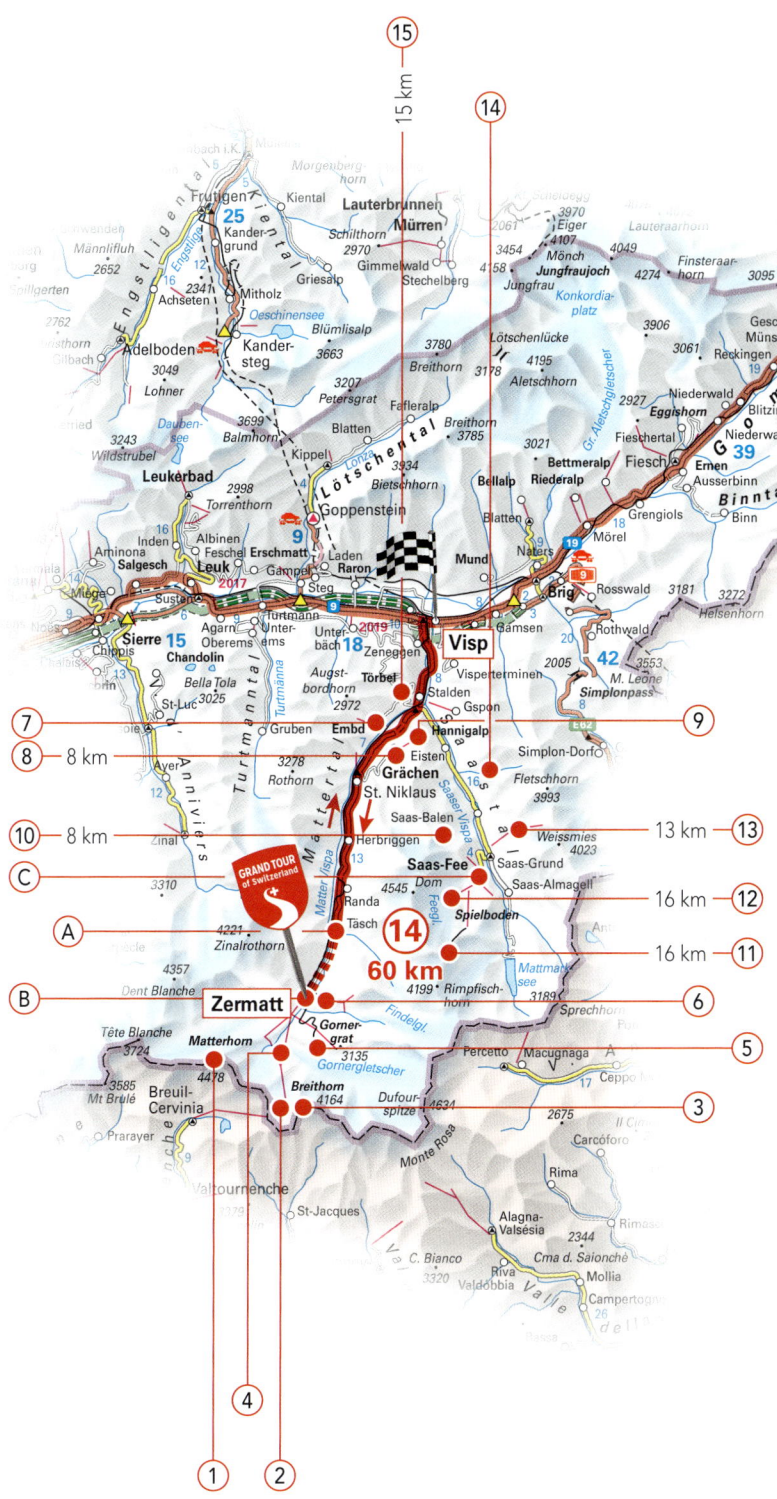

Zermatt, the Visp and Saas Valleys
Valais region

Visperterminen (1)

Southern Lötschberg Ramp (2)

The Lötschberg RegioExpress train

Meier pork butchers, Turtmann

The two churches at Raron (3)

Leg 15

Visp – Martigny

Highways and byways in central Valais

Only a few dozen kilometres separate the towns of Visp and Martigny as the crow flies, but we strongly recommend that you spend at least a day on this leg. At Visperterminen you can visit the highest vineyard in the Alps with its famous "Heida" and at Raron, not far from Visp, the grave of the poet Rainer Maria Rilke and the Church of St. Michael dating from 1974 and carved out of the rock. Don't miss the most famous of Valais pork butchers, Meieir, in Turtmann, nor the 400-year-old ossuary in Leuk under the former church, with its memento mori: "What you are, we once were. What we are, you will become".

There's a lot to see so you won't make fast time. In Varen, you mustn't miss the view over the Rhône and Pfyn Forest before crossing the Salgesch vineyard as you approach the language border. We now leave Walser German behind us and French becomes the main language.

Historic irrigation channels run parallel with the road as far as Martigny. They are known as "bisses" in Valais. Even today they are used to carry water to fields and vineyards in this canton which receives more than its fair share of sunshine. The Musée des Bisses in Ayent retraces their history, and Nendaz has the most extensive network of "bisses" still in use. Contact local tourist offices for information about walks along the "bisses".

① Visp and Visperterminen

If the Grand Tour takes you to Visp on a Friday afternoon, seize the opportunity to taste local Valais specialities at the Pürumärt (farmers' market) and buy provisions. A little further on you can taste some Heida, the famous fruity, spicy white wine from the highest vineyard in the Alps. You can learn all about it at a tasting at the St. Jodern wine cellar or on a walk following the themed trail. —> 5 km

② Southern Lötschberg Ramp

On the road towards central Valais you might spot a RegioExpress train high up on your right on the Southern Lötschberg Ramp, a railway line which was put into operation by the cantons of Bern and Valais in 1913. A hiking trail runs parallel with the railway line between Hohtenn and Brig. The bridges and tunnels are spectacular and you don't have to be a railway enthusiast to find them fascinating! —> 6 km

③ Raron church: The grave of Rainer Maria Rilke

Born in Prague, René Karl Wilhelm Johann Josef Maria Rilke settled in Switzerland at the age of 44. Before he fell ill he lived for several years at the Château de Muzot above Sierre. He was buried in Raron cemetery, just next to the baroque church, in accordance with his wishes. The Maison Pancrace de Courten in Sierre houses a permanent exhibition devoted to the poet featuring letters, manuscripts, books and photographs.

Lötschental, Bietschhorn (4)

Leukerbad (6)

View of the Gemmi (6)

At Lake Dauben, Gemmi (6)

On the language border, Leuk

Pfyn Forest (7)

Leuk ossuary

Leg 15

④ Lötschental: Tschäggättä and its terrifying masks

The villages in this archetypal alpine valley, surrounded by stunning mountain scenery, have preserved some archaic traditions. At carnival time some terrifying figures roam the villages in the Lötschental: the Tschäggätta, clothed in furs and wearing strange masks sculpted from wood. At Ferden you can learn to sculpt your own mask. You can draw inspiration from the Lötschentaler Museum in Kippel!—> 19 km

⑤ Erschmatt: endangered species garden and rye bread

In Switzerland, growing rye is a time-honoured tradition. The endangered species garden preserves and grows not only old varieties of rye but also local wildflowers such as corncockle, love-in-the-mist and larkspur. The rye is ground at the village mill and used to make the traditional Valais bread. On certain days visitors can watch the grain being turned into flour and make their own Valais bread. —> 11 km

⑥ Leukerbad: the Gemmi Pass

If you feel like relaxing, you'll find the Alps' largest thermal facility in Leukerbad. Four million litres of water at 51°C gush from the mountain to fill public and private pools. Relax and enjoy the benefits of the water while looking out at the stunning mountain scenery. You might notice the old path leading up to the Gemmi Pass, the old route to the Bernese Oberland, which can be reached more comfortably nowadays by cable car from both sides. —> 17 km

⑦ Pfyn Forest and the free-flowing Rhône

Between Leuk and Sierre the Grand Tour crosses the language border between German and French. Stop just beyond the church in Varen to enjoy the view over the Rhône and Pfyn Forest from the church terrace. This is the only place where the river has not been canalised. It provides shelter for beavers, kingfishers, little ringed plovers and other rare animals.

⑧ Salgesch: winegrowing centre and nature reserve visitors centre

Vineyards stretch as far as the eye can see on the slopes and around the villages. This is where a very good pinot noir called Pfyfoltru (meaning butterfly in local dialect) is made. To learn more, visit the Valais Museum of Wine and Winegrowing at the Zumofenhaus in Salgesch. While you're there, don't forget to pay a visit to the Pfyn-Finges nature reserve visitors centre installed in a 300-year-old former commandery of the Knights of St. John.

⑨ The Valais Wine Trail from Leuk to Martigny

The Grand Tour now largely follows the Valais Wine Trail. Opened a few years ago, this route offers three separate itineraries: a footpath, a cycle trail and a road. The routes are all way-marked and pass through small winegrowing villages where you might be able to take part in an impromptu wine tasting.

Sion, the capital of Valais, with Valère (15)

The Vallon de Réchy between Val d'Anniviers and Val d'Hérens (13)

Leuk town centre

Grimentz, Val d'Anniviers (11)

Vineyard between Sierre and Sion (9)

Near Granges, between Sierre and Sion

Leg 15

⑩ Sierre: swimming in the Lac de Géronde
Located in town yet surrounded by vines, the Lac de Géronde is a former arm of the Rhône. It lies very close to our route. On one side it offers swimming pool facilities with a huge water slide, but you can swim at any point around the lake.

⑪ Val d'Anniviers and the village of Grimentz
Val d'Anniviers is worth a visit. Driving along the excellent mountain road which lies above it is a very enjoyable experience in its own right, heightened by the sight of snowy peaks at the end of the valley. Thousands of bright red geraniums bring a cheerful touch to the sun-scorched wooden façades of the houses in the car-free main street of Grimentz. The Maison Bourgeoisiale houses the Bishop's Barrel containing the famous Glacier wine, a very special white wine which used to be reserved for leading dignitaries. —> 22 km

⑫ Chandolin, the Illhorn and the Illgraben trench
Did you know that you can see the Matterhorn from the Val d'Anniviers? Stand in front of Chandolin church and look southwards. The Matterhorn's sharp peak can be seen at the end of the valley above Zinal. If you climb up above the holiday hamlets you can enjoy this alpine view to the full. You'll find another impressive natural phenomenon three kilometres to the north of Chandolin. The spectacular Illgraben trench almost seems to echo with the mass of stone that has collapsed into it. —> 25 km

⑬ Vercorin and Vallon de Réchy
Off the beaten track: Leave the Val d'Anniviers by the small road which goes through Pinsec (worth a visit). Stop in the small resort of Vercorin and take the gondola lift to the Crêt du Midi. Continue climbing upwards on foot for about an hour. The four-thousanders will suddenly appear at the end of the valley while to the west lies the Réchy Valley, preserved from all human activity, which has been awarded national natural landmark status. —> 13 km

⑭ Crans-Montana: the Plaine Morte Glacier plateau
On the other side of the Rhône, the Crans-Montana resort is well-known for its golf tournaments and mountain bike trails. You can reach the glacier, which straddles the Rhône Valley, Valais and the Bernese Simmental, in about 30 minutes with a gondola lift and funitel. —> 14 km

⑮ Sion: the Old Town with Valère and Tourbillon
The capital of Valais is easily recognisable with its two distinctive hills, Tourbillon and Valère. The oldest town in Switzerland (although some people think that Chur holds this honour) has a superb Old Town with an abundance of cafés and restaurants. The fortified Church of Notre-Dame de Valère is famous for its 15th century swallow's nest organ, which is perhaps the world's oldest functioning organ. The world's greatest organists meet here every summer for the Organ Festival.

Grande Dixence Dam (16)

"Bisses" at Nendaz (17)

Derborence (18)

The counterfeiter Farinet (19)

Saillon thermal baths (19)

Leg 15

⑯ Grande Dixence and the pyramids of Euseigne

The next large valley in southern Valais is Val d'Hérens with the villages of Evolène and Les Haudères where local traditions are still very much alive. The Grande Dixence dam, the interior of which can be visited, lies in a side valley to the west. Near Euseigne, where the two valleys meet, stand the famous pyramids formed through erosion of moraine erosion, each one protected by a rock cap. —> 28 km

⑰ "Bisses" at Nendaz: historic irrigation channels

Throughout Valais, from the Goms Valley to Lake Geneva, farmers built irrigation channels known as "bisses". Nendaz, where apricots and raspberries are grown on a large scale, has the most extensive network of "bisses" still in use. There are many lovely walks without much of an incline along these peaceful artificial streams. —> 15 km

⑱ Derborence: the Diablerets rock fall

This is a dream for lovers of picturesque mountain roads. Just after Aven the road heads into a narrow valley interspersed with tunnels and windows in the rock. This dramatic and wild landscape inspired the author C.F. Ramuz to write his famous novel "Derborence". A massive rock slide in the Diablerets range buried the fertile pastures beneath it in 1749. —> 16 km

⑲ The Saillon and the Ovronnaz baths

In the Rhône Valley and 800 metres higher up at the foot of the Muverans range, you will find two thermal centres for a relaxing break. The Saillon thermal baths offers four pools, a spa and a thermal river. Saillon is also famous for providing refuge to the counterfeiter Farinet in the 19th century. The Thermalp thermal centre in the peaceful mountain resort of Ovronnaz offers two outdoor pools and a complete range of wellness treatments. —> 0/8 km

Visp – Martigny
Valais region

The route

A fairly busy main road to Leuk, then by-roads to the right of the Rhône until you reach Sierre. The main road via Sion to Ardon, then by-roads once more through winegrowing villages towards Fully and Martigny.

Distance: 75 kilometres

Photo opportunity: The section between Leuk and Salgesch with a view of Pfyn Forest followed by the vineyard route (NB: take care to follow the road via Leuk and Varen).

Did you know? Until the last century nomadic farmers in Val d'Anniviers had several homes. They took their cattle up to the mountain pastures in summer and grew rye in the valley on their way up and back. In the Rhône Valley they grew fruit trees and vines. The hay for winter was also stored in different places. Lastly, Glacier wine was left to age (as it still is) in cellars in old larch barrels containing wines from different years.

Worth a detour

(A) **Leukerbad:** holiday resort and thermal baths – www.leukerbad.ch

(B) **Saint-Léonard:** underground lake with boat trip – www.lac-souterrain.com

(C) **Ayent:** Musée des Bisses, exhibition and information – www.musee-des-bisses.ch

(D) **Dixence:** power plants, lake, dam, guided tours – www.grande-dixence.ch

Tourist information

Visp Tourismus
Balfrinstrasse 3, 3930 Visp
+41 (0)27 946 18 18; www.vispinfo.ch

Office du Tourisme de Sierre et environs
Place de la Gare 10, 3960 Sierre
+41(0)27 455 85 35; www.sierretourisme.ch

Office du Tourisme de Sion
Place de la Planta 2, 1950 Sion
+41 (0)27 327 77 27; www.siontourisme.ch

Valais/Wallis Promotion
Rue Pré Fleuri 6, 1951 Sion
+41 (0)27 327 35 90; www.valaistourism.ch

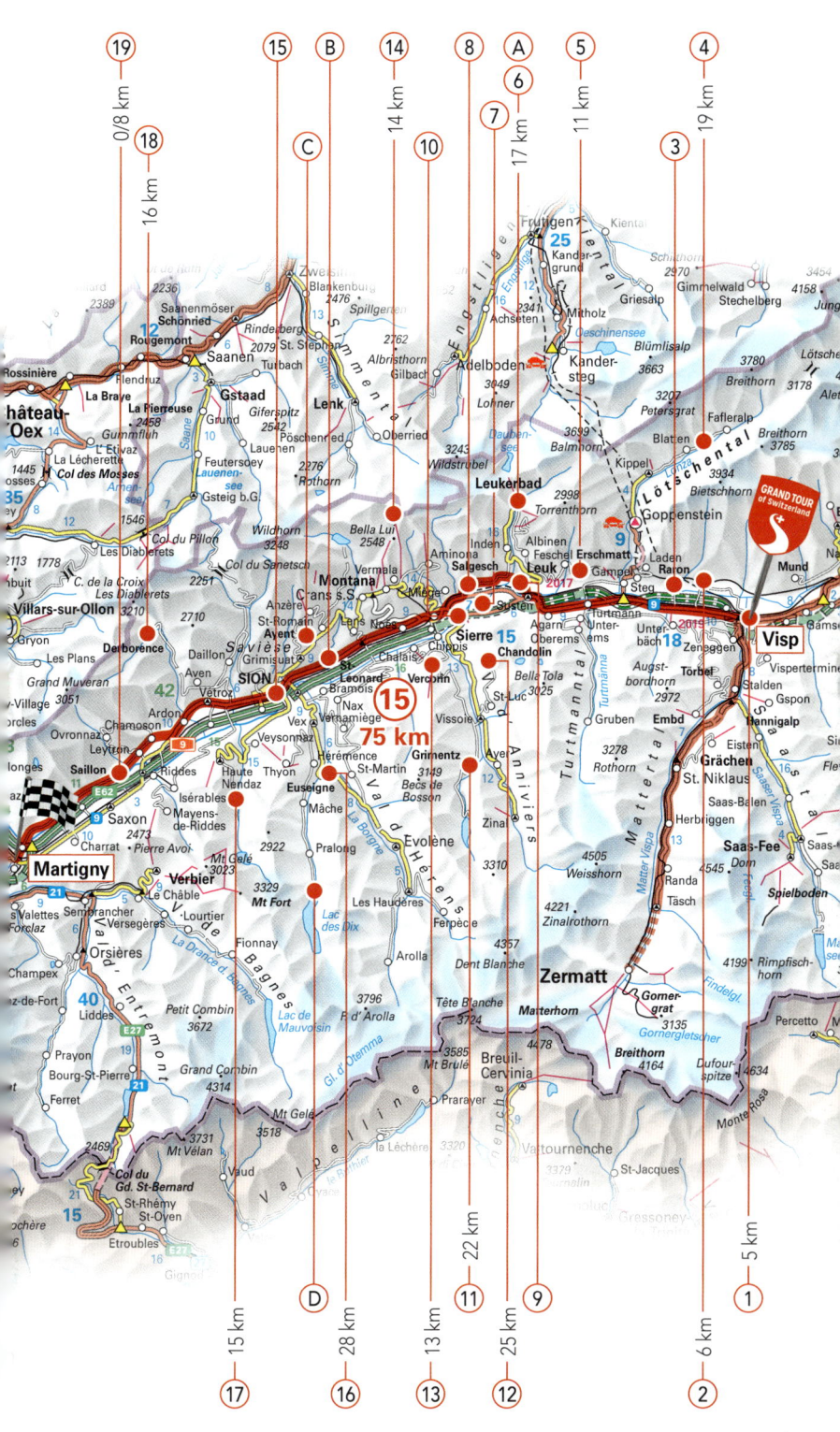

Visp – Martigny
Valais region

Romandy – Geneva region

Romandy belongs to the Francophone world through its language, culture and mentality. Encompassing the Jura Mountains, Lake Geneva and its vineyards and terraces and the glaciers of the Diablerets range, the region offers landscapes which are every bit as rich and varied as the rest of Switzerland.

Lavaux, Lake Geneva

Yvorne near Aigle, the Tour d'Aï in the background

Vineyard at Martigny (1)

Roman amphitheatre (2)

St. Bernard dogs, Martigny (4)

The Fondation Gianadda Museum (3)

Leg 16

Martigny – Montreux

From the Rhône bend to Lake Geneva

Martigny stands at the crossroads of the roads to the Great St. Bernard Pass (and Aosta in Italy) and to the Forclaz Pass (and Chamonix in France). Many different cultures have left their mark here since Gallo-Roman times. Take the road towards Lake Geneva and make a right-angle turn in relation the Rhône, which has been our companion since the Furka Pass.

Travel past the Saint-Maurice Gorge, then Europe's oldest inhabited monastery before reaching the vineyards of Bex, Aigle and Yvorne. You then enter the canton of Vaud, while on the left bank of the Rhône the canton of Valais continues right up to Lake Geneva, which we will reach at the end of this leg.

This section offers numerous excursions to the resorts of Val d'Illiez (Portes du Soleil, a mountain biking park) or to the Vaud Alps towards Leysin, Villars-sur-Ollon and Les Diablerets (Glacier 3,000 cable car station).

① Martigny

Surrounded by vineyards and orchards, the town lies in a bend in the Rhône and is renowned for its gastronomy and its strawberries, apricots, grapes and asparagus which thrive in the warm Valais sunshine. Celtic tribes, the Romans and even Napoleon's troops passed through here.

② Roman amphitheatre

Martigny was already an important crossroads for trade during Roman times. Don't miss the remains of the Roman baths, temples and residential quarters, and above all the restored amphitheatre which could seat 5,000 spectators.

③ The Fondation Gianadda Museum

Built on the remains of a Roman temple, the building houses a Gallo-Roman museum and car museum and also hosts temporary exhibitions (renewed every six months) of work by world-class artists. The Foundation's large park also contains a fine collection of sculptures by leading 20th century artists.

④ The Grand-Saint-Bernard Pass and Martigny: St. Bernard dogs

The famous hospice in which an exhausted Napoleon and his soldiers found respite from battle stands in the barren alpine landscape of the Grand-Saint-Bernard Pass. This is also where monks bred St. Bernard dogs, initially to carry loads and subsequently to rescue avalanche victims. You can still admire these fine animals here and even go hiking with them – a memorable experience.

The dog museum in Martigny (the Fondation Barry) is full of anecdotes and information about St. Bernard dogs. —> 45/0 km

Lac des Chavonnes, Villars-sur-Ollon (11)

View from the summit of Mont-Fort (5)

Pierre Avoi (6)

Alpine flower garden, Pont de Nant

Amusement park, Emosson (8)

Pissevache (7)

Leg 16

⑤ Mont-Fort: panorama and mountain biking

Drive from Verbier or Nendaz (Siviez) to the Col des Gentianes, where you can catch a cable-car to the summit of Mont-Fort. Steps lead up to a cross on the very top of the summit 20 metres above, offering a vista over the surrounding glaciers and mountains. Mountain bikers will enjoy the long downhill stretches and some spectacular sections on the Tour du Mont-Fort (tdmf.ch). —> 27 km

⑥ Verbier: Pierre Avoi, a rock with a view

This peak with magnificent views lies to the east of Martigny. Climbing the Pierre Avoi from Savoleyres (particularly the last 50 metres which include ladders with hand rails) is not advisable for vertigo sufferers. Access from Verbier or La Tzoumaz, then gondola lift and chairlift to Savoleyres. —> 27 km

⑦ Trient Gorge and Pissevache

Now we're back on the Grand Tour's main route, heading for Saint-Maurice and Lake Geneva. You reach the next points of interest at Vernayaz. This is where the Mont-Blanc Express starts its spectacular climb up the Trient Valley towards Salvan, Les Marécottes, Le Châtelard and Chamonix.

Bridges and footways provide access to the 200-metre-deep gorge dug out of the crystalline rock by the Trient River and crossed by two dizzyingly high bridges. A little further north the Pissevache waterfall plunges from a height of 114 metres into the Rhône Valley; Goethe was so impressed that he wrote about it in 1779.

⑧ Le Châtelard – Lac d'Emosson

Further up the Trient Valley you come to the Emosson dam. A two-and-a-half hour walk will take you to dinosaur footprints left on the shores of an ocean before the Alps were formed, 240 million years ago.

The dam can be reached by car from Finhaut (Martigny – the Forclaz Pass) or from the Parc d'Attractions du Châtelard amusement park via funicular (87% slope, 60 cm gauge rails) and the "Minifunic" funicular/cable car hybrid up to the 180-metre-high crest of the dam. After Le Châtelard, continue via the Forclaz Pass or take the train from Martigny towards Chamonix. —> 25 km

⑨ Saint-Maurice: treasures of religious art in the abbey basilica

We now set off towards Saint-Maurice Gorge. The monastery, which is exactly 1,500 years old, displays some masterpieces of religious silverware in the basilica. In 515, Sigismund, son of Gundobad (King of the Burgundians) founded the abbey on the site where martyrs where buried. Not far from here you can explore the first 500 metres of the Fairies' Cave in Saint-Maurice Gorge, as far as the 50-metre-high underground waterfall.

The Peak Walk suspension bridge, Glacier 3000 (14)

Aigle Castle, wine museum (12)

Bex salt mine (10)

The Fairy's Cave, Saint-Maurice (9)

Saint-Maurice (9)

Kuklos, Berneuse, Leysin (13)

Leg 16

⑩ Bex: tour of the salt mine
After the Saint-Maurice Gorge the Rhone Valley widens out. The Bex salt mine covers a total of 50 kilometres and still produces 30,000 tons of salt per year. A train takes visitors 400 metres into the heart of the mountain and the museum tells the story of the mine from 1684 to the present day, and explains how salt arrived in the mountain 200 million years ago when the sea receded.

⑪ Villars-sur-Ollon: from the funicular to mushroom omelette
Legend has it that Lac des Chavonnes, which lies above the valley near Bretaye, hides a hoard of hidden treasure. The mushroom specialities and raspberry desserts served in the mountain restaurant are just as legendary. Since 1913 a funicular has linked Bex to the Bretaye Pass (in the GA zone). The first rail connection between Gryon and Villars-sur-Ollon dates from 1905. —> 16 km

⑫ Aigle Castle: The Vine and Wine Museum
Aigle Castle stands in state surrounded by the vineyards on the slopes of the Vaud Alps about a dozen kilometres before the Rhône reaches Lake Geneva. The building dates from the 12th century and now houses the Vine, Wine and Label Museum.

⑬ Leysin: the Kuklos revolving restaurant on the Berneuse
The mountain overlooking Leysin and Aigle is well-known for its mountain restaurant Kuklos (meaning "circle" in Greek). This gleaming and futuristic panoramic restaurant takes 90 minutes to complete a full rotation thanks to the solar energy produced on site. Diners enjoy a unique view which includes the Eiger, Mont-Blanc and Lake Geneva. —> 15 km

⑭ Glacier 3000: a world of snow and ice
The Diablerets Glacier plateau is a playground for devils: on stormy days they throw stones in an effort to topple the 40-metre-high Quille du Diable (Devil's skittle), a peak also known as Tour Saint-Martin, spreading trepidation in the Derborence Valley 1,500 metres below. The cable car from the Col du Pillon provides access to some easy walks in the snow, the impressive Peak Walk suspension bridge and the Alpine Coaster toboggan run. Take the road from Aigle to the Col du Pillon or, as for leg 24, from Saanen/Gstaad. —> 24 km

⑮ The Col des Mosses: the home of Etivaz
Small cheese dairies throughout the Vaud Alps produce this cellar-matured alpine cheese with a distinctive flavour. At Lioson d'en Bas (the Col des Mosses, between Aigle and Château-d'Oex) this long-established expertise is preserved and perpetuated: every day from late May to mid September, from 9.30 to 10.30 am, the cheese is made is the traditional way using large copper cauldrons over a wood fire. —> 19 km

The route

The by-road from Martigny to the shores of Lake Geneva, surrounded first by tall mountains and then by the vast plain on the right bank of the Rhône.

Distance: 46 kilometres

Photo opportunity: Steep slopes until you reach the impressive Saint-Maurice Gorge. Vista of vineyards around Aigle Castle and the Yvorne.

To savour: The Chasselas grape used to make Les Murailles wine is grown around Aigle and Yvorne. You can taste Switzerland's most popular white wine, accompanied by a selection of "fromage à rebibes" (finely shaved cheeses), in the region's wine cellars.

Worth a detour

(A) **Evionnaz:** maze and adventure park – www.labyrinthe.ch

(B) **Lavey-les-Bains:** thermal baths at the Grand Hôtel – www.lavey-les-bains.ch

(C) **Val d'Illiez / Portes du Soleil:** excursions, hiking, mountain bike park – www.portesdusoleil.com

(D) **Le Bouveret:** Swiss Vapeur Park with miniature trains and Aquaparc – www.swissvapeur.ch / www.aquaparc.ch

Tourist information

Office de Tourisme Martigny
Avenue de la Gare 6, 1920 Martigny
+41 (0)27 720 49 49; www.martigny.com

St-Maurice Tourisme
Avenue des Terreaux 1, 1890 Saint-Maurice
+41 (0)24 485 40 40; www.saint-maurice.ch

Chablais Région
Place du Marché 1, 1860 Aigle
+41 (0)24 471 15 15; www.chablais.ch

Bouveret Tourisme
Bâtiment CFF, 1897 Le Bouveret
+41 (0)24 481 51 21; www.bouveret.ch

Martigny – Montreux
Romandy – Geneva region

Cully, Lavaux, Lake Geneva (11)

Montreux (1)

Chillon Castle (2)

Freddie Mercury, Montreux (1)

Steam boat on Lake Geneva (3)

Leg 17

Montreux – Saint-George

Picturesque roads above Lake Geneva

Don't hesitate to linger awhile in Montreux. If you didn't have time to visit Chillon Castle yesterday, do it this morning, following the beautiful flower-lined promenade along the lake to the famous castle. You can return to town by trolley bus and then you'll be all set to start leg 17, heading for Saint-George. The name isn't familiar? At the foot of the Col du Marchairuz, the access road from Geneva and Saint-George will take us into the Jura uplands.

But before that, today's journey is full of contrasts. Firstly you cross the Lavaux vineyard (a World Heritage Site) on winding and occasionally narrow roads. You will have the opportunity to taste local wines (in moderation, if you are getting back behind the wheel) in winemaking villages which exude southern charm, and enjoy a delicious meal. There is however little accommodation, and it's advisable to continue to Lutry, Pully or Lausanne for the night. The Grand Tour then takes you along the shore of the lake to the Olympic museum and Ouchy harbour. Park here and take the metro, which somewhat resembles a mountain train. In just a few minutes you arrive in the city centre of Lausanne, the sparkling capital of the canton of Vaud. The shores of the lake are built up as far as Morges, where we turn off towards the Jura.

① Montreux: flowers and a stroll on the shores of Lake Geneva

In 1987 Freddie Mercury sang "This could be heaven", and he was right! Apart from leading jazz musicians during the Montreux Jazz Festival, the town also offers Switzerland's most beautiful lakeside promenades and just a stone's throw away, one of the country's most photographed landmarks: Chillon castle, built on an island in Lake Geneva. The car-free promenade stretches for over seven kilometres from Clarens to Chillon and the lakeside restaurants around Villeneuve, via Montreux and its impressive statue of Freddie.

② Chillon Castle

At the end of the flower-lined promenade at Montreux stands the very famous Chillon Castle. Its turbulent history and spectacular position on a rocky island make it one of Switzerland's most visited monuments. For almost four centuries the castle was a residence and very lucrative toll station for the Counts of Savoy, before falling into the hands of the Bern authorities in 1536 and finally the Vaud authorities in 1798. The damp dungeons at lake level always make visitors shudder.

③ Steam tour on Lake Geneva

As you stand by the lake at Chillon or on the promenade at Montreux, sooner or later you're bound to feel an urge to take an excursion on the Upper Lake between Vevey, Montreux, Chillon, Villeneuve and Le Bouveret. The CGN's Belle Époque paddle steamers have plied the waters of central Europe's largest lake for 130 years. They offer tours between France and Switzerland and between Geneva and the upper part of the lake.

Le Dézaley, Lavaux (11)

GoldenPass Panoramic, with Montreux in the background (6)

Glérolles Castle, Lavaux (11)

Nestlé head office, Vevey

On the shores of Lake Geneva

Les Pléiades (8)

Leg 17

④ Montreux – Chauderon Gorge

The impressive and wild Chauderon Gorge above the town is still little-known by tourists. The Chauderon, which flows down from the Col de Jaman continues peacefully through the town. However, on entering this magical gorge (the entrance is located under the motorway bridge) you turn your back on civilisation; an hour's walk takes you to the panoramic terrace at Glion.

⑤ The Rochers de Naye: Montreux and Lake Geneva at your feet

The rack-and-pinion railway takes you on an interesting itinerary leaving from the station, via Glion to the Dent de Jaman and then around the mountain to one of Montreux's emblems. The Rochers, which overlook the town from a height of 1,650 metres, are as much part of Montreux as Chillon and the jazz festival. The restaurant Plein-Roc, clinging to the rock face, offers a superb view of Lake Geneva.

⑥ MOB (the Montreux – Oberland-Bernois railway): express train to the Bernese Oberland

The Panoramic Express awaits you at Montreux railway station for a journey to the Bernese Oberland. The GoldenPass-Line is one of the world's most spectacular railway lines. Leaving the palm trees of the French-speaking "Vaud Riviera" behind, the panoramic train climbs up through the vineyards to the meadows and hills of the Pays-d'Enhaut before continuing to the Saanen area and the German-speaking Simmental.

⑦ The Blonay – Chambly museum railway

The old Blonay – Chamby railway line above Clarens now operates as a railway museum. It has the second largest collection of metre gauge rolling stock in Switzerland. The two exhibition halls in Chaulin present more than 60 heritage vehicles in working order, from a steam locomotive to an electric tram. Closed in winter. —> 5 km

⑧ Les Pléiades: amongst the stars and the narcissi

At the level of the N12 motorway junction for Fribourg, on the wooded hills of Les Pléiades there is a belvedere with an open air exhibition devoted to the universe. The Astro-Pléiades educational trail guides visitors from observation on earth to the solar system and fixed stars and ends with the extragalactic universe. In springtime, a host of narcissi adorns the surrounding fields, making this a very popular setting for wedding photos. —> 15 km

⑨ Towards Mont Pèlerin

To reach the mountain above Vevey by car or funicular you have to pass through the Chardonne vineyard. When you reach the upper station or the Monts de Chardonne, continue on foot for about an hour until you reach the television transmission tower, then by lift up to the Plein Ciel panoramic viewing platform, 770 metres above Lake Geneva. Open to the public since 1995, this 64-metre tower can be visited from Easter to October. —> 8 km

Lavaux terraced vineyard (11)

Vevey (10)

Saint-Saphorin

Notre-Dame Cathedral and metro, Lausanne (13/14)

Lausanne (12)

Leg 17

⑩ Vevey: Charlie Chaplin and the shores of Lake Geneva

You'll meet a celebrity on the shores of Lake Geneva: Charlie Chaplin, who settled in Corsier with his family; his children attended the local school. A statue on the promenade at Vevey commemorates the 25 years that the actor, scriptwriter and producer spent here. The Chaplin's World museum is to open in spring 2016 at Manoir de Ban, former home of the Chaplin family.

⑪ Lavaux terraced vineyard, a World Heritage Site

After Vevey, the Grand Tour climbs up to the vineyard. The route passes through the World Heritage Site of Lavaux, with its terraced vineyards set against the lake below and snowy summits behind, until it reaches Lutry. With 830 hectares, this is one of Switzerland's largest winegrowing regions. The landscape is as delightful as the wines you will find in the region's many wine cellars. Narrow streets and picturesque winegrower's houses contribute to the charm of villages such as Saint-Saphorin, where the ancient Auberge de l'Onde serves delicious local specialities on its three floors.

⑫ Lausanne: a town with three hills

The capital of Vaud was built on three hills on the north shore of Lake Geneva. This means that the alleys of the old town are sometimes quite steep, like Rue du Petit-Chêne, and the metro resembles a mountain train. The town centre lies above the railway station, around Place Saint-François; the carfree historic heart of the city is studded with monuments and exudes Mediterranean charm. Take the time to wander through the medieval town with its delightful cafés and shops. Don't forget to savour regional specialities such as "Papet Vaudois", made from saucisson, potatoes and leeks.

⑬ Lausanne: Notre-Dame Cathedral

The cathedral is undoubtedly the highlight of the old town. One of the most noteworthy features of this Gothic masterpiece is an early 13th century rose window over the transept. Its iconography includes earth and heaven, air and fire, the four seasons, the months and signs of the zodiac as well as monsters. Ever since 1405 a night watchman has called the hour from the clock tower from 10 pm to 2 am and the tradition continues to this day.

⑭ The Lausanne metro: metro or mountain train?

Every few minutes a metro leaves the Lausanne-Ouchy station to climb silently to the CFF mainline station, the town centre (Flon) and further on, Epalinges-Croisettes. This six-kilometre line covers a record climb of 336 metres with a maximum incline of 12%. It is entirely automatic so has no driver; feel free to sit at the very front and fulfil a childhood dream!

On the shores of Lake Geneva, Tour d'Aï and Tour de Mayen

Ouchy harbour, Lausanne (16)

Vufflens Castle, Morges (18)

École Polytechnique (EPFL) (17)

Lakeside promenade at Nyon

Olympic Museum, Lausanne

Leg 17

(15) Sauvabelin Forest and Lausanne Vivarium

Leisure time just outside the city. Lausanne residents love to go swimming in this woodland lake, and relax in its friendly restaurant. Not far from here is a 35-metre viewing tower, with a staircase which was inspired by the one designed for Chambord by Leonardo da Vinci.

The Parc de l'Hermitage and its famous art museum lies nearby, while the Lausanne Vivarium can be found north of the motorway. It houses one of Europe's largest reptile and insect collections, with snakes, lizards, crocodiles, tortoises, amphibians, scorpions, tarantulas, etc. —> 6 km

(16) Ouchy Lausanne's port on Lake Geneva

Return to Ouchy to savour the lakeside atmosphere to the full with the Olympic Park, Ouchy Castle (which is now a hotel) and the paddle steamer landing stage. Before taking to the road again, treat yourself to a coffee in the Watergate Lounge at the Voile d'Or, between the beach and the marina. Sit back in its white wicker furniture and enjoy the stunning view and sophisticated ambience.

(17) EPFL: Rolex Learning Center

It would be hard to miss the unique, wave-shaped building which houses the Ecole Polytechnique Fédérale de Lausanne (EPFL) on the Lausanne-Dorigny campus. In the space of a few years the campus has become an international centre for communication, culture and learning. The Rolex Learning Center impresses visitors with its disconcerting and spectacular shape, designed by internationally acclaimed Japanese architects. Lovers of modern architecture will be pleased to learn that the building is open to the public!

(18) Vufflens Castle

In Morges, the Grand Tour leaves the densely populated shores of Lake Geneva around Lausanne. Our route takes us under the motorway and railway and the dramatic outline of Vufflens Castle, with its 60-metre-high keep, soon appears in the distance. Built on the site of a medieval castle (and no doubt inspired by the design of Piedmontese castles) it occupies an idyllic position on the banks of the River Morges, right in the middle of the vineyard. The castle is privately owned and not open to visitors, but we can admire it nonetheless!

(19) L'Isle: a French chateau in the foothills of the Vaud Jura

It might not be Versailles, but there is a resemblance. Built in 1696 by Charles de Chandieu, a lieutenant-general in the service of Louis XIV, the chateau was inspired by the French classical style. It has belonged to the town since 1877 and is used for school administration. Unfortunately it is not open to the public. It's nonetheless worth making a short detour below the Col du Mollendruz to see the park and its pools, filled with water from the River Venoge. —> 12 km

The route

Take the by-road from Montreux to Vevey, then small rural roads through the Lavaux vineyard to Lutry. Continue parallel to the lake towards Lausanne and Morges, then go via Aubonne in the foothills of the Vaud Jura to Saint-George.

Distance: 62 kilometres

Photo opportunity: Crossing the Lavaux World Heritage Site is a delightful experience which offers several opportunities to stop and enjoy the finest vistas over the lake.

To savour: "Pâté vaudois", which you will find almost everywhere, should be made in the Vaud region to be authentic. It is even better when accompanied by a glass of white wine from the slopes of Lake Geneva. Our favourite: game pâté.

Worth a detour

(A) **Vevey:** The Alimentarium, a food museum opened by Nestlé in 1985; the giant fork standing in Lake Geneva – www.alimentarium.ch

(B) **Lausanne:** Lausanne: the Olympic museum, history of the games from Antiquity to the present day – www.olympic.org/museum

(C) **Lausanne:** Fondation de l'Hermitage, temporary art exhibitions in a 19th century villa – www.fondation-hermitage.ch

(D) **Lausanne:** Musée de l'Elysée, a photography museum featuring permanent and temporary exhibitions – www.elysee.ch

(E) **Aubonne:** Arboretum with trees and shrubs from all over the world; wood museum – www.arboretum.ch

Tourist information

Montreux-Vevey Tourisme
Rue du Théâtre 5, 1820 Montreux 2
+41 (0)848 86 84 84; www.montreuxriviera.com

Lausanne Tourisme
Gare CFF, 1003 Lausanne
+41 (0)21 613 73 73; www.lausanne-tourisme.ch

Morges Région Tourisme
Rue du Château 2, 1110 Morges
+41 (0)21 801 32 33; www.morges-tourisme.ch

Office du Tourisme du Canton de Vaud
Avenue d'Ouchy 60, 1001 Lausanne
+41 (0)21 613 26 26; www.region-du-leman.ch

Montreux – Saint-George
Romandy – Geneva region

2 FOR 1-OFFERS
Savings of up to CHF 4000.–

SWISS COUPON PASS

85 DINE & EXPLORE COUPONS
Enjoy culinary treats and discover great attractions in 11 destinations along the Grand Tour of Switzerland.
www.swisscouponpass.com

stc
switzerland travel centre

DINE & EXPLORE IN 11 DESTINATIONS

- Restaurants (Swiss, Italian, Asian, Indian cuisine)
- Lunch & dinner cruises
- Dining in mountaintop restaurants
- City tours (by foot, coach, mini-train, segway)
- Rentals (boats, cars, motorcycles, sports equipment)
- Entrance to tourist attractions and fun&adventure parks
- Shopping vouchers (souvenirs, watches, chocolate, fragrances)
- First-class upgrades on trains and boats
- Airport transfer and fuel vouchers
- Mountain railways

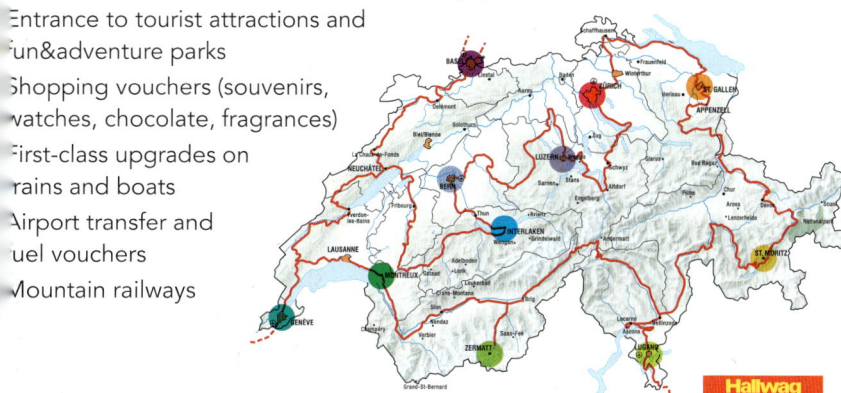

Hallwag Kümmerly+Frey

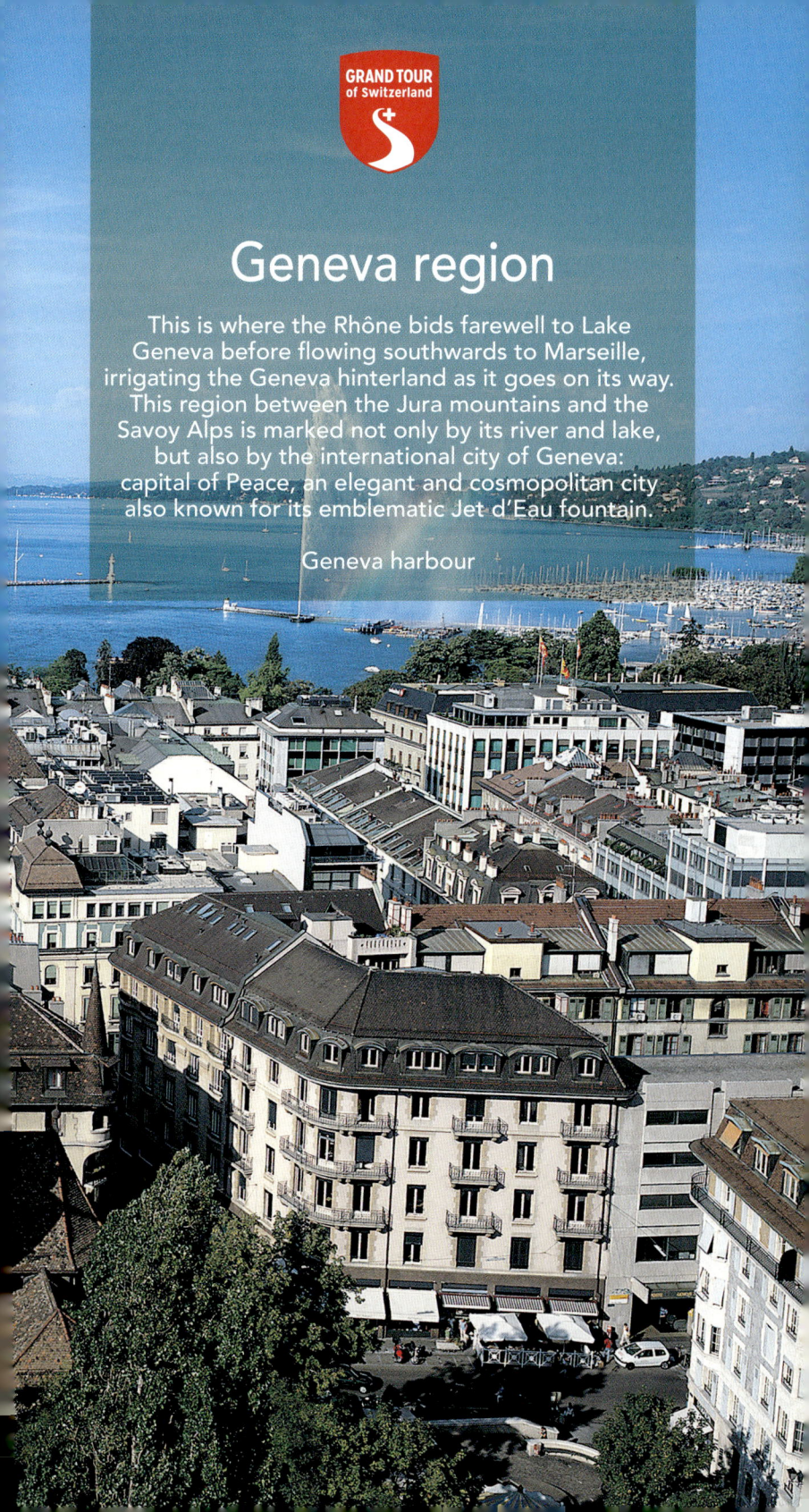

GRAND TOUR of Switzerland

Geneva region

This is where the Rhône bids farewell to Lake Geneva before flowing southwards to Marseille, irrigating the Geneva hinterland as it goes on its way. This region between the Jura mountains and the Savoy Alps is marked not only by its river and lake, but also by the international city of Geneva: capital of Peace, an elegant and cosmopolitan city also known for its emblematic Jet d'Eau fountain.

Geneva harbour

The Salève, just outside Geneva, seen from St. Pierre Cathedral (1)

Geneva city centre

View from the Salève over the Geneva hinterland (1)

Patek Philippe Museum, Geneva

The Forces Motrices converted power station (6)

Leg 18

Road from Geneva to Saint-George

Joining the Grand Tour at Geneva

If you are arriving from France, your Grand Tour of Switzerland starts when you cross the border at Saint-Julien. On your right lies Mont Salève, which is in France but the Genevans have annexed it after a fashion. You arrive via Carouge, a charming town in its own right on the edge of Geneva, near the Reformation Wall which commemorates some of the major figures of the Reformation including Jean Calvin, who marked the city's history. It is advisable to leave your car in a covered car park near the itinerary to continue your visit of the old town. You can absorb the city's atmosphere in the streets around the cathedral and on the Rhône Islands.

The Bains des Pâquis swimming baths offer an unusual choice of activities with not only a pool in the lake but also a steam bath, a restaurant and programme of cultural events. If you turn left a little further on you reach the Palace of Nations and the International Red Cross and Red Crescent Museum.

The road leading from Geneva to join the Grand Tour follows the built-up shoreline to Nyon and then branches off towards the Jura foothills and Saint-George, where it joins the central loop. The main points of interest by the lake include Madame de Staël's chateau at Coppet, the former Roman city of Nyon and the Swiss National Museum at the Chateau de Prangins.

The Salève: the "Balcony of Geneva" located in France

(1) As soon as you cross the border at Saint-Julien you see the Grand Salève on your right. Although it lies in France, the Genevans consider it to be their own official mountain. In 1887 a steam train was put into operation between the city and the Salève and in 1894 an electric rack-and-pinion railway (now replaced by a cable car) gave visitors access to the summit. Hiking trails and steep, narrow paths lead to some spectacular rocky stretches. —> 5 km

Carouge market

(2) Before reaching the cosmopolitan city of Geneva, stop off at this small town on the east bank of the River Arve, preferably on a Wednesday or Saturday morning for the market. You're bound to find what you're looking for in the Place du Marché with its small shops, craftsmen and artists.

Rafting on the River Arve

(3) The River Arve rises in the Mont Blanc region, crosses the Savoy Alps and ends its 100-kilometre journey when it joins the Rhône in the outskirts of Geneva. An eight-kilometre rafting route including six rapids offers an original way to discover the area surrounding Geneva in just three hours. —> 5 km

Place des Nations in front of the Palace of Nations (10)

Rousseau Museum, Geneva

Geneva old town (4)

Quai du Mont-Blanc

Reformation Wall (5)

St. Pierre Cathedral (4)

Leg 18

Geneva: old town and St. Pierre Cathedral

④ Old Geneva and its busy shopping district make up the heart of the city. This is where the Rhône leaves Lake Geneva to continue its journey to Marseille. St. Pierre Cathedral stands on a small hill overlooking the historic city centre with its wine bars, galleries and antique shops. If you make the effort to climb the 157 steps leading to the top of the bell tower you will be rewarded with a magnificent view over the roofs of the old town and the Lake Geneva basin. The archaeological excavation site at the foot of the cathedral is also worth a detour.

Geneva and the Reformation

⑤ The history of Geneva is closely intertwined with that of reformer Jean Calvin. The International Museum of the Reformation makes history come alive with a clear and detailed narrative of the reform from its early days to the present time. It was awarded the Council of Europe's Museum Prize in 2007. An underground passageway links the museum to the archaeological site under St. Pierre Cathedral.

The famous Reformation Wall, which pays tribute to Calvin and other figures of Protestant Geneva, stands not far from here in the Parc des Bastions, near the University of Geneva.

The city's islands

⑥ This place is charged with history. The islands, which are partly natural, house fortifications, bridges, mills and workshops, public baths and even a hydraulic power station. The former Forces Motrices hydroelectric power station has been turned into an impressive cultural centre with exhibition halls and a theatre which can seat an audience of 950 people. The Cité du Temps on Pont de la Machine houses a watch exhibition and a gourmet restaurant, while Ile Rousseau pays tribute to the famous Genevan philosopher with a statue.

Some odd birds: Mouettes Genevoises (Geneva seagulls)

⑦ Popular with tourists and Geneva residents alike, these boats are part of the public transport network and provide a shuttle service from shore to shore every 10 minutes. They are omnipresent in Geneva harbour, around the Jet d'Eau and on the adjacent Rhône.

The Jet d'Eau

⑧ The famous Jet d'Eau fountain is a prominent feature of Geneva harbour. Originally a safety valve for the high-pressure water systems used for machinery in the watchmaking industry, it can reach 140 metres in height. In 1891 the decision was taken to increase its height and illuminate it at night. It became the town's emblem and now disgorges 500 litres of lake water per second at a speed of 200 kilometres per hour, representing five tons of water spurting continuously into the air.

Bains des Pâquis with Jet d'Eau (8/9)

International Red Cross Museum (11)

UN European headquarters (10)

Nyon (13)

Nyon old town (13)

Chateau de Nyon (13)

Nyon–St-Cergue railway (14)

Leg 18

⑨ Bains des Pâquis: a swim in the city centre

When you make your way towards the Palace of Nations you pass a swimming pool built on 448 stilts. The fashionable Bains des Pâquis swimming pool reflects the Genevan way of life to perfection – whether swimming in the lake, relaxing in the steam bath or simply enjoying the view of the Jet d'Eau and Mont Blanc. Park your car at the car park in front of the baths or in an adjacent street.

⑩ Palace of Nations: UN European headquarters

Each year the United Nations Geneva headquarters in the Parc de l'Ariana (to the west of the botanical gardens) hosts 8,000 events including 600 major conferences. But if you take a guided tour you can nonetheless visit some parts of the Palace of Nations. Many peace treaties have been signed here, so a tour is of great historical interest!

⑪ The International Red Cross Museum: emotionally engaging and thought provoking

The headquarters of the International Committee of the Red Cross stand opposite the Palace of Nations. The modern museum located a little further down offers insight into the humanitarian work undertaken by the International Red Cross and the Red Crescent. An audio guide in several languages is available for visitors. The presentation breaks with traditional concepts of museum display. When visitors step through the door they are immediately struck by the architecture which showcases the "Petrified" sculpture piece and the organisation's flags.

⑫ Coppet: château and Madame de Staël's home

Madame de Staël's former residence looks like a museum, but it is in fact a home which is open to the public. The château in which the famous authoress used to live is the only one in the Geneva region to have preserved its period furniture. Its authentic atmosphere takes visitors straight back to the 18th and 19th centuries.

⑬ Nyon

You mustn't leave the shores of Lake Geneva for the Jura without visiting the historic town of Nyon. The old town has Bern-style arcades and in the gardens near the shore three Corinthian columns evoke Roman times. Nyon castle, with its distinctive round towers, houses the history and porcelain museum.

In a more light-hearted vein, visitors can use a mini-guide to follow in the footsteps of Tintin, Snowy and Captain Haddock as they search for Professor Calculus.

⑭ Nyon – Saint-Cergue railway

Each year in July this small railway carries out an important mission: it carries festival-goers to the Paleo Festival. The first electric train to Saint-Cergue, put into operation almost 100 years ago, was used by visitors to the health resort. As the narrow-gauge railway twists and turns up the mountain it gives passengers superb views over Lake Geneva, the Vaud Alps and Mont Blanc.

The route

From Saint-Julien-en-Genevois via Carouge to Geneva harbour. Take the main road along the shore until you reach Nyon and Gland, then continue directly to Saint-George via Begnins.

Distance: 53 kilometres

Photo opportunity: Sights as you cross the city of Geneva, the Pont du Mont-Blanc, the harbour with the Jet d'Eau and the Bains des Pâquis are worth capturing for posterity. The road which climbs up through La Côte vineyard to the Col du Marchairuz passes through some delightful scenery.

To savour: The traditional Genevan "longeole" is thought to have been brought here by the Huguenots who sought refuge in Geneva. The fairly fatty meat of this sausage is flavoured with fennel seeds and white pepper. Once a year, market gardeners and pork butchers in Geneva organise a "longeole night".

Worth a detour

Geneva: The Patek Philippe Museum, a watchmaking museum with some outstanding exhibits – www.patekmuseum.com

Geneva: International Museum of the Reformation, from 1536 to the present – www.museereforme.ch

Château de Prangins: Swiss National Museum, life in an 18th century chateau. www.nationalmuseum.ch/d/prangins

Vaud: La Garenne animal park, mainly European fauna – www.lagarenne.ch

Tourist information

Ville de Carouge
Place du Marché 14, 1227 Carouge
+41 (0)22 307 89 87; www.carouge.ch

Genève Tourisme
Rue du Mont-Blanc 18, 1201 Genève
+41 (0)22 909 70 00; www.geneve-tourisme.ch

The United Nations Office in Geneva
Palais des Nations, 1211 Genève
+41 (0)22 917 12 34; www.unog.ch

Morges Région Tourisme
Av. Viollier 8, 1260 Nyon 1
+41 (0)22 365 66 00; www.nyon-tourisme.ch

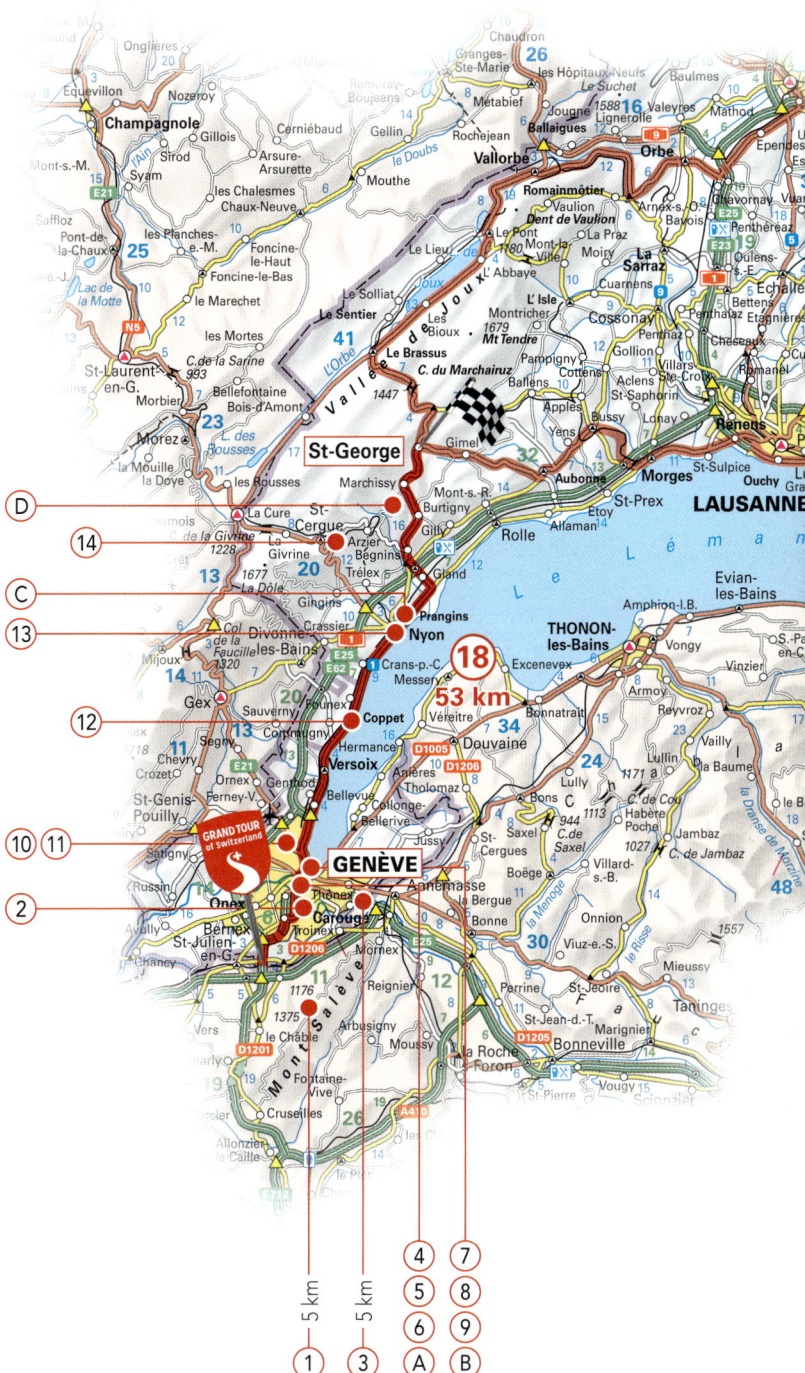

Road from Geneva to Saint-George

Geneva region

Southern Jura

For anyone arriving from Lake Geneva or the Swiss Plateau, the Jura range gives the impression of being an impregnable fortress. The passes might only be 1,000 metres high, but they are reached by true mountain roads with hairpin bends. Behind this long, limestone massif lie remote valleys which shelter picturesque villages.

Col du Marchairuz, Mont Blanc

Pré d'Aubonne, not far from the Col du Marchairuz (3)

The Jura regional park near Vallorbe

Joux Valley (6)

Road to the Col du Marchairuz (3)

Leg 19

Saint-George – Yverdon-les-Bains

Exploring the Vaud Jura

You really mustn't forget to make a stop on the road up to the Col du Marchairuz to enjoy the view which has opened up behind you. You'll see a superb panorama to the east and west. The green and rural landscape studded with vineyards in the foreground gives way to a view of Lake Geneva and snow-capped Alpine peaks in the background with Mont Blanc (4,810 m) as the centrepiece. This is just one of the wonderful views the Grand Tour has to offer.

On the north side of the pass the scenery is worthy of a picture postcard. Travelling down seemingly endless roads lined with traditional dry stone walls we now cross vast pastures interspersed with tall pines. The Joux Valley is home to the workshops and headquarters of watchmakers Audemars Piguet, Patek Philippe and Blancpain. For 150 years Jura residents have specialised in producing small masterpieces of precision engineering. Even today they are still amongst the most sought-after watchmakers in the world. After the very pretty and interesting road to Vallorbe (Juraparc, caves and iron museum) and Orbe (Roman mosaics) we round off this leg with a visit to Romainmôtier.

The Vaud Jura nature park

A karst topography, vast pastures, mysterious wetland landscapes and the northern Joux Valley with its eponymous lake: welcome to the Vaud Jura regional nature reserve which stretches from La Dôle to Romainmôtier. Dry stone walls are a typical feature of Haut-Jura landscapes. Cheese dairies and mountain inns provide refreshment and local food.

Saint-George ice cave

This is a little-known curiosity. The temperature in Jura ice caves remains constant all year long, keeping the natural ice there frozen even in summer. You can get to the Saint-George ice cave via either a forest road or the route from the Col du Marchairuz. Visitors climb down ladders to reach the layer of ice which was once used to supply local restaurants.

Col du Marchairuz and Mont Tendre

On the road which leads up to the Col du Marchairuz you must stop to enjoy the view over Lake Geneva to Mont Blanc and the Valais Alps, which is far too spectacular to be consigned to the rearview mirror! At the Col you'll find a mountain inn and several hiking trails. Choose the one which leads along the ridge to Mont Tendre (1,679 m), the Jura's highest peak, a two-and-a-half hour walk through picture-postcard scenery. You can take a break at the Chalet du Mont Tendre for refreshment while you enjoy the breathtaking view.

The Orbe, a small river flowing into Lac de Joux (6)

In the Combe des Amburnex region (5)

Le Pont, a village on the shore of Lac de Joux; the slope on the right leads to the Dent de Vaulion (6/7)

Le Sentier watch museum

Vallorbe (9)

Leg 19

④ 300 million inhabitants

The Col du Marchairuz is home to one of Europe's largest wood-ant colonies. There are an estimated 1,200 anthills, all linked together by hundreds of kilometres of "ant motorways", scattered over a 70-hectare area. You can observe these tireless workers near the main car park.

⑤ Combe des Amburnex and the Pré-aux-Veaux mountain inn.

After crossing the pass the road branches off on your left to the Combe des Amburnex. The landscape features a characteristic terrain in which generally wooded ridges run parallel to elongated depressions (the "combes"). Dry stone walls mark the boundaries between pastures. Don't miss a stop at the Pré-aux-Veaux mountain inn, which serves delicious local produce in a pastoral setting.

⑥ Joux Valley and lake

Vallée de Joux (a closed high-altitude valley) backs onto the north side of the Col du Marchairuz and contains the largest lake in the Jura mountain range. In summer it offers a scheduled boat service. The river flows out underground and only appears again at Vallorbe. The valley is famous for its watchmaking industry and of course, creamy Vacherin Mont d'Or cheese, kept in place with a band of spruce bark.

⑦ Dent de Vaulion

To take a last look at the lake, the entire Vallée de Joux and in clear weather the Alps 80 kilometres away, follow the narrow mountain road which leads to Dent de Vaulion. And as fabulous views and great food go hand in hand, a restaurant serving regional specialities opens during the summer. —> 12 km

⑧ Vallorbe: the Orbe caves

You can reach the Juraparc animal park via the Col du Mont d'Orzeires. The caves and the "source" of the Orbe (in fact the resurgence of the water flowing out of Lac de Joux) are to be found further down the valley after a few hairpin bends. A path along the underground river leads you to a world of stalagmites, stalactites and other formations, once thought to be the home of fairies. Closed in winter.

⑨ Iron museum and Fort de Pré-Giroud

The presence of iron ore and significant timber resources gave early impetus to the Orbe Valley's industrial development. The Iron Museum in the former village forge in Vallorbe retraces the history of ironwork and the railway. The Second World War fort, used by Swiss artillery units to protect the nearby border, is also open to the public.

Between Vallorbe and Orbe with the Alps in the background

Romainmôtier (11)

Château de la Sarraz (12)

Orbe town centre (14)

The small town of Orbe (14)

Leg 19

⑩ Ballaigues: historic rutted road
Routes between Vallorbe and France existed long before the era of railways and motorways. In the forest to the west of Ballaigues, ruts in the rock testify to the existence of an ancient trade route; these grooves provided a way to guide the horse-drawn carts. Although it is sometimes called a Roman road it might not in fact be one, but what is certain is that until the mid 19th century it was used to carry highly prized salt from French salt works to Bern and French-speaking Switzerland. —> 5 km

⑪ Romainmôtier: abbey and prior's house
This small detour is well worthwhile. Romainmôtier abbey was built around the year 1000 on the Cluny model. It is one of Switzerland's oldest Romanesque buildings. The 13th century prior's house near the church has been entirely restored. Its superb halls with large fireplaces, coffered ceilings and frescoes can be rented for receptions.

⑫ Château de La Sarraz: horse museum and Centre of the World
The venerable La Sarraz château hosts a variety of events and also houses an enchanting horse museum in the stables, which tells visitors about stagecoaches, jobs with horses, the army, harnesses and saddles, toys and also the arts.

The "Centre of the World" can be found in the pond by the mill, not far from the château. The water here flows towards the North Sea via Lake Neuchâtel on one side and towards the Mediterranean via the Rhône on the other: this is the watershed. —> 7 km

⑬ The Canal d'Entreroches: linking the Rhône and the Rhine
The watershed gave rise to an epic undertaking. The dream of a navigable waterway from the Mediterranean to the North Sea almost became reality. But although the Canal d'Entreroches linked Lake Neuchâtel to the River Venoge, the section to Lake Geneva was never completed. The only remaining evidence of this great project is a small stretch of canal between Entreroches and Eclépens in the middle of the countryside. —> 11 km

⑭ Orbe: Roman mosaics
Before continuing onwards to Lake Neuchâtel, stop for a while in the small medieval town of Orbe. Another sight not to be missed is the Gallo-Roman villa to the north of the town. It has the finest collection of Roman mosaics north of the Alps. These mosaics paved the floors of 8 of the 100 rooms in this immense and luxurious Gallo-Roman villa built around 160 AD. Destroyed during the Barbarian invasions, its stones were used for building in the Middle Ages and there is now nothing left of its superstructure.

The route

Cross the Col du Marchairuz by the pass road to Le Brassus in the Vallée de Joux. After driving along the shore of Lac de Joux, head down into the Orbe Valley. Follow the by-road from the small town of Orbe to Yverdon-les-Bains on Lake Neuchâtel.

Distance: 70 kilometres

Photo opportunity: The Col du Marchairuz offers two vistas. On one side you have a view of Lake Geneva and the Alps and on the other, to the north, a typical Jura landscape. The road down to Vallorbe and the Orbe Valley is very picturesque.

To savour: Legend has it that the recipe for Vacherin Mont d'Or was brought to the Vallée de Joux by a soldier from Bourbaki's army in 1871. This soft cheese is only made in winter. Its round pine box and band of spruce give it its distinctive woody aroma.

Worth a detour

(A) **Le Brassus:** Audemars Piguet museum; the new spiral building can be visited by appointment – www.audemarspiguet.com

(B) **Le Sentier:** Espace Horloger de la Vallée de Joux, museum of watches and the history of watchmaking – www.espacehorloger.ch

(C) **Vallorbe (Mont d'Orzeires):** Juraparc animal park with American bison, bears and wolves – www.juraparc.ch

(D) **Vallorbe:** Iron and Railway Museum: exhibitions, working forge and miniature railway – www.museedufer.ch

Tourist information

Parc Jura vaudois
Rte du Marchairuz 2, 1188 St-George
+41 (0)22 366 51 70; www.parcjuravaudois.ch

Vallée de Joux Tourisme
Rue de l'Orbe 8, 1347 Le Sentier
+41 (0)21 845 17 77; www.myvalleedejoux.ch

Office du Tourisme de Vallorbe
Grandes-Forges 11, 1337 Vallorbe
+41 (0)21 843 25 83; www.vallorbe-tourisme.ch

Office du tourisme d'Orbe et environs
Grand-Rue 1, 1350 Orbe
+41 (0)24 442 92 37; www.orbe-tourisme.ch

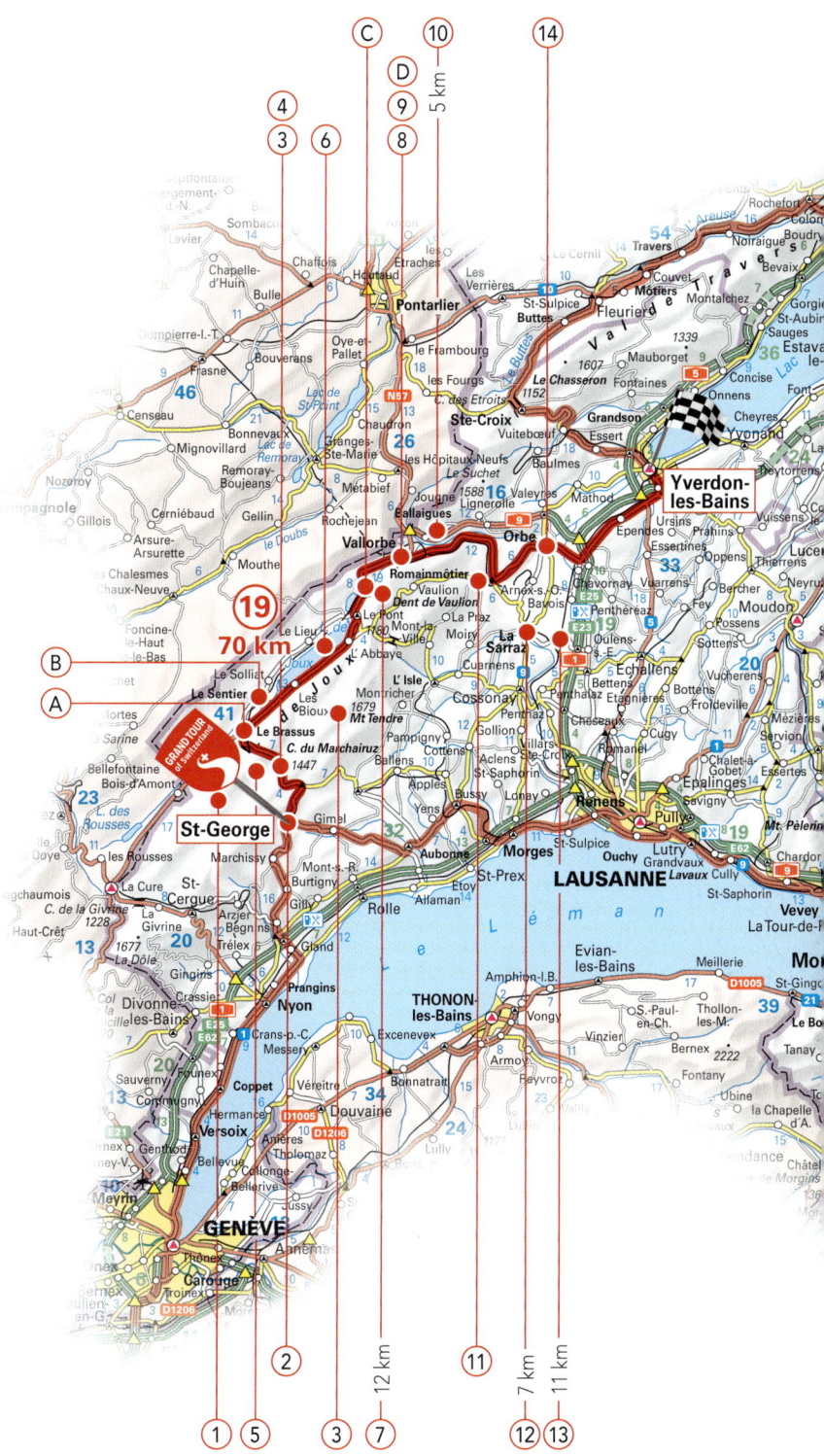

Saint-George – Yverdon-les-Bains
Southern Jura

Sainte-Croix with Covatannaz Gorge in the background (6) and the Alps

Yvonand, Lake Neuchâtel

Yverdon-les-Bains health spa (1)

Grand Hôtel des Bains, Yverdon-les-Bains (1)

Leg 20

Yverdon-les-Bains – Neuchâtel

Music boxes, the "green fairy" (absinthe), asphalt and rocky cirque

Tourists are very well catered for at Yverdon-les-Bains, which offers everything from a health spa to a picturesque old town with interesting museums and excellent restaurants serving good quality local cuisine.

But we now leave the town and follow the twisting but well-built road which climbs 500 metres in altitude to reach Sainte-Croix. Here too it's a good idea to stop along the way to enjoy the view which opens up behind us. After wooded landscapes and a small tunnel, we reach Val-de-Travers. This peaceful valley holds some spectacular surprises, such as Europe's only asphalt mines and Creux du Van. This immense rocky cirque, with 200-metre-high cliffs, can be reached on foot or by a narrow mountain road. The Ferme du Soliat has made a name for itself throughout Switzerland for its fondue, and yet again the view is spectacular.

Just one more tip before you make your way down to Lake Neuchâtel: park your car on the western edge of the village of Rochefort and follow the dirt road which climbs gently up the hill to the south. After a five minute walk you will see the lake below and in clear weather Mont Blanc 130 kilometres to the south and the Glärnisch 170 kilometres to the east. Your photos will be worth their weight in gold.

Yverdon-les-Bains health spa

The Romans were already aware of the virtues of sulphur- and magnesium-rich springs. The remains of ancient Roman baths testify to Yverdon's longstanding thermal and medical heritage. The modern public health spa, with an adjacent 4-star hotel, is located to the south of the town centre.

Lake Neuchâtel's sandy beach

Yverdon-les-Bains owes its name to the hot springs which rise there, but the clear waters of Lake Neuchâtel are just as tempting for a swim. One of the Swiss Plateau's largest and most beautiful stretches of sandy beach lies just next to the camp site and offers greenery, picnic tables, children's play areas, restaurant, football pitch and beach volleyball area.

History, fashion and science fiction museums

Yverdon-les-Bains is a culturally active town and you might be surprised by its unusual array of museums. The 13th century Château de Savoie, which looks out over the old town, houses an exhibition which retraces the region's history. The building is also home to the Swiss Fashion Museum and its collection of over 5,000 items of clothing. The Maison d'Ailleurs, for its part, is the only European museum to be entirely devoted to science fiction.

Val-de-Travers (11)

The train to Sainte-Croix (7)

Grande Cariçaie, Lake Neuchâtel (4)

Concise, Lake Neuchâtel

The road up to Sainte-Croix (6)

Sainte-Croix, Bietschhorn and Balmhorn (8)

Road to Saint-Croix

Leg 20

④ Grande Cariçaie and the centre for environmental protection

Grande Cariçaie is a vast nature reserve made up of wetlands, alluvial forests and reed beds located to the east of Yverdon. It stretches for 40 kilometres along the southern shore of Lake Neuchâtel as far as Grand-Marais. Visitors can follow hiking trails and cycle paths to explore the nature reserve, where they will even find small beaches for swimming. At Champ-Pittet there is an information centre with a two-kilometre educational trail and an observation tower on the shore of the lake.

⑤ Battle of Grandson, monastery and Gallo-Roman quarry

The north shore of the lake is charged with history. This was where the famous battle of Grandson took place in 1476, during which the Confederates inflicted defeat on the army of Charles the Bold. Not far from there, in the charming hamlet of La Lance, is a former monastery which is now a winegrowing estate highly popular with connoisseurs. A little further east, along the old railway line, is a Gallo-Roman quarry whose stones were sent by boat to build the amphitheatre at Avenches (Aventicum). —> 12 km

⑥ Covatannaz Gorge: on the road to Sainte-Croix

As you climb up from Vuiteboeuf to Sainte-Croix you will come across the most spectacular system of rutted roads in Switzerland. Several dozen of these roads were made between the 13th and 18th centuries, with ruts for guiding horse-drawn carts.

⑦ A train journey to Sainte-Croix

On the other side of the gorge you come across a different kind of way: the metre-gauge Yverdon – Sainte-Croix railway, inaugurated in 1893, was used mainly to carry labourers working in the world capital of music boxes. Although steam trains no longer operate on this route (they were replaced in 1945) the section which runs more than 300 metres above the Orbe plain never fails to impress!

⑧ Sainte-Croix: world capital of music boxes

Today, the town is no longer a busy city. Residents commute the other way to work in Yverdon-les-Bains. It was, however, at Sainte-Croix that Genevan watchmaker Antoine Favre-Salomon invented the music box in 1796. The town then became the world's largest manufacturer of music boxes and automatons up until the end of the 19th century. The CIMA (international centre for mechanical art) museum exhibits a unique collection of this musical art form. You can visit another museum devoted to music boxes not far from here in L'Auberson.

⑨ The Chasseron

In summer, the Chasseron (1,607 m) can be accessed by a narrow road from Sainte-Croix – Les Rasses. Cable cars operate in winter. A welcoming little hotel stands at the summit, offering simple accommodation and a spectacular view over the Alps and half of Switzerland. Hikers and mountain bikers will love the Jura ridges which they can follow as far as Creux du Van. —> 8 km

The Chasseron, view to the north (9)

Môtiers, Val-de-Travers (12)

Le Soliat, Creux du Van (14)

Creux du Van (14)

Saint-Sulpice near Fleurier (11)

Poëta Raisse, Val-de-Travers (12)

La Robella, Buttes (10)

Leg 20

⑩ Buttes-La Robella: activities and adventure
After Sainte-Croix and the marshy plain of L'Auberson, the landscape becomes less open and the road twists and turns through the Vallon de Noirvaux. You then reach Buttes and La Robella. Hikers and mountain bikers can take a chairlift to the Jura uplands before making an exhilarating descent. Kick-scooters (and toboggans in winter) are also available. Near the lower station, the bends and loops of the Féeline toboggan run stretch over a kilometre.

⑪ Val-de-Travers: hydraulic museum and steam trains
You might already have passed through the valley of fairies, asphalt and absinth in a high-speed train. However, this valley in the Neuchâtel Jura mountains is really worth a stop. The Haute-Areuse ecomuseum near Saint-Sulpice gives visitors a chance to learn about the history of the two hydraulic plants, and the railway depot holds Europe's largest collection of steam locomotives.

⑫ Môtiers: former capital of the canton, hike in the Poëta Raisse Gorge
In spite of its slightly dull appearance, the former capital of Val-de-Travers has much to offer. A museum reminds us that Jean-Jacques Rousseau lived here for a short time before being driven away by local residents and taking refuge on St. Peter's Island. Other museums, a delicious sparkling wine which can be tasted in the former Benedictine monastery and Poëta Raisse Gorge are all also worth a detour.

⑬ Travers: a tour of the asphalt mines
The asphalt which paves the roads of Paris, London or New York might well have come from the mines at Travers. More than 100 kilometres of galleries were excavated near the hamlet of La Presta between 1711 and 1986. A one-kilometre stretch of the mine is open to visitors, who can also enjoy the famous ham cooked in asphalt which features on the menu at the Café des Mines.

⑭ Creux du Van: rocky cirque
Don't stint on photos of this natural phenomenon of precipitous cliffs towering over an abyss. You get the most spectacular view from the very top, on the edge of the rocky rim (which can be reached by a mountain road from Couvet), and an opportunity to observe chamois, marmots and birds of prey. —> 12 km

⑮ Areuse Gorge
As Val-de-Travers lies behind the first hills of the Jura, railways and rivers have to make deep cuttings through the mountain to reach Lake Neuchâtel. The Areuse surges through a spectacular gorge which can be viewed from a precipitous path which runs alongside. —> 5 km

The route

Mountain road to Sainte-Croix, then the narrow Vallon de Noirvaux to Val-de-Travers. On leaving the valley take the by-road to Rochefort before descending to Lake Neuchâtel, then continue to Neuchâtel through the outskirts.

Distance: 67 kilometres

Photo opportunity: The road through the forest to Sainte-Croix twists and turns dramatically above Covatannaz Gorge. After the music box village, the picturesque route continues through the narrow valley to Val-de-Travers.

Did you know? In 1796 the Genevan watchmaker Antoine Favre-Salomon invented a pocket watch with a musical mechanism. In the late 19th century as many 40 businesses employing 600 workers produced mechanical singing birds and musical automats, making Sainte-Croix the capital of music boxes.

Worth a detour

(A) **Château de Grandson (13th century):** weapons collection and vintage car museum – www.chateau-grandson.ch

(B) **Sainte-Croix:** music boxes and CIMA (international centre for mechanical art) – www.musees.ch

(C) **Môtiers:** winetasting, guided tours and production of sparkling wine at the former Benedictine monastery – www.mauler.ch

(D) **Val-de-Travers:** the "green fairy", tasting in absinth distilleries, Môtiers absinth museum – www.val-de-travers.ch

Tourist information

Office du Tourisme et du Thermalisme
Av. de la Gare 2, 1401 Yverdon-les-Bains
+41 (0)24 423 61 01; www.yverdonlesbainsregion.ch

Office du Tourisme de Sainte-Croix/Les Rasses
Rue Neuve 10, 1450 Sainte-Croix
+41 (0)24 455 41 42; www.sainte-croix-les-rasses-tourisme.ch

Buttes – La Robella
Place de l'Abbaye, 2115 Buttes
+41(0)32 862 22 22; www.robella.ch

Val-de-Travers Tourisme
Place de la Gare 1, 2103 Noiraigue
+41 (0)32 889 68 96; www.val-de-travers.ch

Yverdon-les-Bains – Neuchâtel

Southern Jura

Basel region – northern Jura

This city nestling in a bend in the Rhine is noteworthy for the architectural heritage of its protected historic centre and for its 40 or so museums. Switzerland's oldest university town is also renowned for its modern architecture. The nearby Jura, stretching to the picturesque River Doubs and the Franches-Montagnes, offers an opportunity to relax in the countryside.

Mittlere Brücke, Basel

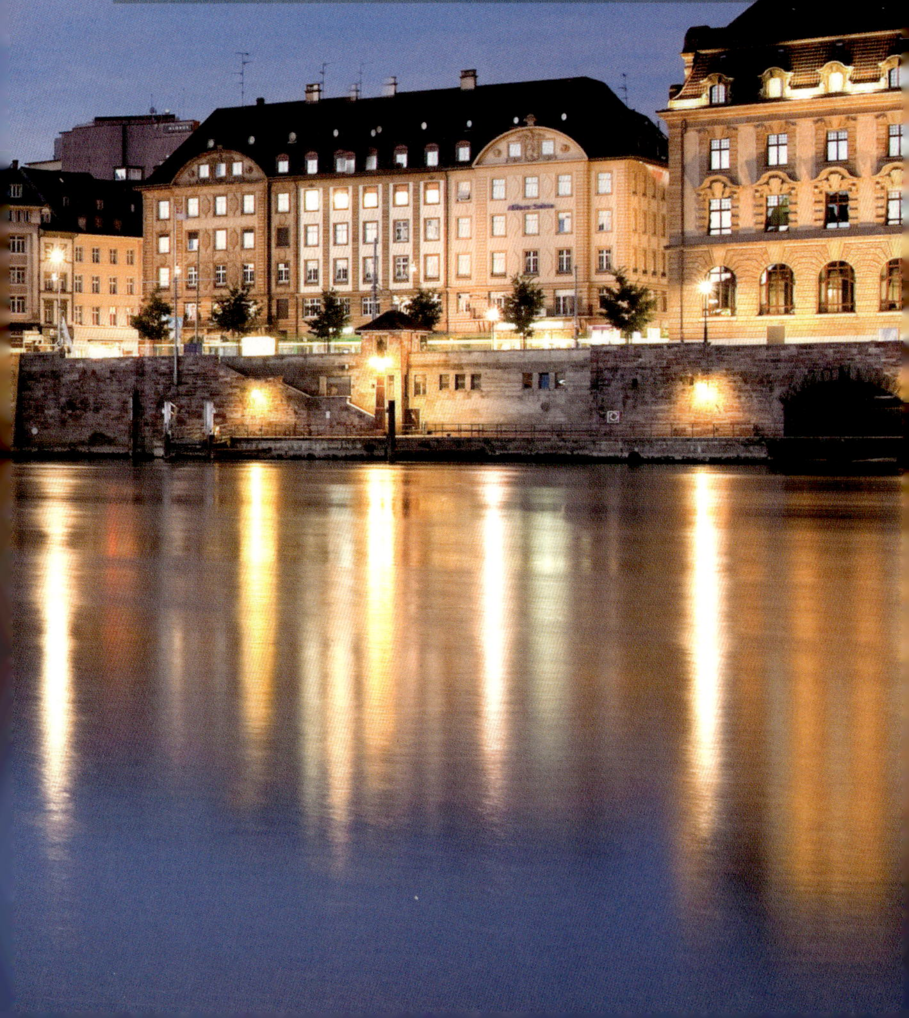

Mittlere Brücke, Basel (2)

Barfüsserplatz

Basel Rathaus (1)

Basel Minster (2)

Tinguely museum (3)

Leg 21

Road from Basel to Neuchâtel

Joining the Grand Tour via Basel and the Jura

Access to the Grand Tour via Basel starts either at the German border (Weil am Rhein), or the French (Saint-Louis). From Kleinbasel the road crosses the Rhine over Wettstein bridge, passes in front of the SBB railway station and heads towards the Birsig Valley. But first of all, let's take some time to visit Basel. A prominent cultural hub and centre for contemporary architecture, the city also offers simple yet memorable pleasures such as a stroll through the Spalenberg quarter or up to the Pfalz overlooking the Rhine.

We take a road running parallel to tram line 10, the former Birsig Valley railway, and leave the city behind us as we head for the Jura capital Delémont through a region which is little known to tourists. After Saint-Ursanne we cross the wild and majestic landscapes of the Doubs regional nature park, followed by the Franches-Montagnes and their distinctive eponymous race of horses (also known as Freibergers). At Saignelégier, make a small detour to Etang de la Gruère and its mysterious peat bog in the heart of a forest.

In terms of culture, two towns with UNESCO World Heritage status are the highlights of this leg: La Chaux-de-Fonds and Le Locle. A detour via Col des Roches and its underground mills to Lac des Brenets will allow you to take one last look at the River Doubs before joining the central loop of the Grand Tour at Neuchâtel, via Vue-des-Alpes.

Basel: a city with cultural activities to suit all tastes

Located in a bend of the Rhine, this city has no shortage of emblematic landmarks including the market square, the town hall built in ornately decorated red sandstone, the old streets of the Spalenberg quarter and the Romanesque and Gothic minster. But historic monuments are not all the town has to offer. It also has a significant number of modern buildings built by world-class architects such as Herzog & de Meuron and Mario Botta. Bar Rouge on the 31st floor of the Messeturm has become a highly popular place to relax.

Around the minster

The minster hill is one of the places you mustn't miss. The Romans set up a military post at this strategic location, and the view is just as impressive today from the Pfalz, a terrace behind the minster which overlooks the Rhine. Steps lead down to the ferry jetty, and a small door takes you into a peaceful cloister. After climbing one of the minster towers, go to the Zum Isaak restaurant.

Art museum, Tinguely museum and Cultures museum

No other town in Switzerland has as many museums as Basel. There are 40 of them, including the Art Museum (Kunstmuseum Basel) which has the world's largest collection of paintings by Holbein, the Tinguely museum with its large glass gallery designed by Ticino architect Mario Botta, and the Cultures museum devoted to the peoples of Europe and elsewhere.

Rhine port (4)

Klingental ferry "Vogel Gryff" crossing the Rhine at Basel (4)

Augusta Raurica (5)

Bottmingen Castle (6)

Mariastein Abbey (8)

Historic town of Laufen (9)

Leg 21

④ On the river: cable ferries and the Rhine port

You can't imagine Basel without the Rhine. Four cable ferries cross the river, guided by steel cables and propelled by the strength of the current. The ferrymen continue the tradition of recounting anecdotes to liven up the crossing. You can swim in the river in summer and from April to October take a boat trip to explore the town and port or the locks which lie upstream, as far as Rheinfelden.

⑤ Augusta Raurica: Roman town

2,000 years ago as many as 20,000 people lived near Augst and Kaiseraugst in this ancient Roman city which owes its name to a Celtic tribe, the Rauraci, and the emperor Augustus. With a mysterious well, the best preserved Roman theatre north of the Alps, the largest silver treasure in late Antiquity, workshops, public baths and homes, it offers a spectacular insight into life in Roman times. Switzerland's largest open-air museum is open all year long. —> 9 km

⑥ Bottmingen Castle: a picturesque and gourmet experience

Surrounded by water and a delightful park, this 14th century castle was recently beautifully renovated. The restaurant is now highly regarded for the standard of its cuisine. Elegant and stylish function rooms are an ideal venue for special occasions. This romantic setting is particularly popular for weddings.

⑦ Seewen: museum of musical automatons

The museum displays barrel organs, orchestrions, musical watches and jewellery and 600 music boxes dating from the 18th century to the present day. Figures start to dance on their own, invisible hands press the keys on a piano and a large barrel organ suddenly strikes up a tune. It isn't done by magic, but visitors are nonetheless enchanted and bowled over by the refinement and playful sophistication of these instruments. —> 14 km

⑧ Mariastein Abbey: chapel, basilica and convent

Mariastein Abbey near Einsiedeln is Switzerland's second most popular Marian pilgrimage. Each year, 150,000 visitors travel to this holy place to seek comfort in the smiling Virgin's presence. The sanctuary is in a cave under the convent, which also has a late Gothic basilica and baroque church. From here, the Grand Tour takes us across the Blauen uplands which separate the Leimental and Laufental valleys (respectively in the canton of Solothurn and the canton of Basel-Landschaft).

⑨ The small historic town of Laufen

Since our route passes nearby, we mustn't miss the opportunity to explore the medieval old town with its partially intact ramparts and three gates, in particular the southern gate known as the Zeitturm (time tower) with its large astronomical clock. The museum near the Church of St. Katharina exhibits archaeological artefacts from different eras.

Excursion in a horse-drawn wagon or a holiday in a gypsy caravan in the Franches-Montagnes and Ajoie areas

Delémont (10)

Relaxing on the banks of the Doubs (13)

Near Saint-Ursanne

Saint-Ursanne (14)

Leg 21

⑩ Delémont: capital of the canton of Jura

In this section we move from one canton to another quite frequently since the canton of Solothurn forms enclaves within the canton of Basel-Landschaft. At Ederswiler we finally reach the canton of Jura, and shortly afterwards its capital, Delémont. The Jura museum of art and history offers a predominantly cultural perspective of the canton's history, but does not neglect social, political and economic aspects.

⑪ Porrentruy: the region's cultural centre

In 1527, after the town of Basel underwent Protestant reform, Porrentruy became the seat of the prince-bishops of Basel. The town went through a prosperous period and the castle was enlarged. The oldest keep, dating from 1271, offers a magnificent view over the Ajoie region and the very attractive old town with its fine Gothic, Baroque and Neoclassic houses. —> 14 km

⑫ Réclère caves

This is another site which you must see during our small detour through the Ajoie region. The Réclère caves open up a fascinating subterranean world with extraordinary concretions such as the "Dom", a 15-metre stalagmite which is thought to be Switzerland's largest. You can explore a 1.5 kilometre-section of the caves with a group guided tour. Closed in winter. Access from Saint-Ursanne via a picturesque route along the River Doubs across the border in France, or from Porrentruy. —> 25 km

⑬ The Doubs: picturesque scenery along the river

After crossing the well-hidden motorway access road at Saint-Ursanne, we catch our first sight of the River Doubs at the bottom of a wooded gorge. It is popular not only with canoe and kayak enthusiasts, but also hikers, anglers and gourmets. The quiet road which runs parallel to it will take you to the Tariche fish restaurant before you rejoin the Grand Tour via the Clos du Doubs.

⑭ Saint-Ursanne

The charming little medieval town of Saint-Ursanne, with its three superb gates, narrow streets and impressive Romano-Gothic church and cloisters, lies in a large bend in the Doubs, which now continues its journey to France. The almost untouched historic centre contains imposing houses built between the 14th and 16th century and you get a wonderful view of the town from the four-arched bridge.

⑮ Franches-Montagnes and Etang de la Gruère

After crossing the Doubs once again, the road climbs up to the Franches-Montagnes. Take a deep breath and enjoy the spirit of liberty which is no doubt shared by the horses which live on this vast plateau. Etang de Gruère, in the middle of a peat bog, offers a unique wetland environment which is well worth exploring.

Étang de la Gruère, Franches-Montagnes (15)

Lac des Brenets, Doubs (19)

Via ferrata above the Doubs

La Chaux-de-Fonds, UNESCO World Heritage Site (17)

Old mill at Le Theusseret, Doubs nature park

Leg 21

⑯ The Sommêtres: cliff overlooking the Doubs

If you're not afraid of heights, you will love this. After Saignelégier (capital of the Franches-Montagnes district) you reach the Sommêtres, a rocky ridge with a commanding view over the River Doubs as it flows through the idyllic landscape of the valley far below.

⑰ La Chaux-de-Fonds and Le Locle: a World Heritage Site since 2009

The Neuchâtel region of Jura was an important hub for the watchmaking industry for many years. So don't be surprised to find not just one, but two museums devoted to the history of timekeeping: the international museum of watchmaking in La Chaux-de-Fonds and the Château des Monts museum in Le Locle. The town of La Chaux-de-Fonds, Corbusier's birth place, has a distinctive grid street plan worthy of a great metropolis.

⑱ Col des Roches: underground mills

As water pierced its way through the karst rock to Lac des Brenets, it formed subterranean rivers. These rivers were put to use 400 years ago, creating a system of mills, wells, canals, waterwheels and sawmills. Restored by volunteers, this underground factory unlike any other in Europe is now open to the public at Col des Roches. —> 11 km

⑲ Lac des Brenets: boat trip to the Saut-du-Doubs

After Col des Roches, Lac des Brenets is also worth visiting. 14,000 years ago a rockslide formed a natural dam, giving the River Doubs a somewhat fjord-like aspect over a four-kilometre stretch. Boats take visitors to the lower end of the lake, from which point the famous Saut-du-Doubs waterfall is quite close. —> 11/3 km

⑳ Vue-des-Alpes: as its name implies, a view of the Alps

The most direct route from La Chaux-de-Fonds to Lake Neuchâtel goes through this pass. At its highest point, which is reached shortly after leaving the town, it offers a panorama in clear weather which encompasses the Swiss Plateau and the Alps. Tourists are catered for at the pass with walking trails, a hiking path to the Tête de Ran, a year-round toboggan run and a hotel which offers rooms of all sizes.

The route

From the Birsig Valley to the first Jurassic range, the Blauen mountains. Small roads to Delémont then Saint-Ursanne, and via Clos du Doubs on small roads to the Franches-Montagnes. Main road to La Chaux-de-Fonds and then via Vue-des-Alpes to Neuchâtel.

Distance: 157 kilometres

Photo opportunity: In the Blauen range, Mariastein Abbey and the Challpass. Road leading from Saint-Ursanne to the vast open plateau of the Franches-Montagnes, crossing the River Doubs twice.

To savour: "Tête de Moine" (monk's head) is a semi-cooked pressed cheese, 10 to 15 cm in diameter. Served in thin rosettes, legend has it that the monks of Bellelay Abbey already cut it this way 800 years ago by skimming the surface with a knife.

Worth a detour

A **Riehen:** Fondation Beyeler, art collection in a building designed by Renzo Piano – www.fondationbeyeler.ch

B **Basel:** Basel zoo, more than 7,000 animals and considerable success in reproduction – www.zoobasel.ch

C **Arlesheim:** hermitage, large landscaped garden with lakes, hill fortress, caves – www.ermitage-arlesheim.ch

D **Mariastein:** the Burg Rotberg youth hostel with guestroom in the keep, wall-walk, armoury – www.youthhostel.ch/mariastein

E **Valangin NE:** Château de Valangin museum, armoury, kitchens, furnished bedrooms, paintings, arms, tools, tableware – www.chateau-de-valangin.ch

Tourist information

Basel Tourismus
Stadt-Casino am Barfüsserplatz, 4051 Basel
+41 (0)61 268 68 68; www.basel.com

Baselland Tourismus
Altmarktstrasse 96, 4410 Liestal
+41 (0)61 927 65 44; www.baselland-tourismus.ch

Jura Tourisme
Delémont, Porrentruy, Saint-Ursanne, Saignelégier
+41 (0)32 420 47 70; www.juratourisme.ch

Tourisme neuchâtelois - Montagnes
Espacité 1, 2302 La Chaux-de-Fonds
+41 (0)32 889 68 95; www.ville-de-la-chaux-de-fonds.ch/tourisme

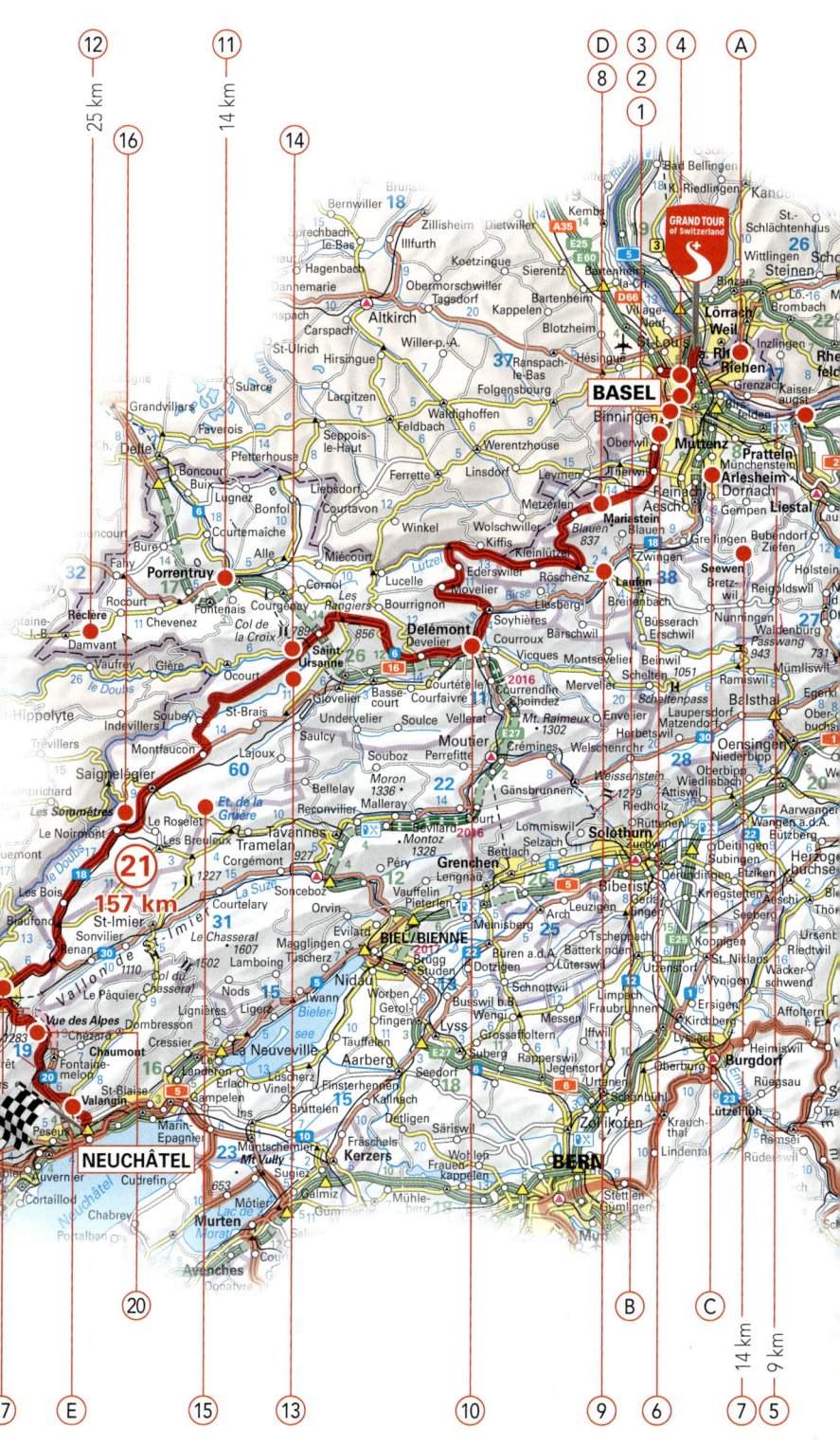

Road from Basel to Neuchâtel
Basel region – northern Jura

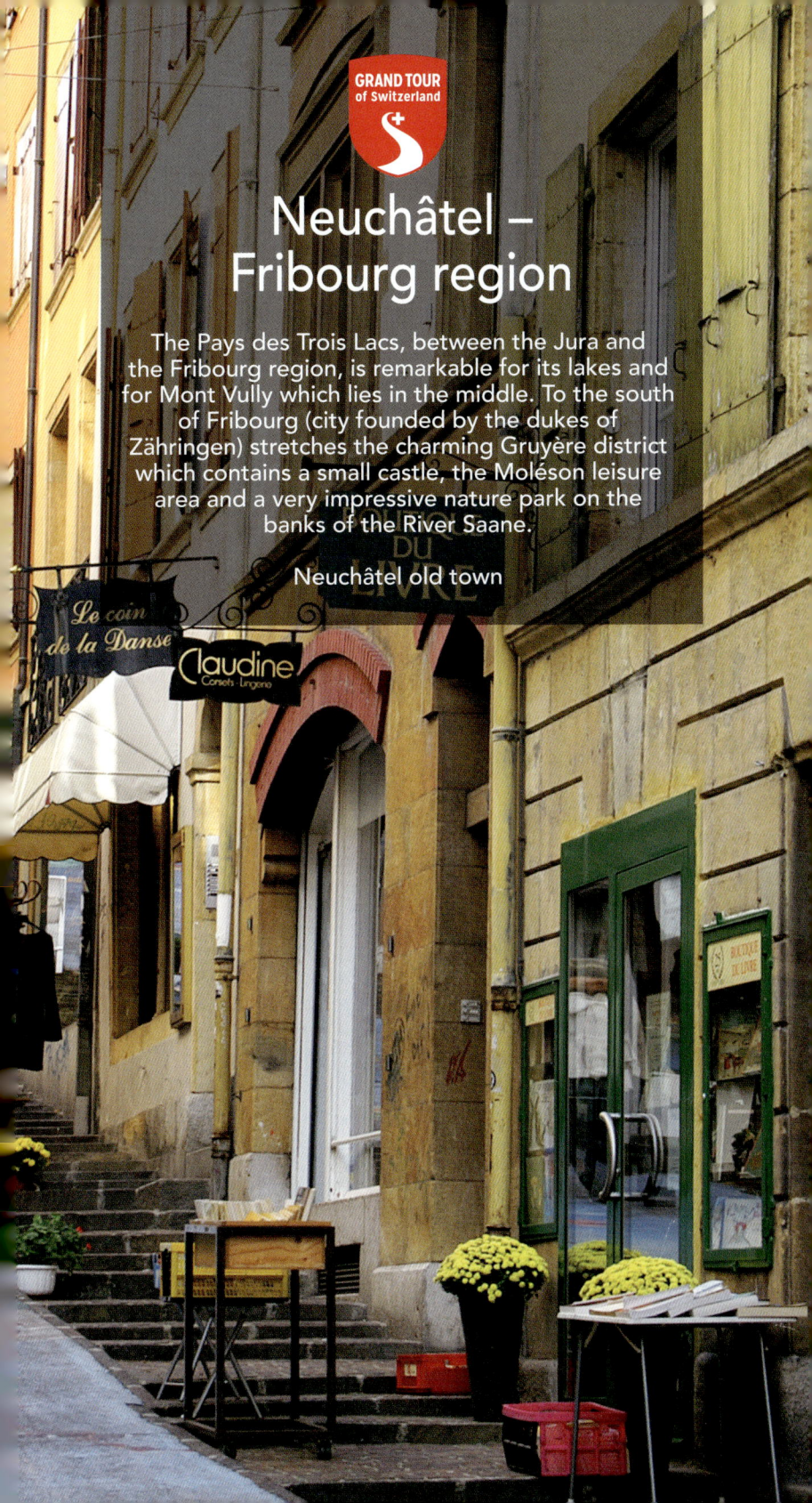

GRAND TOUR of Switzerland

Neuchâtel – Fribourg region

The Pays des Trois Lacs, between the Jura and the Fribourg region, is remarkable for its lakes and for Mont Vully which lies in the middle. To the south of Fribourg (city founded by the dukes of Zähringen) stretches the charming Gruyère district which contains a small castle, the Moléson leisure area and a very impressive nature park on the banks of the River Saane.

Neuchâtel old town

Hôtel des Postes, Neuchâtel (1)

Tour de Chaumont (3)

Lake Neuchâtel, the Eiger and the Mönch (2)

Three-Lakes boat crossings (2)

Paper Kite butterfly at the at Papiliorama in Kerzers

Leg 22

Neuchâtel – Fribourg

Pays des lacs, Mont Vully and Lake Morat

There could hardly be a greater contrast between the venerable past of this old university town and the youthful energy it exudes today! Its ochre-coloured sandstone buildings, café terraces and the blue waters of its lake call out to you to spend at least one night here – especially as thanks to its very liberal regulations it is the only Swiss town where you can have a hot meal at three in the morning.

Taking the route via Grand Marais and the Fanel birdwatching tower, we reach Mont Vully which lies between the three lakes of the Seeland (Pays des lacs) region. The road takes us through pretty winegrowing villages on the southern slopes of the hill, right down to the shore of Lake Morat.

Before we visit the former city of the dukes of Zähringen, we stop off at the historic fortified town of Morat. Traffic is permitted here, even in the old town. Don't miss a walk on the ramparts, or a taste of local fish specialities in the Old Town or on the shores of Lake Morat.

Neuchâtel

The charming medieval city centre in yellow sandstone, with its many cafés, bistros, museums and theatres, is a lovely place to linger. It is dominated by a 12th century castle and church. This French-speaking university town is also known for its research facility and observatory which for many decades gave the precise hour to one tenth of a second on Swiss radio. A weekly market with an almost Mediterranean vibe is held three times a week in Place des Halles.

Boat services on the three lakes

Thanks to the canals linking Lake Neuchâtel, Lake Bienne and Lake Morat, tourist excursions on these three lakes in the Jura foothills provide an opportunity to explore the whole region by boat. From Neuchâtel port you can sail to Morat, St. Peter's Island and Bienne amongst other destinations. On some days the Neuchâtel, a recently-restored old steam boat dating from 1912, is put into service on these routes.

Chaumont: the tower above the lake

Located between Lake Neuchâtel and Val-de-Ruz, this summit is an ideal starting point for hikes across the Jura. Near the La Coudre funicular station stands a 100-year-old observation tower which offers a superb view over the Pays des Trois-Lacs to the Alps. You can return to Neuchâtel railway station via the Time Trail, a 4.5-kilometre themed walk evoking the evolution of life on earth, each metre of which represents a million years. The hotels in Chaumont can be reached by road via Pierre-à-Bot.

Erlach and St. Peter's Island (5)

The watchmaking city of Biel/Bienne (6)

Former monastery, St. Peter's Island (5)

Grand-Marais (7)

Bernese Seeland (7)

Môtier (10)

Leg 22

④ Laténium: archaeology museum

As you leave Neuchâtel you pass Switzerland's largest archaeology museum to your right, on the shore of the lake. Some 3,000 artefacts in a 2,200 m² exhibition area tell the story of our ancestors' daily lives, from Neanderthal times to the Middle Ages, not forgetting life in Neolithic lakeside villages.

⑤ St. Peter's Island and Lake Bienne

"Of all the places I have lived in, none have made me so truly happy nor left me with such affectionate regret as St. Peter's Island in the middle of Lake Bienne", wrote Jean-Jacques Rousseau shortly before his death, as he remembered his short stay there in the autumn of 1765. Today the peninsula can be reached on foot from the charming little town of Erlach by the Heidenweg path (4 kilometres), by shuttle bus from Erlach, or boat from La Neuveville and Ligerz (Lake Bienne) or by the Thielle Canal from Neuchâtel. The monastery founded in 1127 is now an award-winning hotelrestaurant. —> 6 km

⑥ Biel/Bienne: a watchmaking city on the language border

Another detour, slightly longer this time, takes us along the shore of Lake Bienne to the town of Biel/Bienne, renowned for its longstanding watchmaking tradition and bilingualism. Major companies such as Swatch, Rolex, Omega, Tissot, Movado and Mikron have their headquarters here and the Omega museum (opposite the company's head office) is really worth a visit. This unique museum exhibits 4,000 pieces of just one brand. Macolin (Magglingen), which is a true Mecca for sports enthusiasts, is located in the surrounding hills and can be reached by funicular. —> 23 km

⑦ Grand-Marais

This former wetland area between Kerzers and Lake Neuchâtel is known for vegetable farming. As well as a wide variety of vegetables, the Seeland region also grows fruit, wheat, beetroot and grapes. It alone produces a quarter of the vegetables grown in Switzerland. The straight, flat and often tarmacked or concrete-surfaced farm tracks are popular with rollerbladers.

⑧ La Sauge: Fanel and Chablais de Cudrefin reserves, observing fauna

Located near the Broye Canal, the La Sauge nature reserve offers exhibitions, an environmental laboratory and a very instructive educational trail which includes three perfectly camouflaged observation huts. Rare species such as the kingfisher and the European tree frog have taken up residence in the reserve and with a bit of luck you might catch sight of a wild boar or even, at dusk, a beaver.

Neuchâtel – Fribourg
Neuchâtel – Fribourg region

View from Mont Vully towards Lake Morat and the Alps (9)

Morat (11)

Avenches amphitheatre (12)

The Ryf, an emblematic street in Morat (11)

Mont Vully: a spectacular view

⑨ Although it is more a hill than a mountain, Mont Vully (which lies between Lake Neuchâtel and Lake Morat) nonetheless offers a superb panorama of the lakes; in clear weather you can see as far as the Alps, from the Finsteraarhorn to Mont Blanc. As the Rhône glacier retreated it left behind and pared down this sandstone ridge whose shape now evokes a whale. It also left behind some blocks of granite such as the Agassiz stone, named after a Neuchâtel-born naturalist.

Caves and tastings on Mont Vully

⑩ The southern face of Mont Vully is fairly steep. The caves that are to be found there were once used by the army and are nowadays an ideal playground for children and young explorers. The sunny slopes, which were already popular with the Celts and the Helvetii (as archaeological remains show) are now home to Switzerland's smallest vineyard. The cellars are open for wine tastings every Saturday, or by appointment.

Morat

⑪ Pretty arcades, narrow, twisting streets, historic façades and gables: there's plenty to see in the charming town of Morat. A walk along the ramparts of the medieval town makes history come alive: this is where Charles the Bold was conquered by the Confederates in 1476. Before you leave, treat yourself to a piece of "Nidelkuchen", a pastry speciality from the town.

Avenches: capital of Roman Switzerland

⑫ Welcome to Aventicum, a Roman town on the shore of Lake Morat. Baths, temples and 70 towers bear witness to the importance of this ancient capital of Roman Switzerland, which had more than 20,000 residents. Well-preserved remains, archaeological discoveries and treasures such as a gold bust of Marcus Aurelius give us an insight into this prosperous era. The impressive amphitheatre is still used for opera festivals and plays during the summer.
—> 7 km

Schiffenensee

⑬ Just before we reach Fribourg we arrive at Schiffenensee, a reservoir formed in 1963 which is fed by the River Saane. This 13-kilometre fjord-like artificial lake is surrounded by steep rocky slopes. Barberêche, Grand-Vivy and Petit-Vivy castles overlook it as if they had always been standing on the shores of a lake.

Grandfey railway bridge and Hermitage of St. Magdalena

⑭ The upper part of Schiffenensee offers two tourist attractions of very different sorts. The Grandfey railway bridge (on the Fribourg to Bern line) was not built for the train alone. A footbridge for pedestrians and cyclists passes below the railway. Not far from here, at Räsch, is the Hermitage of St. Magdalena where, over the centuries, a dozen or so rooms have been dug out of the cliff above the River Saane.

The route

Main road and a small section of motorway to the bridge over the River Thielle, then Grand-Marais. Via Mont Vully along the shores of Lake Morat to the town of Morat. Main road to Granges-Paccot and over the new Pont de la Poya to the eastern side of Fribourg.

Distance: 51 kilometres

Photo opportunity: Grand-Marais offers an impressive landscape. The route across Mont Vully, with its steep cliffs rising from the lake, and the small town of Morat are also very pleasant.

To savour: "Nidelkuchen" from Morat was in fact originally from Mont Vully. Three fine layers of cream are applied to a light dough during cooking and two more layers of Gruyère double cream after cooking. More than just a dessert, this cake also makes an ideal accompaniment for a glass of Mont Vully white wine as an aperitif.

Worth a detour

Kerzers: Papiliorama, butterflies, small animals and tropical plants – www.papiliorama.ch

Romont: Vitromusée, museum of stained glass and painting on glass at Romont Castle – www.vitromusee.ch

Granges-Paccot: Kaeserberg model railway, 1:87 scale trains – www.kaeserberg.ch

Tourist information

Tourisme neuchâtelois
Hôtel des Postes, 2001 Neuchâtel
+41 (0)32 889 68 90; www.neuchateltourisme.ch

Société de Navigation sur les lacs de Neuchâtel et Morat SA
Port de Neuchâtel, 2001 Neuchâtel
+41 (0)32 729 96 00; www.navig.ch

Tourisme Bienne Seeland
Bahnhofplatz 12, 2502 Bienne
+41 (0)32 329 84 84; www.bienne-seeland.ch

Vully Tourisme
Route Principale 69, 1786 Nant
+41 (0)26 673 18 72; www.levully.ch

Morat Tourisme
Franz Kirchgasse 6, 3280 Morat
+41 (0)26 670 51 12; www.rnurtentourismus.ch

Neuchâtel – Fribourg
Neuchâtel – Fribourg region

Fribourg – Freiburg (1)

Tinguely fountain

Auge quarter/Rue des Forgerons

Rue de Romont, Fribourg (1)

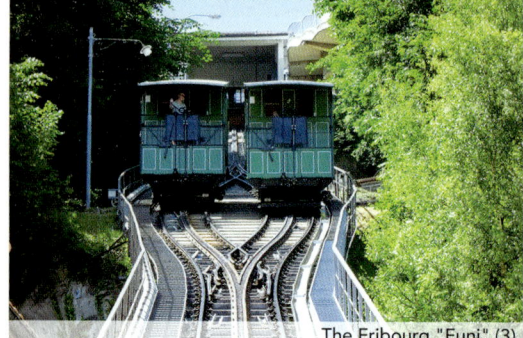
The Fribourg "Funi" (3)

Leg 23

Fribourg – Château-d'Oex
Crossing the Fribourg Alps

After exploring Fribourg old town and enjoying a meal in one of its excellent little restaurants, we're ready to head off for Lake Gruyère and the small town of the same name. Well, almost ready, as before we leave we really must visit the Cailler chocolate factory in Broc. The entrance ticket includes tasting!

The town of Gruyères and its castle stand on a rocky spur below the Moléson (2,002 metres). This remarkably well preserved medieval town is well worth a visit. We mustn't pass over the opportunity to taste a local cheese speciality or a meringue with Gruyère double cream, or to visit to the Hans Rudolf Giger museum near the castle. You might not know the name of this artist who died in 2014, but you will certainly know his creations: Hollywood's aliens. Be prepared for a futuristic experience, which continues in the trendy bar opposite. The road through Upper Gruyère is very pleasant but the real gems are houses decorated with "poyas" (traditional paintings) on the other side of the valley at Estavannens, Grandvillard and Lessoc.

When you turn towards the Pays-d'Enhaut area you might catch sight of hot-air balloons in the sky: Château-d'Oex is a popular destination for balloonists. During the International Balloon Festival the sky is filled with a host of balloons in every shape and colour.

1. Fribourg – Freiburg
Bilingualism is routine in this medieval city founded by the dukes of Zähringen on the banks of the River Saane. "Un petit verre de vin" or "ein Gläschen Wein"? French and German are used indiscriminately and the two cultures fuse together to produce a very pleasant way of life. The old town, with its 200 Gothic facades dating from the 15th century, holds unique charm.

2. Espace Jean Tinguely – Niki de Saint Phalle
Art lovers should not miss the exhibition area in the former tramway depot near Fribourg's museum of art and history. Devoted to Jean Tinguely and Niki de Saint Phalle, it pays tribute to these leading figures in the art world of the mid to late 20th century.

3. An urban mountain train
The "Funi", a funicular which connects the upper town with the lower part of the city on the banks of the Saane, is a feat of engineering. This listed historic monument is the last funicular in Switzerland to use water as a counterweight. It is not powered by a motor but by wastewater from the upper town (which explains the unusual odour when the 3,000 litre reservoir is filled at the upper station).

Pont de la Poya (5)

Cailler chocolate factory

Moléson cable car (10)

The Moléson

Musée Gruérien (8)

Leg 23

Urban golf in Fribourg
(4) This is an original way to explore the various quarters of the picturesque old town on the banks of the River Saane. Using a three-sided golf club (available from the tourist office, Place Jean Tinguely), a golf ball and a map, all you have to do is take aim and tot up your score.

The new Pont de la Poya
(5) With a main span of 196 metres, Pont de la Poya is Switzerland's longest cable-stayed bridge. It continues Fribourg's long tradition of suspension bridges and features a wide sidewalk for pedestrians and cyclists.

Ile d'Ogoz and its two towers
(6) The only buildings on this small island in Lake Gruyère are a ruined castle and chapel, which make a perfect setting for a romantic wedding. The small town of Pont-en-Ogoz stood here until the middle of the 15th century. When the reservoir was filled in 1947, its ruins were submerged. This idyllic islet is all that remains.

La Berra: a small and tranquil mountain
(7) The range of hills to the east of Lake Gruyère is accessible by cable car from the holiday resort at Le Brand, above La Roche. From its highest point (1,719 m) (which possess two panoramic signs) you can see the whole range of the Jura in clear weather as well as the Eiger, the Wildhorn, some of the peaks in the canton of Valais and even Mont Blanc.

Bulle: Musée Gruérien (museum of the Gruyère region)
(8) The museum of folk art and traditions in Bulle is worth a detour. Visitors learn all about the Gruyère region's customs and rich cultural heritage: "poyas" (folk paintings), carved spoons, wardrobes and costumes are cleverly presented with a contemporary slant through scenic representations, interactive audio-visual displays and picture albums. Don't miss it!

Fribourg – Château-d'Oex
Neuchâtel – Fribourg region

Rapido Sky cable car to Vounetz, Charmey

Château de Gruyères (12)

Panoramic platform on the Moléson (10)

Modern cheese dairy (11)

Jogne Gorge (9)

Wood shingle roof, La Berra (7)

Making wood shingles (13)

Broc–Charmey: Jogne Gorge

⑨ To reach the Jogne Gorge follow the hiking trail from Gruyères which leads to the Pont qui Branle (shaking bridge) and the chapel of Notre Dame des Marches. After taking you through the wild Jogne Gorge, with its limestone cliffs, glacial potholes and galleries hollowed out of the rock, the trail climbs up to Lake Montsalvens, crosses a suspension bridge and arrives in Charmey.

The Moléson

⑩ Fribourg residents are so attached to this mountain that they have composed an anthem to it, "A Moléson". Take the road to Moléson-sur-Gruyères, a model resort built for Expo 1964 (the Swiss National Exposition). A modern funicular (a large stretch of which is on raised track) then takes you up sweeping curves at a speed of 10 metres per second to Plan-Francey, where you can take a cable car to the summit. When you reach the Moléson, just step out onto the panoramic viewing platform on the roof of the upper station to enjoy an unobstructed view over the Fribourg mountains to the Bernese and Valais Alps and to Mont Blanc, and over the Fribourg and Vaud plateaus to Lake Geneva and the Jura.
—> 7 km

The Maison du Gruyère and the Moléson mountain cheese dairy

⑪ At Pringy, not far from the town and the castle, you can see modern cheese-making techniques in action and the cheese wheels maturing in a cellar as you learn all about the world-famous Gruyère AOP (protected designation of origin) cheese. The restaurant also has a terrace and serves local gruyère-based specialities. You can buy cheese, and of course a wide variety of other regional products, in the shop. The Moléson-sur-Gruyères mountain cheese dairy, on the other hand, uses traditional methods. You can also watch cheese being made here, taste their produce and buy local products. —> 7 km

Château de Gruyères

⑫ The former home of the Counts of Gruyère occupies a unique location. This 13th century castle stands on a rocky spur at the spot where the River Saane leaves the Intyamon Valley in the Fribourg Pre-Alps, and stands out from a distance. The castle museum presents eight centuries of the region's architectural, historic and cultural heritage, while the small flower-bedecked town is well worth a long stop. Don't miss the opportunity to taste one of the delicious local deserts made with Gruyère double cream.

Paintings on wood and wood shingle roofs

⑬ In local dialect the word "poya" means not only the journey up to the mountain pastures but also the naïve paintings on wood which still decorate the lintels of many cowsheds in the Intyamon Valley. In the Fribourg and Vaud Alps, roofs were traditionally covered with wooden tiles. They are still used on mountain chalets to the present day, and also very decoratively embellish the vast chimney stacks.

Moléson mountain cheese dairy (11)

Village fountain, Lessoc

Poya painting on wood (13)

Wooden bridge in Lessoc (14)

The Grand Chalet (16)

Leg 23

⑭ Bridges in the Gruyère area
There are three gems of bridge engineering straddling the River Saane between Broc and Montbovon: an old stone bridge built in 1580 near Broc castle, a covered wooden bridge (known as "the shaking bridge") near Gruyères, and the prettiest of the three, a small bridge covered with a wooden tiled roof, tucked away in the forest between Lessoc and Montbovon.

⑮ Buvette des Moilles
You'll find mountain chalets all over the Fribourg Alps, where you can enjoy delicious local dishes on a sunny terrace or in a cosy room by a fire. The Buvette des Moilles above Albeuve, which can be reached by a mountain road, is an excellent example. —> 7 km

⑯ Rossinière: the Grand Chalet
Nobody can fail to be impressed by this chalet with a floor surface of 500 m², five floors, 60 rooms, 113 windows, an ornately decorated façade and immense hip-end roof partly covered in wood shingles. Built between 1752 and 1756, it was first turned into a hotel before becoming the home of the painter Balthus. The privately-owned Grand Chalet is not open to the public, but there are plans for the Grand Salon to be used to host art exhibitions.

The route

Main road past the Gotteron Gorge to Marly, then towards La Roche, Broc and Gruyères. Via the Upper Gruyère region to Montbovon then westwards to Pays-d'Enhaut and Château-d'Oex.

Distance: 61 kilometres

Photo opportunity: The detour to Lake Gruyère via the Pont-la-Ville golf course offers wonderful scenery. There is a good road from Gruyères but the typical houses of Intyamon Valley are on the other side of the River Saane. The Defilé de la Tine, which played a strategic part in defending the Swiss National Redoubt (a line of fortifications), is highly impressive.

To savour: Originally, the "Bénichon" was a parish festival in the Fribourg area. Traditionally, people would eat "cuchaule", a saffron brioche with sweet-and-sour "Bénichon mustard", on that day. Nowadays, the mustard and bread are sold all year long.

Worth a detour

(A) **Broc:** Tour of Cailler chocolate factory – www.maisoncailler.ch

(B) **Gruyères:** H.R. Giger museum and its bar – www.hrgigermuseum.com

(C) **Moléson-sur-Gruyères:** toboggan run, Devalkart downhill karting, trottinerbe downhill kickscooters – www.moleson.ch

(D) **Charmey:** Vounetz treetop and adventure park – www.charmeyaventures.ch

Tourist information

Fribourg Tourisme et Région
Place Jean-Tinguely 1, 1701 Fribourg
+41 (0)26 350 11 11; www.fribourgtourisme.ch

La Gruyère Tourisme
Place des Alpes 26, 1630 Bulle
+41 (0)848 424 424; www.la-gruyere.ch

Office du Tourisme de Moléson
Place de l'Aigle 6, 1663 Moléson-sur-Gruyères
+41 (0)26 921 85 00; www.moleson.ch

Fribourg Région Information
Rte de la Glâne 107, 1701 Fribourg
+41 (0)26 407 70 20; www.fribourgregion.ch

Fribourg – Château-d'Oex

Neuchâtel – Fribourg region

GRAND TOUR of Switzerland

Bernese Oberland region

The Eiger, the Mönch and the Jungfrau are the three legendary mountains which watch over this region. But the Oberland offers many other treasures, from Saanenland on the language border to the Simmental with its pretty farms, the very rural Haslital, and the Grimsel and Susten Passes. And we mustn't forget Thun, which is perhaps Switzerland's most beautiful town.

Lake Thun, near Saint Beatus caves

Château d'Oex, balloonists' paradise

Near Moulins, Gruyère Pays-d'Enhaut nature park (1)

Rougemont (5)

Paper cutting (2)

Leg 24

Château-d'Oex – Interlaken

Pays d'Enhaut, Saanenland, Simmental, Lake Thun

It's well worth spending a little extra time in the western part of the Bernese Oberland. Take your time to stroll through the traffic-free main shopping street in Gstaad, crossed only by the MOB (Montreux-Oberland Bernois) railway on its high bridge. Make a few excursions in Saanenland, to Lauenensee and Arnensee or to the Turbach Valley. And if you wish to take one last look at the canton of Valais, go to the Col du Pillon and take the gondola lift up to the Glacier 3000 plateau.

But we must move forward nonetheless. So off we go… but not too fast! For how can you resist the temptation to stop and photograph this enchanting landscape chock-full of the famous Simmental cows? And how can you not want to visit all those mountain peaks with panoramic views and the flower-bedecked villages in the Simmental? In Schönried, for example, you can take a cable car to the Rellerli opposite the Hornflue, while at Erlenbach you can look out over the Swiss Plateau from the Stockhorn, with its two distinctive "eyes" in the rock face. We must also take our time because the Simmental is a long valley with twisting roads.

After passing through the narrow passage at Wimmis we arrive at Lake Thun. Yet again the landscape is stunning: the port and pretty village of Spiez, with its castle and chapel against the backdrop of the vineyard. A road along the shore of the lake finally leads us to Interlaken.

① Gruyère Pays-d'Enhaut nature park

The nature park which we cross almost as far as Saanen starts south of Gruyères Castle. Straddling the cantons of Fribourg and Vaud, the park stretches southward to the Col des Mosses and Chillon Castle and is remarkable for its alpine and agricultural economy which has remained intact thanks to a centuries-old symbiosis between man and the environment.

② Châteaux-d'Oex: paper-cutting in the Pays-d'Enhaut

The Musée du Vieux Pays-d'Enhaut in Château-d'Oex is a true gem. In addition to furniture you will also find an old forge, bells and weapons and more than 60 very well preserved traditional paper cuttings. These extremely delicate and beautiful pieces of craftsmanship are a pleasure to the eye and at the same time tell stories. You can find out all about the history of this form of folk art and will perhaps be surprised to learn that it originated in towns and not in these rural areas.

③ La Braye: mountain adventure park

From Château-d'Oex a cable car takes you to the other side of the River Saane, where you continue in a gondola lift. A treasure hunt narrates the expeditions of explorer Mike Horn, a themed trail devoted to ants gives you an insight into the fascinating world of these small six-legged creatures and at the upper station those in search of excitement can try a 250-metre long zip wire.

Saanen church, Gstaad in the background (6)

Lauenensee (8)

La Pierreuse region (4)

Saanenland

Sanetsch Pass region (9)

Leg 24

④ La Pierreuse nature reserve

The steep limestone faces of the Gummfluh in the south of the Pays-d'Enhaut and the Rubli to the east mark the boundaries of this deep and untouched valley. The largest nature reserve in Frenchspeaking Switzerland can be reached on foot from Videmanette or via the main valley. —> 5 km

⑤ Rougemont: church and castle

In the 11th century the Cluny monks built a monastery and church on land provided by the Count of Gruyère. 500 years later the Bernese bailiff decided to make his permanent home at the exact spot where the former priory was built. Today the charm of this photogenic village lies in its church, castle and traditional chalets. Located on the border between the cantons of Vaud and Bern, the village population is still mainly French-speaking.

⑥ Gstaad – Saanenland

The diversity of its visitors no doubt contributes to the charm of this region which has become holiday destination. Celebrities gather at Gstaad, while the surrounding villages provide a more family-oriented offer. The main street in Gstaad is now an elegant pedestrian shopping thoroughfare; it might be the shortest in Switzerland, but it is certainly one of the most desirable. At Saanen, the region's capital, the landscape museum devoted to the history of Saanenland is worth a visit.

⑦ Saanenland "shaving cheese"

This cheese from the mountain pastures is ripened for a minimum of two years, but only reaches maturity after three years. During the first year, this famous "shaving cheese" from Saanenland is very carefully tended. From then on it ripens as it dries out almost without any further human intervention. As it is too hard to cut with a knife it has to be shaved using a special tool into thin slices which can then be rolled to a greater or lesser extent according to the type and age of the cheese.

⑧ Lauenensee

From Gstaad a small road winds peacefully through the mountain pastures to the picturesque Lauenensee at 1,380 metres above sea level. Hikers can leave from the Wispile for a three-hour walk with panoramic views to Lauenensee, immortalised as "Louenesee" by the Swiss rock group Span. You can return to Gstaad from the lake or the village of Lauenen by CarPostal bus. —> 15 km

⑨ To the source of the River Saane

After Gsteig, the cable car (which used to be run by the power station) takes you up to the Sanetsch reservoir lake and dam in the canton of Valais. In the Middle Ages the pass which connected Saanenland to the Rhône Valley was used by mule-drivers and troops. Nowadays, the area where the Saane River rises is popular with hikers and mountain bikers. At the upper station the Auberge du Sanetsch offers a tempting break. The larger-than-life owner extends a warm welcome to guests and the auberge serves delicious dishes and excellent Valais wines. —> 15 km

Spiez Castle, Lake Thun (15)

The Niesen funicular (14)

Alpine culture, Lenk (11)

Stockhorn (12)

Seebergsee, Diemtigtal (13)

Summer toboggan run on the Rellerli (10)

Leg 24

⑩ Schönried: gondola lift to the Rellerli

Take a deep breath! This gondola lift with a 16-degree curve runs at full speed; you'll feel as if you're on a rollercoaster! The summit offers a magnificent view of the Alps and a summer toboggan run. Mountain bikers can enjoy a superb and safe single trail down to the valley; others might prefer downhill kick-scooters, or a high-altitude hike to the Hundsrügg/Sparenmoos or Abländschen.

⑪ Lenk

When you reach Zweisimmen, the road and the railway turn south towards Lenk. The Wildstrubel massif which closes off the valley is one of the most beautiful places in the Alps and is also home to the source of the River Simme and the famous Simmenfälle waterfalls. But Lenk is also well known for its springs of sulphurous water, beneficial for rheumatism and respiratory illnesses, as well as its tourist facilities which are particularly well-suited to families. —> 13 km

⑫ The Stockhorn "eyes"

The distinctive rocky "head" which marks the entrance to the Bernese Oberland can be recognised from afar. Its long-distance vision must be good, since you can see as far as Thun, the valley of the Aare, Bern and the Jura from its summit. A cable car in two sections takes you up from Erlenbach via Chrindi and Hinterstockensee to enjoy this panorama over the Alps and the Swiss Plateau.

⑬ Diemtigtal nature park

This valley, which seems to be isolated from the rest of the world, is a 16 kilometre oasis for the natural environment and includes the delightful village of Diemtigen with its charming church and houses. Follow the "house trail" to discover the valley's finest buildings. The Grimmimutz adventure trail offers children an opportunity to relive the adventures of a kind little elf and the wicked witch Pfefferhexe. —> 5 km

⑭ The Niesen: a pyramid with a view

Its almost perfect pyramidal shape has inspired a number of artists including Ferdinand Hodler, Paul Klee and Cuno Amiet. It takes just half an hour to reach the summit (2,362 m) in comfort by funicular railway from Mülenen. Participants in the Niesenlauf, an annual race up the world's longest flight of steps (no fewer than 11,674 steps to which access is prohibited at other times) running parallel to the railway, have to make a bit more of an effort. —> 6 km

⑮ Spiez Castle

When you catch sight of this castle standing atop the Spiezberg, it's impossible to resist the urge to continue down to the small town on the shore of the lake. The vineyard lying on the south-facing slopes behind the castle's pre-Romanesque church and the view over Lake Thun contribute to the charm of this place. The castle illustrates the different stages of transforming a medieval fortress into a patrician residence.

The route

By-road through the Pays-d'Enhaut, from Saanen to Schönried and Saanenmöser. The Simmental road to the Simmenfluh near Wimmis. Link road crossing the River Kander to Spiez railway station. Along the lake on the old main road via Leissigen to Interlaken.

Distance: 78 kilometres

Photo opportunity: The Rougement area of the Pays-d'Enhaut is particularly charming. The road along Lake Thun offers some lovely views of the opposite shore towards Beatenberg and the Niederhorn.

To savour: When alpine cheese is washed at 5 to 7 months to remove the morge (a residue from the cheese-making process) and continues to ripen in a cellar at 12°C with a relative humidity of 70 to 75%, over time it becomes the famous Hobelkäse "shaving cheese". It takes the one produced in Saanenland three years to reach maturity. It is distinctive for its salty, spicy flavour and white spots.

Worth a detour

(A) Rougemont: Videmanette via ferrata, 3 different routes – www.chateau-doex.ch/fr/4saisons/escalade/ferrata

(B) Saanen/Gstaad – Château-d'Oex: Rafting on the River Saane – www.rivieres-aventures.ch /www.swissraft.ch

(C) Lenk: Alpine culture and agriculture in the Simmental – www.alpkultur.ch

(D) Erlenbach BE: the Simmental houses route, houses decorated with remarkable paintings (app available) – www.hauswege.ch

(E) Spiez: museum of local traditions and winemaking, Simmentalerhaus at the Spiezberg near the castle – www.museum-spiez.ch

Tourist information

Pays-d'Enhaut Tourisme
La Place 6, 1660 Château-d'Oex
+41 (0)26 924 25 25; www.chateau-doex.ch

Gruyère Pays-d'Enhaut regional nature park
Place du Village 6, 1660 Château-d'Oex
+41 (0)26 924 76 93; www.gruyerepaysdenhaut.ch

Gstaad Saanenland Tourismus
Promenade 41, 3780 Gstaad
+41 (0)33 748 81 81; www.gstaad.ch

Lenk Simmental Tourismus
Rawilstrasse 3, 3775 Lenk
+41 (0)33 736 35 35; www.lenk-simmental.ch

Château-d'Oex – Interlaken

Bernese Oberland region

Grimsel Hospiz, Guttannen, Bernese Oberland

Lodgings along the Grand Tour.

After a full day of touring, our accommodations along the Grand Tour are perfect for putting up your feet, relaxing and thinking about the highlights of your day.

Those who travel have more fun
The Grand Tour is the key to the treasures of Switzerland. It meanders its way through the lovely countryside from one famous attraction to the next and with a few inside tips adding a special touch.

Camping Delta, Locarno, Ticino

Hotel Meisser, Guarda, Graubünden

Domaine de Châteauvieux, Satigny, Geneva

Rest and relaxation at the end of the day

Choose a cosy inn, a luxury establishment or a peaceful campground along the route to spend a night of pleasant dreams. Wherever you are, you can expect warm hospitality and sometimes a nice surprise, especially for Grand Tour guests, a neck massage, perhaps, a spotless windshield or a packed lunch to enjoy on your trip.

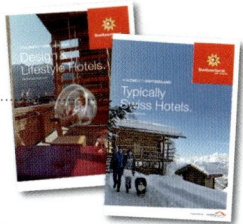

The perfect hotel is just a click away

Exploring your hotel options is an adventure in itself with the Best Swiss Hotels app. The hotels recommended by Switzerland Tourism can now all be booked directly via the app. Download it free of charge from **MySwitzerland.com/best-swiss-hotels**

Brochure

Order the latest "Typically Swiss Hotels" or "Design & Lifestyle Hotels" brochure from Switzerland Tourism on **MySwitzerland.com/brochures**

All accommodations along the Grand Tour of Switzerland are listed at **MySwitzerland.com/grandtourhotels**

Yodellers on the Kleine Sheidegg, facing the north face of the Eiger

Interlaken (2)

Staubbach Falls, Lauterbrunnen (5)

Harder Kulm, Interlaken (1)

Sunset over the Brienzer Rothorn

Leg 25

Interlaken – Bern

The eastern Bernese Oberland to Bern

The economy of the Bernese Oberland's alpine town is based on tourism, and this is very obvious. A Swiss national almost looks out of place here. It should not, however, be missed; for if Interlaken attracts so many visitors there is surely a reason. Its success is no doubt due in part to the many possibilities it offers for excursions. Popular destinations include Grindelwald and the Jungfraujoch, Brienz, the Rothorn's historic rack-and-pinion railway and "Grimselwelt".

We pass Saint Beatus Caves and follow a road running parallel to the lake to Thun, an old and well-preserved town with high pavements (designed to protect shops from flooding by the Aare) which are surprising to say the least.

We are now only 28 kilometres from Bern by the main road, but the Grand Tour takes us on a much more attractive route via the Längenberg. At Seftigen, we cross the Gürbe Valley (well known for its cabbage production). We then climb up to Riggisberg to the Tavel memorial, to enjoy a stunning view of lush green hills with the imposing Stockhorn and Gantrisch mountains in the Bernese Alps in the background. At Kehrsatz we join the Gürbe Valley road which takes us to Bern. And at the Bundesplatz in the old city of Bern, our 1,600-kilometre Grand Tour of Switzerland will have come full circle.

① Harder Kulm: a panoramic viewing platform

This belvedere just above Interlaken is ideal for a short excursion, giving you a first glimpse of the Jungfrau region which will help you decide where you would like to go next. The Harder funicular, which travels up through the forest, has been in operation for over a century. From the upper station it takes just five minutes to reach the restaurant with its small tower and the new aerial viewing platform with a vista over the Eiger, the Mönch, the Jungfrau, Lake Brienz and Lake Thun.

② Interlaken Adventure Sport

Adventure sport lovers will be in their element. Paragliding, rafting, canyoning, bungee-jumping and treetop circuits: Interlaken is proud to be known as "the adrenaline Mecca" and recently received official recognition as Top Region für Sport und Spass (best region for sport and fun). The town between two lakes is also a starting point for excursions to the Jungfrau region, Lake Brienz and the Haslital.

③ Burgseeli: natural beach above Lake Brienz

On the main road to Brienz, between Goldswil and Ringgenberg, lies a small lake (located 50 metres higher than Lake Brienz) which is just perfect for bathing. You can swim amongst the water lilies in Burgseeli and benefit from the properties of its natural waters with a temperature which can be as high as 26°C from May to September. The lawn areas offer some ideal spots for quiet relaxation.

The Great Aletsch Glacier with the Jungfraujoch to the right (4)

Bachalpsee, Grindelwald

Schilthorn cable car (6)

Schynige Platte (7)

Lake Brienz (8)

Brienz-Rothorn steam train (9)

Leg 25

④ Jungfraujoch: a close-up view of the Aletsch Glacier

Between 1896 and 1912 a seven-kilometre tunnel was dug through the rock, with Eigergletscher station as its starting point. Two windows in the north and east faces of the Eiger offer spectacular views over the deep valley and the sea of ice. A gallery leads from the upper station to the Ice Palace and the plateau. You can take a cable car to the Sphinx panoramic viewing platform and the Alpine Sensation circuit. In summer you can also enjoy a 45-minute walk to the Mönchsjoch in the snow and clear mountain air. —> 19 km

⑤ Lauterbrunnen: valley of waterfalls

Not far from Lauterbrunnen the Staubbach Falls, which drop from a height of 297 metres into the valley, inspired Goethe to write that "the soul of man is like water". Half way towards Stechelberg, the underground Trümmelbach waterfalls rumble away under the mountain; they are accessible via a maze of steps and galleries and a lift. —> 13 km

⑥ Mürren: 007 on the Schilthorn

A famous secret agent has passed this way. From the valley of waterfalls you can take a gondola lift via the traffic-free village of Mürren to the famous Schilthorn (2,970 m), which entered film history under the name of Piz Gloria. A permanent exhibition recounts James Bond's adventures and the revolving restaurant serves a champagne breakfast with an idyllic view of the Jungfrau massif. —> 19 km

⑦ Schynige Platte

For the last 120 years a small rack-and-pinion railway has valiantly climbed the steep slope (25% in places) which leads to the Schynige Platte viewing point and mountain hotel. The journey aboard the panoramic train takes an hour, which almost seems to pass too quickly. When you reach the top, the Eiger, the Mönch and the Jungfrau lie before you. A high-altitude trail with a view over Lake Brienz and an alpine garden growing 600 different species of plants are also of interest.

⑧ Boating on Lake Thun and Lake Brienz

Steam and paddle boats dating from the Belle Epoque (the Blüemlisalp, built in 1906, on Lake Thun and the Lötschberg, built in 1914, on Lake Brienz) give passengers a delightfully retro experience. From Lake Thun you have an excellent view of the castles and churches on the shore and an everchanging perspective of the Alps. Lake Brienz, for its part, is surrounded by steep-sided mountains and a relatively untouched natural environment.

⑨ The Brienzer Rothorn

Full steam ahead! Not without effort, a small locomotive takes an hour to push the red panoramic carriages up to the Brienzer Rothorn. When you arrive, a breathtaking panorama spreads out before you: the Bernese Alps, Lake Brienz, the Grimsel region, Mount Pilatus and the Hohgant. Mountain restaurants and a hotel with recently renovated guestrooms allow you to enjoy this place to the full from sunrise to sunset. —> 17 km

One of the two restaurant terraces at the summit of the Brienzer Rothorn (9)

Giessbach Falls and hotel (10)

The Niederhorn with the Eiger, the Mönch and the Jungfrau (11)

Saint Beatus Caves (12)

Suspension footbridge, Sigriswil (14)

Leg 25

(10) Giessbach: waterfall and historic Grand Hotel

On the wooded shore opposite Brienz, a unique place with a romantic atmosphere awaits you. The Grand Hotel Giessbach, which for over a century has received guests in a peaceful, natural environment, nowadays also exudes nostalgic charm. The Giesbach Falls, with a 500-metre drop over 14 levels, are a stunning natural wonder. The hotel even has its own landing stage and historic rackand-pinion train. —> 22 km

(11) Beatenberg and the Niederhorn

A mountain road climbs up from Interlaken to Beatenberg, a linear village which enjoys picture postcard views. A cable car then takes you up to the Niederhorn, with its welcoming inn (restaurant, sunny terrace and accommodation) and view over the Eiger, the Mönch and the Jungfrau. If you're lucky you might come across chamois on the path leading to the Gemmenalphorn. You can also get to Beatenberg by taking the panoramic funicular from Beatenbucht. —> 12 km

(12) Saint Beatus Caves

2,000 years ago, a fearsome dragon led a reign of terror here until a wandering Irish monk successfully drove it away. So nowadays you can enter the accessible part of Saint Beatus Caves without fear. The caves are open during the summer. A safe path with electric lighting takes you from the monk's cell to magical formations and underground waterfalls.

(13) Lake Thun pilgrim's way

On the map, the hiking trail which passes Saint Beatus Caves and continues to Sundlauenen is shown as a pilgrim's way. You can get your pilgrim's "passport" stamped at Merligen church. The wellmaintained path then runs past dry stone walls and climbs 150 metres above the lake before returning to the caves. The trail can be reached by bus.

(14) Sigriswil: suspension footbridge

Sigriswil is worth a detour, mainly for the new 340-metre suspension footbridge connecting Sigriswil to Aeschlen. Originally designed for children to get to school, it offers a spectacular experience for any walker. When you cross it (toll payable) try to overcome your fear and look around you: you will be rewarded by a breathtaking alpine vista.

(15) Thun: old town and castle

Boats arriving from the lake carefully make their way up the Aare and the canal as far as Thun railway station. In the opposite direction, the journey from the town centre to the lake takes half an hour on foot. The crowning glory of this pleasant walk is the view of the Eiger, Mönch, Jungfrau, Blüemlisalp, Niesen and Stockhorn. The towers of the church and castle soar above a charming historic centre dating from the late Middle Ages. The town is also known for the friendly atmosphere of the cafés and restaurants on the banks of the River Aare and for its famous raised pavements which are conducive to shopping.

Scherzlig lock with wooden bridge over the Aare, Thun (15)

Schadau Castle (16)

On the Längenberg (17)

Rüeggisberg monastery ruins (18)

The Gantrisch nature park, peaks of the Nünenen, the Gantrisch and the Bürglen (17)

Leg 25

Schadau castle and the Thun Panorama
(16) A 360° panorama of Thun painted by Basel-born artist Marquard Wocher in 1810 is exhibited in the park of Schadau Castle on the shore of Lake Thun. The artist depicted morning life in the small town of Thun from a rooftop in the town centre, giving us a glimpse into the drawing rooms, classrooms and alleys of the time. This 38-metre circular painting includes more than 300 figures of inhabitants. Schadau Castle, for its part, hosts festivals and conferences. It is also a restaurant and home to the museum of gastronomy.

The Gantrisch nature park
(17) The Gantrisch regional nature park, located in the triangle formed by the towns of Bern, Fribourg and Thun, has an abundance of attractions. Highlights include Schwartzsee, the "Vreneli" hike to Guggisberg, the Gäggersteg raised trail, Gantrischseeli (a mountain lake saved in extremis), a treetop circuit and a hike on the Längenberg. —> 15 km

Rüeggisberg monastery ruins and the Bütschelegg
(18) Rüeggisberg monastery reached its golden age during the early Middle Ages. This former Cluny priory on the Way of Saint James was at the time one of the most important monasteries in Switzerland. Its impressive ruins now host cultural events. They are also popular with hikers, either as a high energy area or as a historic site with a beautiful view of the Bernese Alps.

If you too enjoy this vista, you should now visit the Bütschelegg or the monument which pays tribute to dialectal poet Rudolf von Tavel (1866 – 1934) on the Längenberg to the north of Riggisberg.

Bern Airport
(19) Bern airport (formerly called Bern-Belp international airport) is a medium-sized aerodrome which is worth a visit. You can sit comfortably in the restaurant and watch the ballet of gliders, helicopters, private aircraft and passenger planes as they take off and land. Not far from here the banks of the Aare offer a pleasant place for a stroll, and in the summer the river is a popular swimming spot.

Interlaken – Bern
Bernese Oberland region

The route

By-road from Interlaken to Thun via Beatenbucht, Merligen and Oberhofen. At Steffisburg, through the Aare Valley then the Gürbe Valley towards Wattenwil. The Längenberg panoramic route.

Distance: 62 kilometres

Photo opportunity: Scenery by Saint Beatus Caves and from Oberhofen Castle to Thun, travelling along the river. Scenery on the Längenberg with the Eiger, the Mönch, the Jungfrau, the Niesen, the Stockhorn and the Gantrisch range behind you.

To savour: The rich and fertile soil of the Gürbe valley is ideal for growing white cabbages (chabis in the Bern dialect), which is then made professionally into "suurchabis" (sauerkraut). This has given the valley its nickname of Chabisland (cabbage country).

Worth a detour

(A) **Interlaken:** Jungfrau Park/the great mysteries of the world – www.jungfraupark.ch

(B) **Interlaken:** Heimwehfluh with funicular, summer toboggan run, model railway – www.heimwehfluh.ch

(C) **Interlaken:** Museum of tourism in the Jungfrau region – www.touristikmuseum.ch

(D) **Hofstetten bei Brienz:** Ballenberg open-air museum, Swiss houses, farm animals, crafts – www.ballenberg.ch

(E) **Oberhofen:** castle, lifestyle museum with oriental smoking room, park – www.schlossoberhofen.ch

(F) Riggisberg: Abegg Foundation, collection of textiles from Europe, the Middle East and the silk road – www.abegg-stiftung.ch

Tourist information

Interlaken Tourismus
Höheweg 37, 3800 Interlaken
+41 (0)33 826 53 00; www.interlaken.ch

Jungfrau Region
Untere Bönigstrasse 8, 3800 Interlaken
+41 (0)33 854 12 50; www.jungfrauregion.ch

Thun-Thunersee Tourismus
Welcome Center at the station, 3601 Thun
+41 (0)33 225 90 00; www.thunersee.ch

Naturpark Gantrisch
Schlossgasse 13, 3150 Schwarzenburg
+41 (0)31 808 00 20; www.gantrisch.ch

Interlaken – Bern
Bernese Oberland region

Emmentaler Show Dairy

The birthplace of the „King of Cheese."
Discover our four dairy generations on an audio guided tour or participate in one of our cheese experience offers. Have a taste of the world famous Emmentaler cheese.

The best place for an interesting stay on your Grand Tour!

www.e-sk.ch

Enjoy a typical Swiss dish in our à la carte restaurant. In our two shops you find a variety of Swiss cheeses, Swiss watches and the famous Swiss Army knives. For children there is a new playground and a petting zoo.

Find us in this guide on page 17 point 7 and page 22 point B.

Emmentaler Schaukäserei AG
Schaukäsereistrasse 6, 3416 Affoltern i.E.
+41 34 435 16 11 / www.e-sk.ch

Kambly Experience, Trubschachen

Dive into the world of Kambly, **Switzerland's best known and most popular premium biscuit brand**. At the Kambly visitor centre look over our **master confectioner's** shoulders to discover the secrets of the art of fine biscuit making and take **your pick of over 100 varieties of biscuits**. Enjoy moments of delight!

Further information on **www.kambly.ch**

Tradition and innovation from Trubschachen

Trubschachen is home to internationally **successful and traditional family businesses**. Combine the visit to the Kambly Experience with a **stroll around Trubschachen** and follow the **interactive trail** «Ropes today and yesterday» at Jakob AG, a global leader in rope and hoist systems. Just across the street, you can watch the potters and ceramic painters at work at Aebi Open **Pottery. Entrance is free.** Further information on **www.kambly.ch/tour**

Useful information for the journey

Index of places
My personal impressions of
the Grand Tour

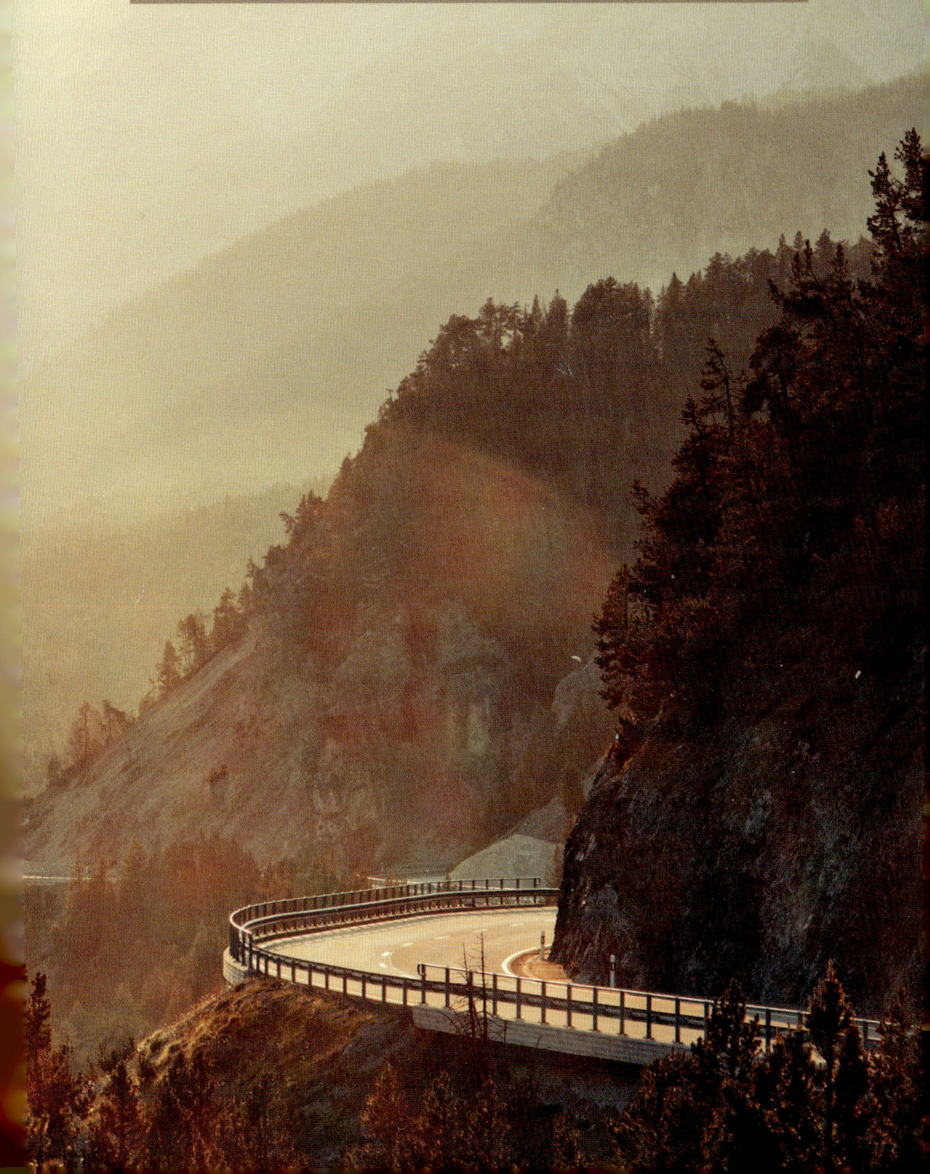

Travel in safety with these useful tips

Technical specifications for the itinerary

Ⓘ The itinerary of the Grand Tour of Switzerland is intended for cars and motorbikes. Larger vehicles will encounter certain restrictions.

Ⓘ Ⓘ The Grand Tour circuit can be travelled in either direction but we recommend that it is followed clockwise. This is particularly relevant in towns with one-way systems and for motorway access roads.

Ⓘ Ⓘ Ⓘ The Grand Tour does not use motorways unless justified by traffic or itinerary constraints. A motorway vignette (toll sticker) is required.

Ⓘ Ⓥ The Grand Tour takes you over five alpine passes at over 2,000 metres above sea level, with the following options:

Flüela:	vehicles can be loaded on a car shuttle at the Vereina Tunnel from Klosters-Selfranga to Sagliains
Julier:	the road over the pass is open all year
San Bernardino:	Road tunnel from Hinterrhein to San Bernardino
St. Gotthard:	new road over the pass, road tunnel from Airolo to Göschenen
Furka:	vehicles can be loaded on a car shuttle from Realp to Oberwald

Ⓥ Lake Lucerne is crossed by car ferry, from Gersau to Beckenried (from late April to late October, www.autofaehre.ch). Alternatively, you can take the road from Gersau to Brunnen.

Ⓥ Ⓘ **Disclaimer:** the Grand Tour is a recommended itinerary which uses the existing Swiss road network. It is followed entirely at the user's own risk. Neither Switzerland Tourism nor the Grand Tour of Switzerland Association can be held liable for any possible structural modifications, diversions, safety alerts and recommendations or any particular incident occurring at any point of the itinerary.

Ⓥ Ⓘ Ⓘ **Explanation of the arrow and km in the guide:** —> 12 km at the end of a paragraph indicates the distance from the main itinerary. Short distances are not indicated.

Useful information for the journey

 Switzerland Tourism Tödistrasse 7, CH-8027 Zurich
Internet: www.MySwitzerland.com, **E-Mail:** info@switzerland.com
Grand Tour of Switzerland: www.MySwitzerland.com/grandtour
Maps: www.MySwitzerland.com/grandtourmap

Service
✆ 00800 100 200 29

 Swisscamps/Swiss camping association Bahnhofstr. 5 / P. O. Box,
CH-3322 Schönbühl-Urtenen, ✆ +41 (0) 31 / 852 06 26, www.swisscamps.ch
Swiss federation of camping and caravanning
Wührestrasse 13, CH-5724 Dürrenäsch, ✆ +41 (0) 62 / 777 40 08, www.sccv.ch
Touring Club Switzerland (TCS) Ch. de Blandonnet 4,
CH-1214 Vernier, ✆ +41 (0) 58 / 827 25 20, www.tcs-camping.ch

 1 Swiss franc (CHF) = 100 cents

CHF

Cents

      0,5 ‰
0,1 ‰

      (CHF 40.–)

  SBB Studded tyres →
✆ +41 (0) 800 140 140   ✆ +41 (0) 900 300 300, www.sbb.ch   24.10.– 30.4. / 80 km/h

Automobile Club of Switzerland (ACS)
Wasserwerkgasse 39, CH-3011 Bern, ✆ +41 (0) 31 / 328 31 11, www.acs.ch
Touring Club Switzerland (TCS)
Chemin de Blandonnet 4, CH-1214 Vernier, ✆ +41 (0) 844 888 111, www.tcs.ch

Road conditions

 ✆ **+41 (0) 58 827 24 24**
for TCS members

✆ **+41 (0) 900 57 12 34**
-.86 CHF per minute

www.inforoute.ch

Polizei   ACS +41 (0) 44 628 88 99
117   **118**   **144**   **1414**   TCS +41 (0) 800 140 140

Index of places (selection)

Leg 1
Berne – Lucerne
Affoltern i.E.	17
Berne	15
Beromünster	19
Burgdorf	17
Entlebuch biosphere	19
The Gurten	17
Lake Hallwil	21
Heidegg Castle	21
Langnau i.E.	17
Lützelflüh	17
Muri AG	21
Solothurn	17
Sörenberg	19
Sursee	19
Trubschachen	19
Willisau	19
Wolhusen	23

Leg 2
Lucerne – Schwyz
Altdorf	35
Bauen	35
Beckenried	33
Brunnen	37
Buochs	37
Bürgenstock	33
Bürglen UR	35
Emmetten	33
Flüelen	35
Gersau	33
Hammetschwand	33
Klewenalp	33
Küssnacht	31
Lake Lucerne	29
Lake Uri	35
Lucerne	29
Morschach	37
Pilatus	31
Rigi	31
Rütli	35
Seelisberg	33
Stanserhorn	31
Tellsplatte	35
Titlis, Engelberg	37
Vitznau	31
Weggis	31

Leg 3
Schwyz – Zürich
Ägerisee	43
Bubikon	45
Einsiedeln	43
Lake Zürich	45
Lützelsee	45
Morgarten	43
Muotatha	41
Mythen	41
Pfäffikon SZ	47
Rapperswil	43
Rotenfluh	41
Rothenthurm	43
Sattel-Hochstuckli	41
Schwyz	39
Seegräben	47
Stoos	41

Leg 4
Zurich – Schaffhausen
Flaach	57
Irchel	55
Kloten	53
Kyburg	53
Marthalen	57
Rheinau	57
Rüdlingen	55
Uetliberg	53
Wildensbuch	57
Winterthur	55
Zürich	51

Leg 5
Schaffhausen – St. Gallen
Altenrhein	67
Arbon	67
Arenenberg, Salenstein	65
Bischofszell	67
Kreuzlingen/ Constance	67
Lake Constance	67
Lipperswil	69
Randen	63
Rhine Falls	63
Rorschach	67
Schaffhausen	63
Steckborn	65
Stein am Rhein	65
Untersee	65

Leg 6
St. Gallen – Wildhaus
Alpstein	73
Appenzell	73
Churfirsten	75
Ebenalp	73
Gäbris	73
Gais	73
Gontenbad	75
Heiden	73
Hoher Kasten	73
Kronberg	77
Ofenloch	75
Säntis-Schwägalp	75
St. Gallen	71
Starkenbach	75
Stein am Rhein	77
Urnäsch	77
Waldegg AR	73
Walzenhausen	73

Leg 7
Wildhaus – Davos
Bad Ragaz	83
Brambrüesch	83
Chur	83
Klosters	85
Madrisa	87
Maienfeld	83
Malans GR	83
Malbun-Steg	81
Partnun	85
Pizol	87
Prättigau	85
Sargans	81
Schiers	83
St. Antönien	85
Tectonic Arena Sardona	81
Toggenburg	79
Triesenberg	81
Vaduz	81
Werdenberg	79
Wildhaus	79

Leg 8
Davos – St. Moritz
Bernina Pass	99
Celerina	97
Cluozza	95
Davos	93
Diavolezza	97
Engadine	99
Flüela Pass	93
Fuorn Pass	95
Guarda	95
Lower Engadine	93
Monstein	93
Muottas Muragl	97
Müstair	97
National Park	95
Parsenn	91
Pontresina	97
S-charl	95
Samnaun	95
Schatzalp	91
Scuol	93
Sertig Dörfli	93
Tarasp	99
Val Roseg	97
Weissfluhjoch	91
Zernez	95
Zügenschlucht	93

Index of places

Leg 9
St. Moritz – Andeer
Albula	105
Alp Flix	103
Alvaneu	107
Bergün / Bravuogn	107
Bivio	103
Celerina	107
Corvatsch	101
Flims	105
Julier Pass	103
Maloja	103
Obermutten	105
Parc Ela	103
Piz Lunghin	103
Riom (Oberhalbstein)	105
Savognin	103
Lake Sils	103
St. Moritz	101
Upper Engadine	101
Val Fex	103
Viamala	105
Zillis	105

Leg 10
Andeer – Bellinzona
Parc Adula	111
Andeer	109
Beverin nature park	109
Juf (Avers)	109
Mesocco/Misox	111
Rheinwald/Hinterrhein	109
Rofla Gorge	113
San Bernardino	111
San Bernardino Pass	111
Splügen	109
Val Calanca	111
Walser trails	111

Leg 11
Road from Chiasso to Bellinzona
Ascona	121
Avegno	123
Bosco Gurin	123
Brissago Islands	121
Breggia Gorge	124
Cardada/Cimetta	121
Denti della Vecchia	121
Gandria	119
Gordola	125
Locarnese national park	123
Locarno	121
Lugano	119
Melide	125
Mendrisio/Mendrisiotto	117
Meride/Monte San Giorgio	117
Mogno/Fusio	123
Monte Brè	119
Monte Generoso	125
Monte Lema	119
Monte Tamaro	121
Morcote	119
Riva San Vitale	119
Rivera	125
San Salvatore	119
Verzasca Valley	123
Muggio Valley	117
Maggia Valley	123

Leg 12
Bellinzona – Furka
Airolo/Pesciüm	129
Andermatt	131
Bedretto Valley	129
Bellinzona	127
Biaschina and Piottino	129
Claro	127
Four Springs Trail	133
Furka steam train	131
Gemsstock	131
Hospental	131
Leventina	129
Monte Carasso/San Bernardo	127
Pizzo di Claro	127
Pollegio	133
Ritom/Piora Valley	129
St. Gotthard	131
Schöllenen Gorge	131
Lago Tremorgio	129
Tremola	131

Leg 13
Furka – Visp
Aletsch Glacier	139
Belalp	141
Bettmeralp	139
Brig	141
Brigerbad	143
Ernen/Binntal	139
Fiesch/Eggishorn	139
Furka Pass	137
Gletsch	137
Goms	139
Grimsel Pass	139
Mund	141
Münster (Goms	139
Niederwald	143
Rhône Glacier	137
Riederalp	141
Simplon Pass	141

Leg 14
Zermatt, the Visp and Saas Valleys
Breithorn	147
Gornergrat	149
Grächen/Hannigalp	149
Jungen, Sparren, Embd	149
Kreuzboden/Hohsaas	151
Klein Matterhorn	147
Matterhorn	147
Mittelallalin	151
Moosalp	151
Saas-Fee	151
Saas-Grund	151
Sunnegga	149
Täsch	153
Törbel	151
Zermatt	147

Leg 15
Visp – Martigny
Ayent	163
Chandolin/Illhorn	159
Crans-Montana	159
Derborence	161
Dixence	161
Erschmatt	157
Euseigne	161
Gemmi	157
Lac de Géronde	159
Grimentz	159
Leuk	157
Leukerbad	157
Southern Lötschberg Ramp	155
Nendaz	161
Ovronnaz	161
Pfyn Forest	157
Plaine Morte	159
Raron	155
Saillon	161
Salgesch	157
Sierre	159
Sion	159
Saint-Léonard	163
Val d'Anniviers	159
Val d'Hérens	161
Valais wineTrail	157
Varen	157
Vercorin/Vallon de Réchy	159
Visp/Visperterminen	155
Wiler (Lötschental)	157

Leg 16
Martigny – Montreux
Aigle	171
Bex	171
Le Bouveret	173
Les Diablerets/Glacier 3000	171
Emosson	169
Evionnaz	173
Great St. Bernard Pass	167
Lavey-les-Bains	173
Leysin/Berneuse	171
Martigny	167
Col des Mosses	171
Pierre Avoi	169
Pissevache	169
Portes du Soleil	173
Saint-Maurice	169
Trient Gorge	169
Val d'Illiez	173
Verbier/Mont Fort	169
Villars-sur-Ollon/Bretaye	171

Leg 17
Montreux – Saint-George

Aubonne	183
Blonay–Chamby	177
Chauderon Gorge	177
Chillon Castle	175
Lake Geneva	175
Lausanne	179
Lavaux	179
L'Isle	181
Les Pléiades	177
Mont Pèlerin	177
Montreux	175
Ouchy	181
Rochers de Naye	177
Vevey	179
Vufflens	181

Leg 18
Route from Geneva to Saint-George

Carouge GE	189
Coppet	193
Geneva	191
Jet d'Eau	191
La Garenne/Vaud	195
Nyon	193
Prangins	195
Rhône	191
Salève	189
Saint-Cergue	193

Leg 19
Saint-George – Yverdon-les-Bains

Combe des Amburnex	201
Ballaigues	203
Canal d'Entreroches	203
La Sarraz	203
Lac de Joux	201
Le Brassus	205
Le Sentier	201
Col du Marchairuz	199
Mont Tendre	199
Orbe	203
Romainmôtier	203
Saint-George	199
Vallorbe	201
Vaud Jura nature park	199
Dent de Vaulion	201

Leg 20
Yverdon-les-Bains – Neuchâtel

Areuse Gorge	211
Buttes/La Robella	211
The Chasseron	209
Concise	209
Creux du Van	211
Covatannaz Gorge	209
Grande Cariçaie	209
Grandson	213
Môtiers	211
Lake Neuchâtel	207
Poëta Raisse	211
Sainte-Croix	209
Saint-Sulpice NE	211
Travers/Val-de-Travers	211
Yverdon-les-Bains	207

Leg 21
Road from Basel to Neuchâtel

Arlesheim	225
Augst/Kaiseraugst	219
Basel	217
Bottmingen	219
Lac des Brenets	223
Delémont	221
Doubs	221
Franches-Montagnes	221
Etang de la Gruère	221
La Chaux-de-Fonds	223
Laufen	219
Le Locle	223
The Sommêtres	223
Mariastein	219
Porrentruy	221
Réclère	221
Rhine	219
Riehen	225
Col des Roches	223
Saignelégier	221
Seewen SO	219
Saint-Ursanne	221
Valangin NE	225
Vue-des-Alpes	223

Leg 22
Neuchâtel – Fribourg

Avenches	233
Biel/Bienne	231
Chaumont	229
Grandfey/Hermitage of St. Magdalena Grand-Marais	231
Granges-Paccot	235
Kerzers	235
La Sauge/Fanel	231
Laténium	231
Mont Vully	233
Morat	233
Lake Morat	233
Neuchâtel	229
Romont	235
Schiffenensee	233
St. Peter's Island	231
Pays des Trois-Lacs	229

Leg 23
Fribourg – Château-d'Oex

Broc	245
Bulle	239
Charmey	241
Fribourg	237
Grandvillard	243
Gruyères	241
Lake Gruyère	239
Intyamon	241
Jogne Gorge	241
La Berra	239
Les Moilles	243
Moléson	241
Moléson-sur-Gruyères	241
Lessoc	243
Pont de la Poya	239
Pont-en-Ogoz	239
Pringy	241
Rossinière	243
Vounetz	245

Leg 24
Château-d'Oex – Interlaken

Château d'Oex	249
Diemtigtal nature park	253
Erlenbach/Stockhorn	253
Gruyère nature park Pays-d'Enhaut	249
Gstaad	251
Gsteig/Sanetsch	251
La Braye	249
La Pierreuse	251
Lauenensee	251
Lenk i.S.	253
Niesen	253
Pays-d'Enhaut	249
Rougemont	251
Saane	255
Saanen	251
Saanenland	251
Schönried/Rellerli	253
Spiez	253
Videmanette	255

Leg 25
Interlaken – Bern

Ballenberg	267
Beatenberg/Niederhorn	263
Belp/Belpmoos	265
The Brienzer Rothorn	261
Lake Brienz	261
Bütschelegg	265
Gantrisch nature park	265
Giessbach	263
Goldswil/Burgseeli	259
Grindelwald	261
Harder	259
Interlaken	259
Jungfraujoch	261
Lauterbrunnen	261
Mürren/Schilthorn	261
Oberhofen	267
Riggisberg	267
Rüeggisberg	265
Saint Beatus caves	263
Schynige Platte	261
Sigriswil	263
Thun	263
Lake Thun	263

Photo credits

Badrutt Andrea 96; Basel Tourismus / Zimmermann Andreas 215; Baumgartner, www.bgr.ch 30, 32, 40, 72, 74, 118, 120, 146, 168, 170, 192, 208, 210, 228, 236, 238, 240, 260; Beatrice Devenes 3; www.beatushoehlen.ch 262; Bern Tourismus 14; Blatter Nadine 138; Braun Thomas 10; www.buergenstock.ch 32; Charmey, Office du Tourisme 240; Davos Klosters Destination / Schlumpf Stefan 84, 90; Emanuel Ammon 20; Emmental Tourismus 16; Fookes Eric 242; Fotolia.com 1, 9, 21, 31, 33, 45, 57, 64, 67, 81, 85, 97, 121, 141, 161, 223, 231, 239, 243, 252, 265, 281, 282, 285; Frei Daniel M. 66; Fribourg Tourisme / Croci Alfredo 236; Furka Dampfbahn / Jossi Urs 130; Giovanoli Gian Andri 100; Grande Dixence / essencedesign.com 160; Greber Markus 100; Gruyère Tourisme 242; www.hohlgassland. ch 30; Harley-Davidson, Schweiz 57; Hostettler Peter 264; Interlaken Tourismus 258; Jungfraubahnen / Lewis Rob 258; Jura Tourisme 222; Kambly Erlebniswelt 18; Keller Heinz 250; www.elgekenneweg.ch 18; Luzern Tourismus 18; Magnani Sebastian 4; Maison Cailler, Broc 238; Maison du Gruyère / Perriard-Benoit 240; Marc Niederhauser 120; Mendrisiotto Turismo 116; MOB - GoldenPass / Schobinger Maurice 176; Monte Generoso 116; Mosimann Peter (Gemälde Giron Charles) 32; Mumprecht Sandra 238, 240; Niesenbahn / Petroni Bruno 252; www.tprnov.ch, Nyon – St-Cergue 192; Office du Tourisme Yverdon-les-Bains 206; Parc d'Attractions du Châtelard 168; Parc Gruyère Pays-d'Enhaut 240; Pays-d'Enhaut Tourisme 240; www. Perretfoto.ch 20, 30, 38, 66; Peter Niederhauser 161; Pfammatter Christian160; Portmann Michael 146; ProWeinland 56; RhB 104; RhB / Keller Tibert 92; RhB / von Blohn Jonas 92; www.ritom.ch 128; Riva Ely 128; www.schatzalp.ch 90; Scherer Evelyne 34; Schmed Patrick 264; Schwyz Tourismus 42, 44, 52; Sciboz Laurent 238; Seyffer Jeroen 154; Shutterstock. com 8, 14, 28, 42, 44, 49, 50, 52, 80, 94, 104, 110, 118, 126, 148, 174, 178, 180, 188, 190, 192, 206, 216, 218, 222, 230, 236; Sonderegger Christof 242; Switzerland Tourism 1, 18, 72; Switzerland Tourism / Bagattini Renato 116; Switzerland Tourism / Christof Schuerpf 180; Switzerland Tourism / Engler Stephan 158, 166, 187, 238; Switzerland Tourism / Gaudenz Danuser 81; Switzerland Tourism / Geerk Jan 14, 50; Switzerland Tourism / Gerth Roland 92, 96, 200, 252, 258; Switzerland Tourism / Gyger Marcus 16, 158; Switzerland Tourism / Hartmann Vera 78; Switzerland Tourism / Mettler Andy 258; Switzerland Tourism / Mizrachi Samuel 50; Switzerland Tourism / Müller Beat 64; Switzerland Tourism / Schaerer Nico 20, 27, 61, 78, 89, 92, 108, 115, 118, 126, 130, 135, 136, 138, 165, 174, 178, 180, 198, 247, 270; Switzerland Tourism / Schmid Max 54; Switzerland Tourism / Schuerpf Christof 190, 192; Switzerland Tourism / Sonderegger Christof 66, 146, 176, 222, 248, 250; Switzerland Tourism / Storto Walter 34, 250; Ticino Turismo 126, 128; Tremorgio 128; Unesco Biosphäre Entlebuch / Bissig Maurin 262; Union fribourgeoise du Tourisme / Sciboz Laurent 236; www.viamala.ch 108; www. fotowalter.ch 148; Wandermagazin Schweiz 13, 14, 16, 18, 20, 28, 30, 34, 38, 40, 42, 44, 50, 54, 62, 64, 66, 70, 72, 74, 78, 80, 82, 84, 90, 92, 94, 96, 100, 102, 104, 108, 110, 116, 118, 120, 122, 126, 128, 130, 136, 138, 140, 146, 148, 150, 154, 156, 158, 160, 166, 168, 170, 174, 176, 178, 180, 188, 190, 192, 197, 198, 200, 202, 206, 208, 210, 216, 218, 220, 222, 227, 228, 230, 232, 240, 248, 250, 252, 258, 260, 262, 264; Winterthur Tourismus 54; Yverdon-les-Bains Centre Thermal / Engler Stephan 206; Zürich Verkehrsbetriebe VBZ 52

More than 5000 hikes in Switzerland.
www.tourfinder.ch

«Arveseeli» near Gemmi pass BE/VS, Picture: Peter-Lukas Meier

My personal impressions of the Grand Tour

Each day is unique. Make a note of the highlights and of your most remarkable experiences on the Grand Tour in case you one day wish to share them with your grandchildren...

My personal impressions of the Grand Tour

My personal impressions of the Grand Tour

My personal impressions of the Grand Tour

GRAND TOUR
of Switzerland

Touring Map to a scale of 1:275 000 laminated, Fr. 19.90

This map is perfect for previewing and reminiscing about the many attractions along the memorable Grand Tour of Switzerland! This route will lead you 1,600 kilometres through four language regions, over five Alpine passes, to eleven UNESCO World Heritage Sites as well as two biospheres and along 22 lakes. The map is a small tour guide in itself! Photos and descriptions in four languages (German, French, Italian and English) complement the cartographical information. This tour provides a concentrated insight into Switzerland, with exquisite scenic views and cultural jewels.

Free download on smart devices with supplied access code included!

The Grand Tour of Switzerland is a unique expedition, which combines the highlights of Switzerland on a journey.

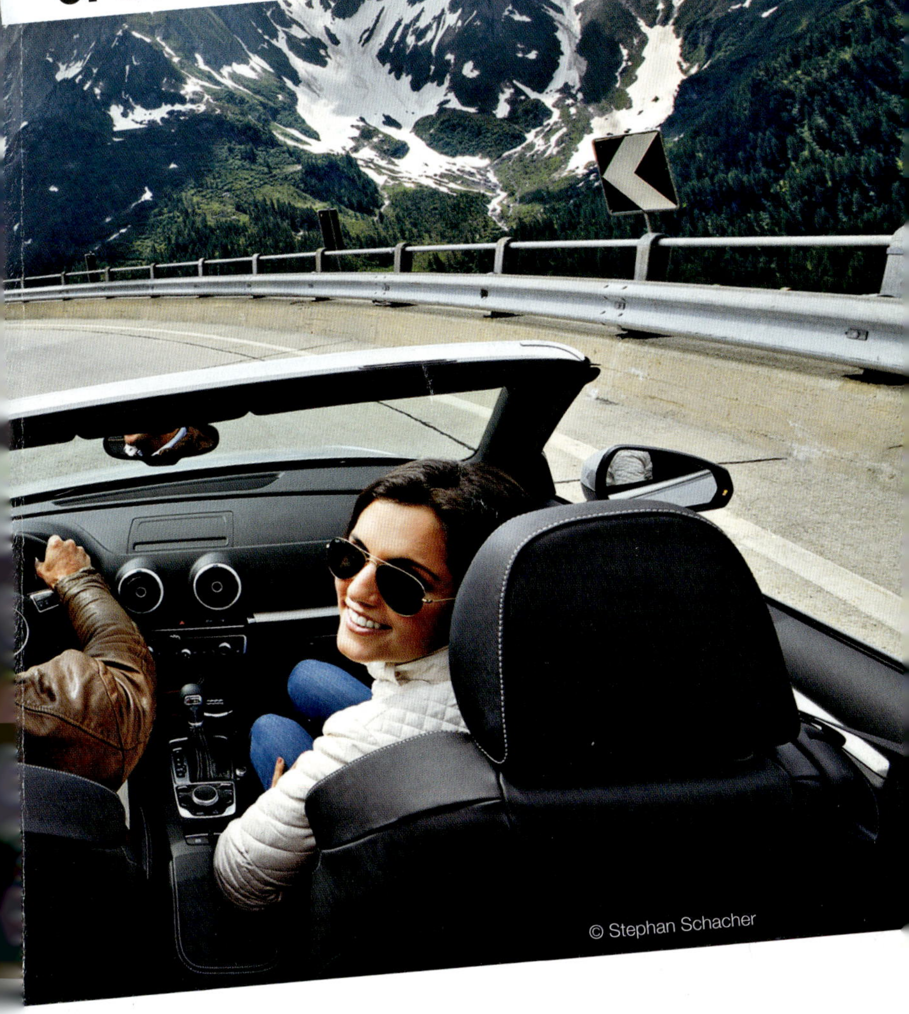

© Stephan Schacher

Hallwag Kümmerly+Frey

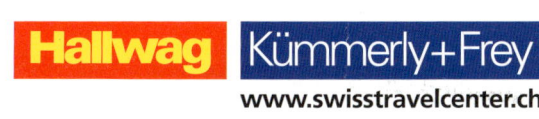

www.swisstravelcenter.ch

Impressum – Legal notice
Grand Tour of Switzerland

First edition 2016

Published by:	Hallwag Kümmerly+Frey AG, CH-3322 Schönbühl-Berne
Authors:	Roland Baumgartner and Peter-L. Meier
In collaboration with:	Switzerland Tourism and the Grand Tour of Switzerland Association
Concept:	Peter Niederhauser
Translation:	Business Editing, Paris
Design:	Funky Strawberry, advertising agency
Proofreading:	Business Editing, Paris / Danielle Zingg
Production:	Hallwag Kümmerly+Frey AG Printed in Italy

Signposts and direction of travel
The Grand Tour can be travelled in both directions, but Switzerland Tourism recommends you make the journey clockwise. This is especially true in cities with one-way streets - and for motorway access roads. Signposts along the route are limited to the clockwise direction of travel on the main route, and to access roads to the main route from abroad.

Suitability of vehicles
The roads chosen for the Grand Tour of Switzerland are suitable for cars and motorbikes. Larger vehicles can expect to encounter restrictions.

Liability disclaimer
The Grand Tour of Switzerland is a recommended itinerary using the existing Swiss road network. Those who use it do so at their own risk. Switzerland Tourism and the Grand Tour of Switzerland Association cannot be held liable for any roadworks, deviations, safety alerts, incidents or safety recommendations at any point of the itinerary.

The information in this book has been scrupulously researched. It is not however possible to guarantee its accuracy. The author is grateful for any information or observations that you may wish to send to info@swisstravelcenter.ch.

All rights reserved. Reproduction in whole or in part by any means whatsoever is subject to the publisher's written approval.

www.swisstravelcenter.ch, www.MySwitzerland.com/grandtour

© Hallwag Kümmerly+Frey AG, Grubenstrasse 109, CH-3322 Schönbühl-Berne

ISBN number: 978-3-8283-0861-9